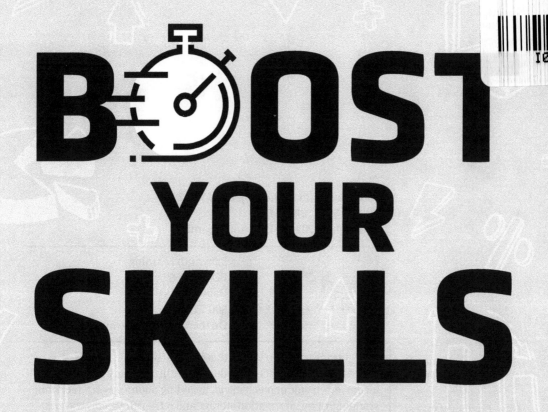

BOOST YOUR SKILLS

in Microsoft® Excel 365/2021

Alex Scott, BBA, MM

LABYRINTH

LEARNING®

Boost Your Skills In Microsoft Excel 365/2021
By Alex Scott, BBA, MM
Copyright © 2024 by Labyrinth Learning

Labyrinth Learning
PO Box 2669
Danville, CA 94526
800.522.9746
On the web at: lablearning.com

Co-Founder:
Brian Favro

Product Manager:
Jason Favro

Learning Solutions Architect:
Laura Popelka

Production Manager:
Debra Grose

Senior Editor:
Alexandra Mummery

eLearning Specialist:
Lauren Carlson

Indexing:
BIM Creatives, LLC

Cover Design:
Sam Anderson Design

Item: 1-64061-576-8
ISBN-13: 978-1-64061-576-2

Contents

Introducing Microsoft Office and Using Common Features

In this chapter, you will be introduced to Microsoft Office and given an overview of the various versions of the software. Understanding what is offered in each will help you make the best decision about which version meets your needs. You'll also practice using some of the features that are common across the Office suite. Once you learn how to use a feature in one application, you can use the same or similar steps in the others.

LEARNING OBJECTIVES

- Describe similarities and differences between Office 2021 for the desktop, Microsoft 365, and Office Online
- Identify uses of cloud storage
- Identify parts of the Office user interface
- Use the spelling checker and other review features
- Identify Office features available through Backstage view
- Use the Office Clipboard
- Format text in Office applications
- Search for Help within Office applications
- Capture a screen in an Office application

CHAPTER TIMING

- Concepts & Practice: 02:00:00
- Self-Assessment: N/A
- Total: 02:00:00

Learning Resources: **boostyourskills.lablearning.com**

Introduction to Microsoft Office

Microsoft Office is a software suite that enables users to create, format, revise, collaborate, and share files quickly across multiple devices. The Microsoft Office 2021 software suite for Windows includes Word, Excel, Access, PowerPoint, Outlook, OneNote, Publisher, Skype, and Teams. A software suite is a collection of applications generally produced by the same manufacturer and bundled together for a better price. Being produced by the same manufacturer also means that each application offers the same user interface. Examples of features shared among the different Office 2021 apps are the Ribbon, Quick Access toolbar, a spelling and/or grammar checker, and collaboration tools.

What Devices Will Microsoft Office Work With?

Microsoft Office works on desktops, laptops/notebook computers, and all-in-one PCs and Macs, as well as Windows, Android, and iOS smartphones and tablets (though some apps, like Publisher and Access, work only on PCs).

If you are writing a paper or preparing a business plan, you probably want to create it on a desktop, laptop, or all-in-one computer. If you want to open, read, share, or make simple changes to a Word document, you can select any device. This chapter assumes you will be using a desktop, laptop, or all-in-one computer.

To learn more about the operating systems (Windows, Android, macOS, or iOS) and types of devices (all-in-one computer, desktop, laptop, smartphone, or tablet) that will run Microsoft Office, do a web search for *Microsoft Office 2021 products*.

What Storage Does Microsoft Office Provide?

Microsoft OneDrive is the cloud storage location included with Microsoft Office 2021 and Microsoft 365, and it provides a convenient way to save, store, and share files, photos, and videos via your computer, smartphone, or tablet anytime, anywhere, and on any device—provided you have an Internet connection or Wi-Fi access. Depending on the Microsoft Office product you use or purchase, you will receive anywhere from five gigabytes to five terabytes of OneDrive cloud storage.

You may want to use cloud storage as your primary saving method so you can access your files at home, at school, at work, or anywhere. Or you may decide to use cloud storage as a backup for files located on your computer's hard drive or your flash drive. Instead of emailing files to yourself, use OneDrive as a faster way to store something in the cloud. To learn more about OneDrive, do a web search for *OneDrive*.

Which Microsoft Office Should I Use?

You may have heard others talk about Microsoft Office 2021, Microsoft 365, and Office Online and are not sure which one is right for you. Base your decision on the apps and features you need, in addition to the pricing structure.

- **Office Online:** This version is free and requires a Microsoft account. It includes limited versions of Word, Excel, PowerPoint, and OneNote. No software is installed on your computer, as the apps are accessed and run in a web browser. The apps are not the same as the full-version apps in the other variations of Office and lack many features of those full versions. This version requires an Internet connection. Office Online is great for simple tasks, like writing a short letter or creating a basic slideshow presentation.

- **Microsoft Office 2021:** This version is software that is purchased once and installed on one PC. It does not require an Internet connection to run. It does not have all the features of Microsoft 365, and you must pay for future major upgrades. Choose from a variety of plans that may include Word, Excel, PowerPoint, OneNote, Outlook, Publisher, Access, Skype, and Teams.

- **Microsoft 365:** Formerly Office 365, this version requires users to pay a monthly or annual subscription fee for installing and using the software on one or more devices (PC/Mac and mobile devices). All upgrades are included, so you always have the latest-and-greatest version, and most Office 2021 apps are included. Microsoft says the Microsoft 365 apps can include features not present in the Office 2021 apps, as Microsoft 365 is updated more frequently than Microsoft Office.

While Microsoft Office has three distinct formats—Microsoft Office 2021, Microsoft 365, and Office Online—and the examples provided in this chapter can work in each of the Office formats, this book assumes you are using Office 2021 on the desktop or Microsoft 365 in a subscription-based plan, as well as Windows 10 or 11. Remember that Microsoft 365 can change at any time. If you are using Microsoft 365, keep in mind that your screen may not match all the illustrations in this book. Changes made to Microsoft 365 after publication of this title may result in additional differences between your book and the software.

What Are the Microsoft Office Apps?

In this chapter, you will learn about four of the Microsoft Office applications included in the Microsoft Office suite: Word, Excel, Access, and PowerPoint.

Application	What It Is Used For
Word	Word-processing software used to create, edit, format, and share documents, such as letters, reports, essays, and business plans.
Excel	Spreadsheet software, arranged with rows and columns, used to perform calculations and analyze numerical data. Use Excel to prepare a budget or income statement, or to determine the amount of interest paid on a loan.
Access	Database software that stores and helps you quickly retrieve data. In Access, you create and enter data into a table and then use forms, reports, and queries to display the desired results.
PowerPoint	Presentation software used to create, edit, format, and share slides designed to tell a story; market a product; or explain a concept.

The Microsoft Office suite may include the following additional applications:

Application	What It Is Used For
OneNote	Note-taking software used to organize notes (handwritten or typed), audio recordings, screen captures, or sketches you have collected or created to share with others.
Outlook	Personal information management software used to create, send, and receive emails, record tasks, maintain one or more calendars, schedule meetings and appointments, manage contacts, and take notes.
Publisher	Desktop-publishing software used to design and lay out text and images, often for newsletters or brochures.
Skype	Internet communication software used to share audio, video, text, messages, files, or desktop screens.
Teams	Communication software typically used in the workforce, providing online video calling, chat features, and sharing options across personalized groups.

Microsoft Accounts

A Microsoft account provides you with access to your Microsoft settings, files, contacts, and more. A valid Microsoft account can include Hotmail, Bing, MSN, Office, OneDrive, Outlook, Skype, Store, Windows, or Xbox Live. Once logged in to your computer, you can log in to your Microsoft account from any Office app. If you do not have a Microsoft account, you can create one for free by doing a web search for *Microsoft account*.

Common Features in Microsoft Office Apps

The Office 2021 applications share some frequently used features. These include the Ribbon, Quick Access toolbar, and common commands.

The Ribbon

Within each application, you will find the Ribbon displayed along the top of the window. The Ribbon contains tabs and commonly used buttons and other icons that are specific to the application. The buttons are arranged in groups within each tab. While the Ribbon changes with each application, some tabs, groups, and commands are common throughout the Microsoft suite. In this chapter, we will look at the Excel Ribbon and, specifically, the File, Home, Review, and Formulas tabs.

> **NOTE!** This course is supported with online resources, videos, quizzes, simulations, and more. When you see the cloud icon, go to the online resources at: boostyourskills.lablearning.com

 View the video "Ribbon Overview."

The Quick Access Toolbar

Each application has a one-line Quick Access toolbar located, by default, below the Ribbon. It's also hidden by default, so if you want to use it, you'll need to enable it first. You can customize the toolbar with the buttons you use most frequently. The settings for each application's Quick Access toolbar work independently; therefore, you need to customize the Word, Excel, Access, PowerPoint, and Outlook Quick Access toolbars separately.

 View the video "Quick Access Toolbar Overview."

Undo/Redo

Within any application, you may type text or perform a command or action and then change your mind about what you did. As long as you have not exited the application, you may be able to undo the action.

> **NOTE!** Some actions, such as saving or sharing, cannot be undone.

You may want to redo an action you just undid. Sounds confusing, right? Use the Redo button to undo the undo, or to reapply the action. This puts the command or action you just undid back into effect.

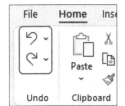

Undo and Redo buttons in the Undo group on the Home tab

Home→Undo ↺ or Redo ↻

In this exercise, you will use the Undo and Redo buttons.

1. Log in to your computer, start Excel, and tap Enter to accept the default template, Blank Workbook.

    A new blank workbook appears.

2. Type the following into **cell A1** and then tap Enter: `My favorite Excel feature is creating formulas.`

    The typed text is inserted in cell A1, but you may notice that the text does not fit in one cell; it appears across multiple columns. The Enter key completes the entry and moves the active cell to cell A2.

3. Type this text in **cell A2** and then tap Enter: `I also like using the Undo button.`

4. Click **cell A1** to select it.

    The cell location is referred to by its column and then its row. Cell A1 is located below the A, for column A, and to the right of the 1, for row 1.

5. Choose **Home→Font→Bold** to apply bold formatting.

6. Now apply **Italic** formatting to **cell A2**.

7. Follow these steps to undo more than one action at a time:

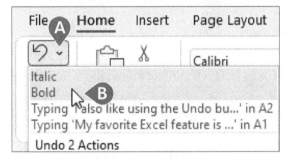

    A. Click the **Undo menu** button ⌄.

    B. Point to the second step, *Bold*, to select both the Bold and the Italic actions, and then click the mouse button. **Cells A1** and **A2** will have the bold and italic formatting removed at the same time.

8. Click the **Undo** button once to remove the text typed into **cell A2**.

9. Click the **Redo** button three times to reinsert the text and reapply the bold and italic formatting to the cells.

10. Keep Excel open.

    Unless otherwise directed, always keep any files or programs open at the end of an exercise.

Common Features on the File Tab

In this section, you will learn about the features on the File tab that are used in a similar manner throughout multiple Microsoft applications, including Word, Excel, and PowerPoint. Here you will use Microsoft Excel 2021 to save, close, and share a file; explore printing options; and open a template.

Backstage View

When you are working in your file and open the File tab, the Backstage view displays. Think of your Backstage view as your personal manager for the open file and application. Use the Backstage view to update file information, select account settings, view program options, open new files, save, print, share, export, provide feedback to Microsoft, and recover unsaved files. These are the "big-picture" items you do to your file and not the specific tasks you perform using the other tabs on the Ribbon.

Program Options

Microsoft provides preference settings that you can customize for each application (that is, Word or Excel) so they are automatically applied each time you use the application on your device. To change your preferences, use the Options feature on the File tab. Some custom options include adding your username and initials so they automatically display in some downloaded templates, displaying formatting marks, correcting spelling, and saving files to a default file location.

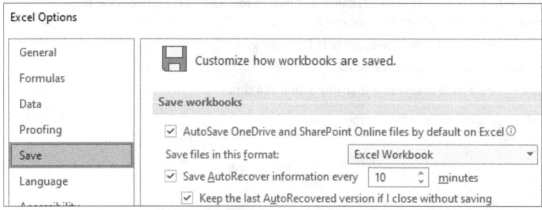

The Save options allow you to set defaults for the file format and the frequency with which documents are automatically saved.

> **File→Options**

Saving Files

As you work in your file, you should save frequently to prevent data or information loss. Some people prefer to save important files every few minutes, while others save at less frequent intervals.

The saving commands are found on the File tab, and you'll see different options, including Save and Save As. You can use the Save command the first time you save a file, and when you do, the Save As screen will appear.

View the video "Using Save and Save As."

You may choose to save files to your device (for example, on the hard drive in the Documents folder), to your flash drive, or to the cloud in OneDrive.

View the video "Saving Files to Multiple Locations."

You can even set Microsoft Office to save your work automatically whenever a specific interval of time has elapsed. A good rule of thumb is to save as often as you can afford to lose data. If you can only afford to lose one minute of data, save your file every minute!

> **File→Save *or* Save As**

DEVELOP YOUR SKILLS: 01-D2

In this exercise, you will use Save As to store an Excel document in a new folder.

Download the exercise files from boostyourskills.lablearning.com and determine your file storage location before starting this exercise.

1. In your open Excel document, choose **File** to display the Backstage view and then click **Save**.

   The first time you save a file, the Save As screen displays. Otherwise, choosing File→Save updates the file with the same name, location, and file type. Once it has been saved you can also use the Save As command if you wish to change the name, location, or file type.

2. Click the **Browse** button and navigate to the **Overview Chapter 1** folder in your file storage location.

3. In the Save As dialog box, click the **New Folder** button.

   The New Folder button is to the right of the Organize button, just under the address bar.

4. Type **My Excel Work** for the new folder name and tap [Enter] twice (once to enter the name, a second time to open the folder).

5. Click in the **File Name** box and type: **01-D2-Features**

6. Verify that *Excel Workbook* displays for Save as Type and click the **Save** button.

7. Close the file.

Finding, Searching, and Opening Files

Files can be opened within an application by using the Open dialog box, choosing from a recently saved files list within the application, using File Explorer, or typing the filename in the Windows Search box. Within Windows, you can use File Explorer to locate and manage your files. You can click the File Explorer icon on the taskbar and then search for files located on your PC, flash drive, or OneDrive.

View the video "Opening Files."

Sharing Files via Email and with People

You can share open files directly from the application to either email or OneDrive. Sharing a file directly to email is usually faster than opening an email application, such as Microsoft Outlook, locating the file to send, and then attaching it. When someone shares a file with you from an application to OneDrive, you will receive a link (in your email account) to access the file.

View the video "Sharing Files via Email."

If the Automatically Share Changes option is set to Always, once the file is shared, anyone who has editing rights to the file can make changes to it.

> **TIP!** You can also use the Share button located in the top-right corner of the application window.

File→Share

Complete this exercise via the online WebSim.

In this exercise, you will share an open Excel file by using the Share with People option that saves to the cloud.

Before You Begin: *Go to the online resources at:* <u>boostyourskills.lablearning.com</u>

1. Click the **View Resources** button under the image of your book cover and then click the **Overview Chapter** tab.

2. Click the link for **WebSim 01-D3**.

3. Follow the on-screen instructions to complete this exercise.

Printing

If you are connected and have access to a printer, you should be able to print. Before printing, you should save your file, run Spelling & Grammar (Word) or Spelling (Excel and PowerPoint), proofread your file, verify formats, and review the file to see if you have used the fewest possible number of pages. Use the Print Preview feature to browse the pages in your file prior to printing so you don't waste time or printing resources, and use the options in the Settings area to adjust elements such as page orientation, paper size, margins, and more.

Keep in mind that you can print to a PDF file if you want to be eco-friendly.

View the video "Printing Files."

> File→Print

Templates

A template is a document, worksheet, or presentation that has the fonts, paragraph styles, and page layout settings such as margins, orientation, and size already built in. Instead of selecting these settings each time you prepare a similar file, you may opt to use a template to save time when you need to add new text, images, and additional formats specific to the file.

Usually an application includes sample templates that are stored on the hard drive of your computer when you install the software. You can also search for online templates using the Search feature available when you create a new document. Templates are arranged according to categories; for example, by business, personal, and industry.

> File→New

DEVELOP YOUR SKILLS: 01-D4

In this exercise, you will open a prebuilt Excel template.

1. If necessary, start Excel. Click **New** at left, scroll down and choose the **Personal Monthly Budget** template, and click **Create**. (If that specific template is not available, choose a different budget template. The templates often change when you launch Excel.)

   Browse through the Excel workbook to view some of the information that you may want to include in a budget of your own.

2. Choose **File→New**, select the **Student Schedule** template, and click **Create**.

You may have to scroll down to find the template. Notice some of the features that are automatically built in, such as Schedule Start and Time Interval, which can easily be adjusted to suit your own schedule. You should also see the current timeslot is formatted with a different color.

3. Choose **File→New** and select the **Welcome to Excel** template or another template of your choice.

Notice the workbook formatting and review the text contained in the file.

4. Close all open files without saving and then exit Excel.

Common Features on the Home Tab

In this section, you will learn about the features on the Home tab that are used in a similar manner throughout multiple Microsoft applications, including Word, Excel, and PowerPoint. You will use Microsoft Excel to Cut, Copy, and Paste with the Office Clipboard, format text, use the Mini toolbar, and find and replace text. Excel is generally used for keying numbers and performing calculations.

DEVELOP YOUR SKILLS: O1-D5

In this exercise, you will open a file created from an Excel template and become familiar with Excel.

1. Start Excel and click the **Open** button on the left side of the window.

2. Click the **Browse** button, navigate to your file storage location, and open the **O1-D5-Clipboard** file.

3. Click **Enable Editing** in the Security Warning bar at the top of the screen, if necessary.

The Security Warning bar may display the first time you open a file. If you know the file sender and trust the content, always choose Enable Content.

4. Scroll down to display **rows 19–25**, if necessary, and then click the **Let's Go** button.

5. Click the various worksheet tabs at the bottom of the Excel window and review the helpful information about Excel on each worksheet.

In this figure, six worksheet tabs are shown:

The Office Clipboard

Located at the far left on the Home tab, the Clipboard group contains the Cut, Copy, Paste, and Format Painter buttons. Selecting the Clipboard dialog box launcher opens the Clipboard pane, which displays at the side of your application. The Clipboard contains thumbnails (small images) of what you have recently cut or copied from your Microsoft Office file(s) during your Windows session, with the most recent item at the top of the list. You can use the Clipboard to quickly paste text, pictures, images, or charts into your file. You can paste all items on the Clipboard into your file(s) as many times as desired, and you can clear all items from the Clipboard.

The Cut feature in the Clipboard group functions much like a scrapbook in which you cut out information, such as newspaper articles about yourself, and then paste it on the desired page(s). When data is cut, the original selection is removed from the source location and is pasted at the target location.

When data is copied, the original selection remains in the source location and a new selection is pasted at the target location.

☁ **View the video "Clipboard Overview."**

CLIPBOARD FEATURES	
Feature	**What It Does**
Cut ✂	**Cut:** Removes the original selection from the *source* location and places the selection on the Office Clipboard.
Copy 🗐	**Copy:** Creates a duplicate of the original selection, which remains in the source location, and places a copy of the selection on the Office Clipboard.
Paste 📋	**Paste:** Inserts a copy of the most recent item found on the Office Clipboard at the *target* location, or destination. Depending on the application, there are usually at least three paste choices, Keep Source Formatting, Merge Formatting, and Keep Text Only. **Keep Source Formatting:** Pastes the text and the formatting (bold, italic, underline) of the selection from the source location to the target location. The selection pasted retains the original formatting from the source location. **Merge Formatting:** Pastes the text and formatting (bold, italic, underline) of the selection from the source location to the target location and combines it with any formatting that is already at the target location. The selection pasted has formats from both the source and target locations. **Keep Text Only:** Pastes the selection from the source location to the target location. The selection pasted takes on the formatting of the target location.
Format Painter 🖌	**Format Painter:** Applies the character and paragraph formatting from the source selection to any characters or text selected. Double-click the Format Painter to apply formats to multiple selections. Click the Format Painter button to turn it off when you are finished.

Home→Clipboard→Cut ✂ | Ctrl+X

Home→Clipboard→Copy 🗐 | Ctrl+C

Home→Clipboard→Paste 📋 | Ctrl+V

In this exercise, you will use Excel to copy data from the source destination to the target destination and cut data from its original location and paste it into the target location.

To begin, you will navigate to the desired tab and locate the range to be copied. Depending on the size of your monitor, you may or may not need to scroll.

1. Click the **2. Analyze** worksheet tab at the bottom of the screen.
2. Follow these steps to view and select a specific part of a worksheet:

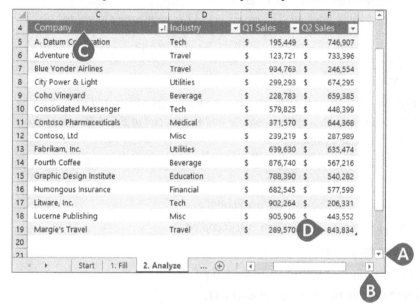

   A. If necessary, scroll down to display **rows 4–20**.
   B. If necessary, scroll right to display **columns C–F**.
   C. Click in **cell C4** to select the Company cell.
   D. Press and hold the Shift key and click **cell F19**.
3. Release Shift and notice that the **range C4:F19** is selected.

4. Choose **Home→Clipboard→Copy** and notice that a moving border displays around the **range C4:F19** to indicate that the selection is copied.

   The copied text is placed on the Office Clipboard and is ready to be pasted in a destination location. The copied text also remains in cells C4:F19 on the 2. Analyze worksheet tab.

5. Click the **New Sheet** button (located below the worksheet, to the right of the *Learn More* tab) to create a new worksheet.

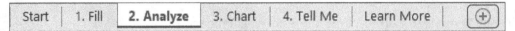

   The new worksheet, called Sheet1 by default, is inserted to the right of the 2. Analyze worksheet. Verify that cell A1 in the new worksheet is selected. The empty cell A1 is your target location.

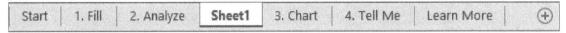

6. Choose **Home→Clipboard→Paste**.

   In Excel, when you copy cell contents, you also can copy the format(s) associated with the cells. In this case, you only copied the cell contents. Anytime you see ##### in a cell in Excel, it means the column is not wide enough to display the cell's contents.

Cut and Paste

7. Click the **2. Analyze** worksheet tab below the worksheet.

   The moving border displays because the selection is still copied.

8. Tap [Esc] to remove the moving border.

9. Select the **range C5:F7** and choose **Home→Clipboard→Cut**.

10. Click the **Sheet1** worksheet tab and then select **cell A17**.

11. Choose **Home→Clipboard→Paste**.

12. Click the **2. Analyze** worksheet tab.

    Notice that the data from the range C5:F7 is no longer there since it was cut, or removed, from the worksheet.

13. Choose **File→Save As** to save the file in your **Overview Chapter 1** folder as:
    `O1-D6-Clipboard`

Drag and Drop

If you want to cut or copy text and then paste it in a different location on the same worksheet, try using drag and drop. Whether you want to cut or copy text, the first step is always to select the desired cell or cells. The difference between cutting and copying in this method has to do with the [Ctrl] key. That is, to copy, you hold down [Ctrl] while moving from one location to the next; when cutting, you do not use [Ctrl].

View the video "Using Drag and Drop."

In this exercise, you will use drag and drop in Excel to cut, or move, data from one group of cells to another location.

1. Save your workbook as: **O1-D7-Drag**
2. Click the **2. Analyze** worksheet tab, if necessary.
3. Click **cell C8**, and then press Shift while clicking **cell F19** to select the **range C8:F19**.
4. Position the mouse pointer over the top border in column C of the selection so the four-headed arrow displays.

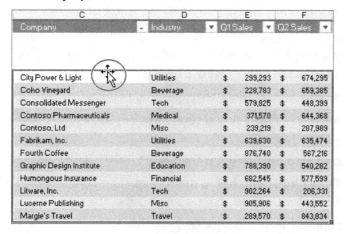

Company	Industry	Q1 Sales	Q2 Sales
City Power & Light	Utilities	$ 299,293	$ 674,295
Coho Vineyard	Beverage	$ 228,783	$ 659,385
Consolidated Messenger	Tech	$ 579,825	$ 448,399
Contoso Pharmaceuticals	Medical	$ 371,570	$ 644,368
Contoso, Ltd	Misc	$ 239,219	$ 287,989
Fabrikam, Inc.	Utilities	$ 639,630	$ 635,474
Fourth Coffee	Beverage	$ 876,740	$ 587,216
Graphic Design Institute	Education	$ 788,390	$ 540,282
Humongous Insurance	Financial	$ 682,545	$ 577,599
Litware, Inc.	Tech	$ 902,264	$ 206,331
Lucerne Publishing	Misc	$ 905,906	$ 443,552
Margie's Travel	Travel	$ 289,570	$ 843,834

5. Click and hold the mouse button, drag up to **cell C5**, and then release the mouse button.

   Using drag and drop to cut removes the range from the original location and pastes it in the new location.

6. Choose **File→Save** to save your changes.

Formatting Text Using Font Group Settings

To make your selection more visibly appealing and easy to read, you may want to use some or all of the font formats available in the Font group or in the Font dialog box. To apply the formats, you must first select a cell or group of cells, words, or phrases.

Use the Font dialog box launcher to open the Font dialog box.

The Format Painter applies multiple formats located in one range to another range within the application. Think of the selected range's original location as your paint can. You apply the formats found in your paint can, the selected range, to another range with the help of the paintbrush, or Format Painter. Whatever cells you click get the formatting. You can use Format Painter to format multiple cells or ranges by double-clicking the Format Painter button. To turn off the multiple-use feature and stop "painting," tap the Esc key.

DEVELOP YOUR SKILLS: 01-D8

In this exercise, you will increase the font size, make text bold, remove the bold, change the font color, launch the Font dialog box, and use the Format Painter.

1. Save your workbook as: **01-D8-Format**
2. At the bottom of the worksheet, click the **3. Chart** worksheet tab and then select the **range C5:D16**.
3. Choose **Home→Font→Increase Font Size** two times to increase the font size of the selection to 14 points.
4. Select **cell C9**, and then choose **Home→Font→Bold**.

   Bold is used to add emphasis to a cell. When a format such as bold is applied, the button on the Ribbon displays a dark-gray background. To turn the format off and remove the dark-gray background behind the button, click the button again. This is known as a toggle format.

5. Select **cell C14**, and then choose **Home→Font→Bold** to toggle Bold to off.
6. Select **cell D6**, and then press and hold the Ctrl key and click **cells D8**, **D9**, **D13**, and **D15** to select multiple cells that are not side by side.
7. Choose **Home→Font→Font Color menu button ⌄** and then select **Red** under Standard Colors.
8. Select **cells C8:D8** and click the **dialog box launcher** at the bottom-right corner of the Font group on the Home tab to open the Font dialog box.
9. Select the **Strikethrough** setting under Effects and click **OK**.
10. With the **range C8:D8** still selected, choose **Home→Clipboard→Format Painter**.
11. Select cells **C10:D10**.

    Notice that the strikethrough format found in cell C8 and the red font found in D8 were applied to cells C10 and D10.

12. Save the file.

The Mini Toolbar

The Mini toolbar is a floating toolbar that contains some of the more commonly used formatting buttons found on the Home tab and specific to the application. The Mini toolbar appears at various times in all the Office applications, giving you a convenient way to choose the most commonly used commands. If the Mini toolbar does not display, right-click the mouse.

The Mini toolbar in Word

The Mini toolbar in Excel

File→Options→General→Check Show Mini Toolbar on Selection

DEVELOP YOUR SKILLS: 01-D9

In this exercise, you will use the Mini toolbar in Excel to apply formatting.

1. Save your workbook as: **01-D9-Toolbar**
2. Click the **Sheet1** tab and then select **cell C4**.
3. Press and hold Ctrl and then select **cell C19** so two cells are selected.
4. Right-click **cell C4** to display the Mini toolbar and the context, or shortcut, menu.
5. In the Mini toolbar, click the **Bold** button and the **Fill Color** button to apply a yellow background color to the two cells (C4 and C19).
6. Click any cell to hide the Mini toolbar again.
7. Save the file.

Find and Replace

Within a document, worksheet, database, or presentation, you may need to locate text quickly. You may also need to substitute one word or phrase, or formatting, for something else. The Find command is used to search for characters, symbols, numbers, words, phrases, or formats that meet the criteria. The Replace command first finds whatever meets the criteria and then replaces it with what you desire.

DEVELOP YOUR SKILLS: 01-D10

In this exercise, you will use the Find command to locate the word Contoso *and then replace each occurrence with* Labyrinth.

1. Save your workbook as: **01-D10-Replace**
2. Choose **Home→Editing→Find & Select** 🔍**→Find**.
3. Type **Contoso** in the Find What box.
4. Click **Find Next** two times.

   The first click finds the first occurrence. The second click finds the next, and final, occurrence.

5. Click the **Replace** tab in the Find and Replace box.

   Verify that the Find What box displays Contoso.

6. Type **Labyrinth** in the Replace With box.
7. Click **Replace All** to change the two occurrences of the word *Contoso* to *Labyrinth*.
8. Click **OK** in the Microsoft Excel message box.
9. Close the Find and Replace box.
10. Save the file.

Common Features on the Review Tab

In this section, you will learn about the features on the Review tab that are used in a similar manner throughout multiple Microsoft applications, including Word, Excel, Access, and PowerPoint.

Spelling & Grammar

Whether you are working in a Word document, an Excel worksheet, an Access database, or a PowerPoint presentation, you should always check the spelling and proofread carefully before you print or share the file with anyone. The Spelling feature reviews the file for misspelled words or words that do not match the Microsoft dictionary for that computer.

DEVELOP YOUR SKILLS: 01-D11

In this exercise, you will use the Spelling feature to correct mistakes.

1. Save your workbook as: **01-D11-Spelling**
2. Insert a new sheet into the workbook.
3. Type **Parctice makes prefect** in **cell A1** and tap ⌷Enter⌷.

   Yes, you are deliberately typing misspelled words so you will have a worksheet that can be spellchecked in the next few steps!
4. Type **Poepple nottace spelling mistakes** and tap ⌷Enter⌷.
5. Choose **Review→Proofing→Spelling** ⌷abc⌷ to launch the Spelling checker.

   Excel asks if you want to continue checking at the beginning of the sheet.
6. Click **Yes**.

   The first spelling mistake is found. Parctice *is not in the dictionary, so the suggested word is* Practice.
7. Click **Change** to accept the suggestion and locate the next misspelled word.
8. Continue correcting two more misspelled words (*People* and *notice*), and then click **OK** when the spell check is complete.

   Since prefect *is a word (just not the correct word for this sentence), it is not identified as a misspelled word when running the spelling checker. You must remember to proofread your work!*
9. Select **cell A1**, then in the Formula Bar double-click **prefect** and type: **perfect**

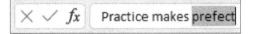

   The figure above shows the incorrectly spelled word selected in the Formula Bar after a double click. The figure below shows the corrected word.

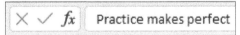

10. Save the file.

Thesaurus

There are times when you end up using a word over and over and over again! Instead of using the same word, you could use a synonym. The Thesaurus provides definitions, word forms, synonyms (words with similar meanings), antonyms (words that are opposite in meaning), and word forms in other languages when dictionaries of other languages are installed on your computer.

In this exercise, you will use the Thesaurus feature to replace a word with one of its synonyms.

1. Save your workbook as: **O1-D12-Proofing**
2. Select the **2. Analyze** worksheet tab and then select **cell D16**.
3. Choose **Review→Proofing→Thesaurus** ▦.
4. In the Thesaurus pane, hover the mouse pointer over the word *Tourism*, (below the *Tourism (n.)* category) click the **menu** button ﹀, and then choose **Insert** to replace *Travel* with *Tourism*.
5. Close the Thesaurus pane.
6. Save the file.

Other Common Features

In the preceding exercises you learned about features found on multiple programs' Ribbons. Here are three additional common features that are available no matter what Microsoft Office program is being used.

Help

When you are working in Microsoft Office, you may need to find out more about a topic as it relates to the application. Located at the top of the application window in the Search box, this box provides a quick way to access help or locate a feature in the application. You'll see different kinds of results depending on what you type in this box. Sometimes you'll see a shortcut to a command or feature, while other times you'll see a definition or a link to the full help page documentation. To view a list of Help topics, tap the F1 function key on the keyboard.

Another Help feature is the *Tell Me More* link that may display at the bottom of a button's help tip. When you click the link, the Help window displays with more information about that specific feature. Using this method, you learn more about the feature without typing any search text. Similarly, right-clicking a cell and choosing Smart Lookup is a fast way to get information about the contents of that cell, such as definitions of a word, website links, or images related to the contents.

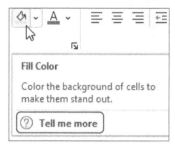

Some buttons display useful help tips with a Tell Me More link when you point to them.

Take a Screenshot

The Screenshot button in Excel allows you to take a picture of anything you see on your screen and insert that picture into any Office program without having to use a separate app (such as the Windows Snipping Tool). The Available Windows gallery gives you the option of inserting any of the open windows on your computer, or, if you only need part of a window, you can use the Screen Clipping option. The Screen Clipping tool returns you to the most recent window, fades the display to white, and changes the mouse pointer to crosshairs that you use to drag and select the area of the window you want to capture.

DEVELOP YOUR SKILLS: 01-D13

In this exercise, you will use the Tell Me More help link and the Search box to learn more about the Insights feature. Then, you will use the Screenshot feature to copy what you found onto a new worksheet.

1. Save your workbook as: **01-D13-Help**
2. On the Ribbon, go to the **Formulas** tab.
3. Point to but don't clck the Insert Function fx button on the ribbon (*not* the Formula Bar) to see the name of the button, the keyboard shortcut, a description of the button, and the Tell Me More link.
4. Click the **Tell Me More** link and then scroll through the content on creating formulas in the Help pane on the right side of the screen; close the Help window.
5. Click in the **Search** box at the top of the Excel window and type: **Smart Lookup**

   Observe the options Microsoft displays in the Search box.
6. From the displayed list, click the **Get Help on "Smart Lookup"** option to display the results in the Help pane.
7. Click the **Get Insights into What You're Working on with Smart Lookup** or similar option.
8. Read about the Smart Lookup feature.
9. Scroll to the bottom of the Help pane and click **Read Article in Browser**.

   Your web browser opens to the Microsoft website and displays the help page.
10. Click the **Excel** button on the taskbar to return to Excel.
11. Insert a new sheet into the workbook.
12. Choose **Insert→Illustrations→Screenshot** 📷.
13. Click **Screen Clipping** to display the browser window with the article in it, and then drag over a portion of the browser window to take a screenshot of it.

    You are returned to Excel and the screenshot is pasted on the new sheet.
14. Save the workbook and then close Excel.

1 Tracking Customer Data

In this chapter, you will use Excel to enter detailed information about customers into a worksheet. You will learn about fundamental Excel features as you create and modify a simple worksheet. By the end of the chapter, you will have a solid grasp of the basic tools used to create worksheets in Excel.

LEARNING OBJECTIVES

- Enter data into a worksheet
- Navigate a workbook
- Format a worksheet
- Apply number and date formats
- Enter a series of related data
- Print a worksheet
- Adjust the view with Zoom tools

CHAPTER TIMING

- Concepts & Practice: 01:10:00
- Self-Assessment: 00:15:00
- Total: 01:25:00

PROJECT: TRACKING CUSTOMER INVOICES

Airspace Travel is a company that provides luxurious travel packages to tropical destinations. It is a small, family-run business, and the owners want your help tracking their customer accounts using Excel.

You will use Excel to enter information about each customer who books a trip. Some of the important information to include for each customer is the airline, destination, number of guests, and cost per person.

Learning Resources: **boostyourskills.lablearning.com**

Introducing Excel

Microsoft Excel is a very popular tool used by millions of people every day. Why do people like it? Partly because it makes work easier! Excel is a worksheet program that allows you to work with numbers and data much more quickly and efficiently than with the pen-and-paper method.

Excel can perform instant calculations and process, analyze, and store large amounts of data. It can perform a variety of tasks such as:

- Creating payment schedules and budgets
- Creating sales reports and performing sales analysis
- Tracking invoices and controlling inventory
- Creating databases or analyzing data imported from a database

The more you learn about and become skilled at using Excel, the more ways you will discover to make work fast and easy.

What Is a Worksheet?

An Excel file is called a *workbook,* and it contains one or more worksheets (also called spreadsheets) that can be used for small tasks or to create large databases of information. Each worksheet is made up of rows and columns of individual cells, into which you can add data. When you open a new blank workbook, the selected cell is A1. The cell is referred to as A1 because this is where column A meets row 1.

The selected cell, also known as the *active cell,* is indicated by the thick box around it. The active cell is where you can type data or insert objects into your worksheet.

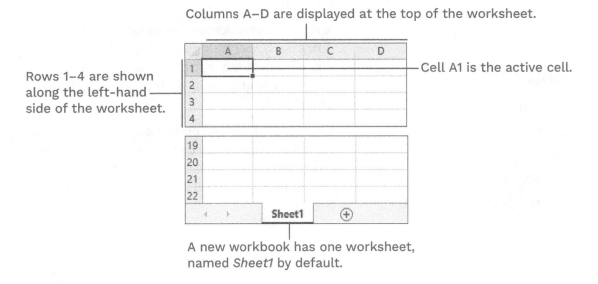

Columns A–D are displayed at the top of the worksheet.

Rows 1–4 are shown along the left-hand side of the worksheet.

Cell A1 is the active cell.

A new workbook has one worksheet, named *Sheet1* by default.

Cell Ranges

For many tasks, you will want to select a group of cells instead of a single cell. A group of cells is referred to as a range. A range is identified by the first and last cell, separated by a colon. The cells in a range are adjacent (side by side), but you can also choose to select two or more nonadjacent ranges.

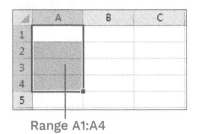

Range A1:A4

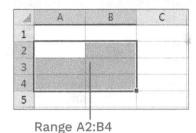

Range A2:B4

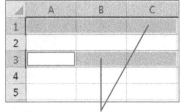

Nonadjacent ranges A1:C1, A3:C3

Cell Selection and the Mouse Pointer

One of the challenges for new Excel users is getting used to the different mouse functions. The shape of the mouse pointer changes as you point to different parts of the Excel window, so pay close attention to the shape of the pointer to ensure you're performing the intended action.

MOUSE POINTER SHAPES	
Pointer Shape	**Task**
⬧	Click to select a cell; drag to select a range of cells
⬚	Drag to move the selected cell contents to another location
I	Enter or edit cell contents in the cell or in the Formula Bar
+	Drag the fill handle to fill adjacent cells with a series of numbers, dates, or formulas
↓ →	Select an entire column or row, such as column A or row 1

Entering and Editing Data

Data is easily entered into Excel by selecting a cell and typing. If a cell already contains data, you can double-click the cell to edit it; or, to replace the existing data, just start typing (no need to delete it first!). Text is used for headings or descriptive data, and numbers can either be typed into a cell or calculated with a formula.

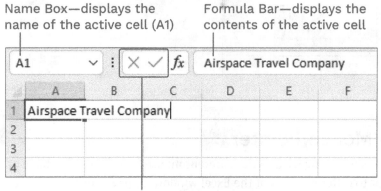

Name Box—displays the name of the active cell (A1)

Formula Bar—displays the contents of the active cell

Cancel and Enter—cancels or completes the entry

Completing Cell Entries

After typing or editing data in a cell, you need to complete the entry before you can continue. The method you use to complete the entry will determine which cell becomes active next.

Excel is in Ready mode when a cell is selected and Enter mode when data is being inserted. The difference between Enter and Ready modes is that many Excel features are unavailable while you are entering data.

Tapping Enter, Tab, or any of the arrow keys (→, ←, ↑, ↓) will complete the entry as shown in the table below. Another option is to use the Enter button on the Formula Bar, which will keep the current cell active.

COMPLETING A CELL ENTRY	
Completion Method	**New Active Cell Location**
Enter	Moves one cell down
Tab	Moves one cell to the right
→ ← ↑ ↓	Moves to the next cell in the direction of the arrow key
✕	Cancels the entry (or modification) and keeps the current cell active
✓	Completes the entry without moving

In this exercise, you will enter the data for your worksheet title and headings.

1. Start Excel.
2. Click **New Blank Workbook** at the top of the Excel Home screen.
3. Save your workbook in your **Excel Chapter 1** folder as: **E1-D1-Invoices**
4. Type **Airspace Travel Company** in **cell A1** and tap ⌷Enter⌷ to complete the entry.

   Notice that cell A2 is now the active cell.
5. Type **Monthly Customer Invoices** in **cell A2** and tap ⌷Enter⌷ to complete the entry.

   So far you've used the ⌷Enter⌷ key to move down column A while entering the data. Now you'll use the ⌷Tab⌷ key to move across row 3 as you enter more data.
6. Type **First Name** in **cell A3** and tap ⌷Tab⌷ to complete the entry, which also moves the active cell one cell to the right.
7. Type **Last Name** in **cell B3** and tap ⌷Tab⌷.

   The First Name text in cell A3 is no longer fully visible because it's wider than column A. Long entries are cut off like this when the cell to their right contains data. You will fix this in a later exercise.
8. Type **Provider** in **cell C3** and tap ⌷Tab⌷.
9. Type **Destination** in **cell D3** and tap ⌷Tab⌷.
10. Type **# of Guests** in **cell E3**, but this time click **Enter** ☑ on the Formula Bar to complete the entry.

    Cell E3 remains the active cell. Use Enter on the Formula Bar to complete entries when you want the current cell to remain active. Your worksheet should now look like this:

	A	B	C	D	E	F
1	Airspace Travel Company					
2	Monthly Customer Invoices					
3	First Nam	Last Name	Provider	Destinatic	# of Guests	

11. Save the workbook.

| **NOTE!** Always leave the file open at the end of an exercise unless instructed to close it.

Navigating Around a Worksheet

Navigating around your worksheet quickly is an important skill to master. The following table lists some useful keystrokes for changing the active cell. You can also click with the mouse to select the desired cell or type a cell name into the Name Box to quickly jump to it. A worksheet has up to 1,048,576 rows and up to 16,384 columns, so for large amounts of data, you definitely want a quicker way to get around than simply scrolling!

NAVIGATION METHODS	
Keystroke(s)	**How the Active Cell Changes**
→ ← ↑ ↓	Moves one cell right, left, up, or down
Home	Moves to the beginning (column A) of current row
Ctrl + Home	Moves to the home cell, usually cell A1
Ctrl + End	Moves to the last cell in active part of worksheet
Page Down	Moves down one visible screen
Page Up	Moves up one visible screen
Alt + Page Down	Moves one visible screen to the right
Alt + Page Up	Moves one visible screen to the left
Ctrl + G	Displays the Go To dialog box

Using AutoComplete to Enter Data

When inputting data, consistency is extremely important. If you are entering employee records in a large database, you want to ensure that information such as department names and position titles is entered accurately; for example, you wouldn't want some employees to be listed in the *Financial* department and others to be listed in the *Finance* department because that would create problems when looking up, sorting, and filtering your data.

Excel has a feature that helps with this problem and also saves you time when repeatedly entering the same text. AutoComplete suggests text for you as you type, using data from the same column. For example, if you type *Accounting* for a department name in one cell, and then farther down in the same column you type the letter *A*, AutoComplete will suggest *Accounting*. You can either accept the suggestion the way you normally complete a cell entry or ignore it and keep typing.

Rearranging Data in Excel

To move or copy content in Excel, you can use the tools in the Clipboard group of the Home tab on the Ribbon, similarly to how you would in other Microsoft Office apps. However, Excel has many unique options for pasting data that aren't available in the other Office apps. The Paste Options are accessible from the Ribbon, the shortcut menu when you right-click a cell after copying, or the Paste Options button that appears after you have pasted something into a worksheet.

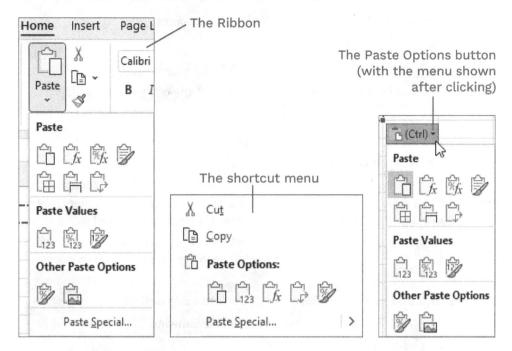

Some of the important paste options unique to Excel that are frequently used include pasting values, pasting formulas, transposing data, or pasting only the formatting from the copied cell or range.

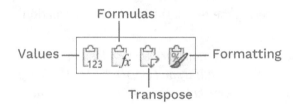

To quickly move data, you can also point to the border of the selected cell (or range), and when the mouse pointer changes to a four-headed arrow, you can then drag the cell's contents to the desired location. To copy instead of move data, hold down Ctrl while dragging. These two methods are best used when the original location and new location are relatively close and both are visible on the same screen.

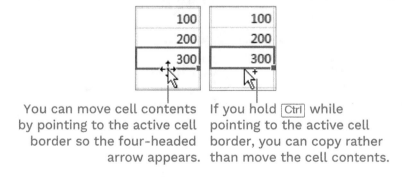

You can move cell contents by pointing to the active cell border so the four-headed arrow appears.

If you hold Ctrl while pointing to the active cell border, you can copy rather than move the cell contents.

DEVELOP YOUR SKILLS: E1-D2

In this exercise, you will enter the customer data below each of the column headings.

1. Save your workbook as: **E1-D2-Invoices**
2. Press Home followed by ↓ to move the active cell to **cell A4**.
3. Enter this data for Eric Snow in **row 4** and press Tab to complete the entry in each cell:

3	First Nam	Last Name	Provider	Destinatic	# of Guest
4	Eric	Snow	Sunwind	Jamaica	

4. Type **2** in **cell E4** and tap Enter to complete the entry.

   The active cell moves to A5, the beginning of a new row. Excel presumes you are finished entering data in the row and wish to start a new row. This is one of Excel's built-in data entry features that make it faster to enter data into a worksheet or database. As long as you enter data using the Tab key continuously from left to right, the Enter key will bring you back to the first column of data to begin the next row. If the active cell does not move from E4 to A5, it is likely because you used the mouse to select a cell rather than Tab.

5. Type **Alison** in **cell A5**, **Lobosco** in **cell B5**, and *only* the letter **S** in **cell C5**.

   In cell C5, Excel's AutoComplete feature prompts you with the name Sunwind.

3	First Nam	Last Name	Provider	Destinatic	# of Guests
4	Eric	Snow	Sunwind	Jamaica	2
5	Alison	Lobosco	Sunwind		

6. Tap Tab to accept the suggestion, then continue entering the rest of the customer information as shown below, starting from **cell D5**.

   As you type the data, use Tab to accept the AutoComplete suggestions for the Provider and Destination columns when possible; the goal is to enter the data quickly and efficiently. Tap Enter at the end of each row to finish one customer's information and begin entering it for the next. Be aware that long entries won't fully display until the column is widened.

	A	B	C	D	E
3	First Name	Last Name	Provider	Destination	# of Guests
4	Eric	Snow	Sunwind	Jamaica	2
5	Alison	Lobosco	Sunwind	Mexico	2
6	Lacy	Henrich	TrueBlue	Dominican Republic	4
7	Will	Johns	Eastjet	Cuba	3
8	Nicki	Hollinger	Sunwind	Mexico	1
9	Lennard	Williams	TrueBlue	Brazil	6
10	Kerri	Knechtel	TrueBlue	Cuba	4
11	Karynn	Alida	Sunwind	Bahamas	2
12	David	Monton	Eastjet	Dominican Republic	2
13	Amanda	Campbell	Sunwind	Jamaica	7

7. Save the workbook.

Adjusting Column Width and Row Height

To create enough space to properly see your text, you may need to adjust the column width and row height. A key step is to select the desired row(s) or column(s) before adjusting the size. Column width and row height can be set precisely using Ribbon commands or adjusted manually by dragging with the mouse. Even better, AutoFit can adjust the size to accommodate the largest entry in the column or row.

In a new workbook, column width is 8.43 and row height is 15.00; however, you might notice that cells are wider than they are tall. This is because column width is measured in characters and row height is measured in points, similar to font size. One character is bigger than one point.

Home→Cells→Format→Column Width ⬚ or Row Height ⬚ | Right-click column/row heading→Column Width or Row Height

Home→Cells→Format→AutoFit | Double-click column/row heading borders

DEVELOP YOUR SKILLS: E1-D3

In this exercise, you will adjust the column widths using various methods to properly display the text in the cells.

1. Save your workbook as: **E1-D3-Invoices**
2. Follow these steps to manually adjust the width of **column A**:

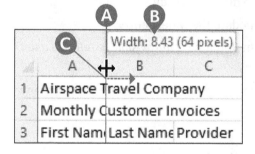

   A. Move the mouse pointer over the line between the column A and B headings to display the adjust pointer.

   B. Press and hold the left mouse button, and notice the ScreenTip displays the current width of column A (the default width is 8.43).

   C. Continue holding the left mouse button and drag right slightly, then release the mouse button. The text *First Name* should now be fully visible in cell A3; if not, keep trying until you get it.

   As you drag, the column width is displayed as it changes. You can set column width to an exact amount this way, but it's difficult to be precise. You'll set precise widths later in this exercise.

3. Widen **column B** until *Last Name* is visible in **cell B3** or try to set the width to 10.00.
4. Widen **column C** slightly or try to set the width to 10.00.

   Now you will use the Ribbon to ensure that columns A, B, and C are all set to exactly 10.00.

5. Follow these steps to select **columns A–C**:

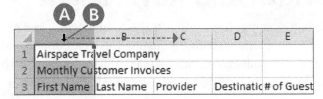

A. Position the mouse pointer on the **column A** heading and then press and hold the left mouse button.

B. Drag right until **columns A–C** are selected and then release the mouse button.

6. Choose **Home→Cells→Format→Column Width** to display the Column Width dialog box.

TIP! You will only see a number in the box if all three columns have the same width; otherwise, the box will be blank.

7. Type **10** in the box and click **OK**, which will set the widths of **columns A–C** to 10.

8. Follow these steps to use AutoFit to adjust the width of **column D**:

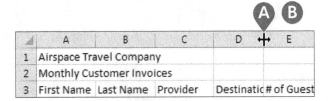

A. Point between the column D and E headings to display the adjust pointer.

B. Double-click to AutoFit **column D** to accommodate the widest entry.

Column D is now wide enough so the text Dominican Republic *is fully visible in cells D6 and D12.*

9. Save the workbook.

Formatting Cells

You may notice that unformatted data does not look very pleasing. The columns are too narrow, and the black-and-white color is plain and boring. Formatting is important not simply to make worksheets more appealing, but also to make it easier to read and interpret the data they contain. A textbook would be very hard to read if all the text were the same font, size, and color on a white page. Likewise, it is much easier to understand a worksheet if it is properly formatted.

Borders and Fill

Adding some color to your worksheet can accentuate the column headings and helps the data stand out. In addition to changing the font, style, and color of the text, you can use Fill Color to add color or shading inside a cell and use Borders to add lines around the cells. The drop-down menu buttons (⌄) give you more choices for lines and colors.

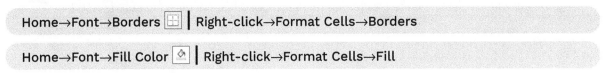

Home→Font→Borders 🔲 | Right-click→Format Cells→Borders

Home→Font→Fill Color 🖌 | Right-click→Format Cells→Fill

In this exercise, you will add color to your worksheet using fill colors, borders, and font colors.

1. Save your workbook as: **E1-D4-Invoices**

2. Follow these steps to select the column headings in the **range A3:E3**:

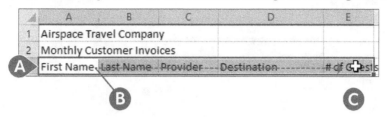

   A. Point to the middle of **cell A3** and then press and hold the left mouse button.

   B. Continue to hold the left mouse button as you drag right, along row 3, until the **range A3:E3** is selected.

   C. Release the mouse button to complete the selection.

3. Follow these steps to explore the Fill Color palette and apply a color:

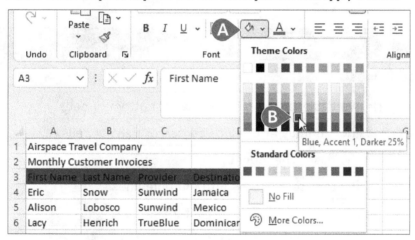

   A. Click the **Fill Color menu** button ⌄ to display the palette and slowly move the mouse pointer around the various colors, pausing on a few.

   When the mouse stops moving, a ScreenTip indicates the name of the color you are pointing at. The top row under Theme Colors gives you ten color options, with different shades for each in the column below.

   B. Choose **Blue, Accent 1, Darker 25%** (fifth column, fifth row).

4. With the range A3:E3 still selected, choose **Home→Font→Border menu button ⌄**.

5. Choose **Thick Outside Borders** to apply a thick border around the selected range.

6. For the same range choose **Home→Font→Font Color menu button ⌄** and choose **White, Background 1** (first column, first row).

7. Use the keyboard shortcut ⌈Ctrl⌉+⌊B⌋ to apply bold formatting.

   Now that you have modified the headings, it's time to work on the titles.

8. Select **cell A1** and choose **Home→Font→Font Size menu button ⌄** and choose **18**.

9. Now select **cell A2** and choose **Home→Font→Increase Font Size** two times to increase the font size to **14**.

10. Select the **range A1:A2** and then apply the **Blue, Accent 1, Darker 50%** (fifth column, sixth row) font color and **Bold** formatting.

11. Select the **range A4:B13** and apply **Bold**.

12. Click anywhere outside your data to deselect it.

	A	B	C	D	E
1	**Airspace Travel Company**				
2	**Monthly Customer Invoices**				
3	**First Name**	**Last Name**	**Provider**	**Destination**	**# of Guest**
4	Eric	Snow	Sunwind	Jamaica	2
5	Alison	Lobosco	Sunwind	Mexico	2

13. Save the workbook.

Cell Alignment

Excel's alignment tools let you adjust the arrangement of entries within cells. The default alignment for text data is left-aligned inside the cell, and the default for numerical data is right-aligned, as you can see in column E of your working file. The Alignment group on the Home tab provides you with the following options:

ALIGNMENT BUTTONS	
Button	**What It Does**
≡ ≡ ≡	Aligns entries vertically at the top, middle, or bottom of cells
≡ ≡ ≡	Aligns entries horizontally at the left, center, or right of cells
← →	Decreases or increases the indent
ab	Wrap Text; splits long text entries into multiple lines
⊟	Merge & Center; combines cells and centers content
≫	Adjusts the angle or rotation of your text

Merge & Center is a one-step method for simultaneously merging multiple cells into one cell and centering the content. This is often used for worksheet titles at the top of your sheet. You can also add an indent to the contents of a cell, which increases the distance of the text from the cell border. This adds more space, making it easier to read the data.

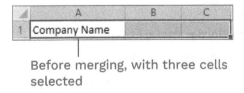

Before merging, with three cells selected

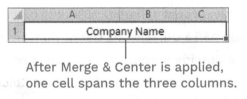

After Merge & Center is applied, one cell spans the three columns.

Home→Alignment │ Right-click→Format Cells→Alignment

Clear Formatting and Clear All

You may want to keep the text in a cell or range but clear all formatting. This is easy to do with the Clear Formatting feature. You can also remove text and formatting at the same time with Clear All.

Home→Editing→Clear ◈

DEVELOP YOUR SKILLS: E1-D5

In this exercise, you will adjust the alignment for your headings and data, and use Merge & Center for your titles.

1. Save your workbook as: **E1-D5-Invoices**
2. Select the **range A3:E3** and choose **Home→Alignment→Wrap Text**.

   Wrap Text takes a long entry and splits it into multiple lines, increasing row height at the same time.
3. With the range A3:E3 still selected, choose **Home→Alignment→Middle Align**.
4. With the headings still selected, choose **Home→Alignment→Center**.
5. Select the **range E4:E13** (the number of guests data) and apply **Center** alignment.
6. Select the **range A1:E1**.
7. Choose **Home→Alignment→Merge & Center** (do not click the menu button ⌄) to center the company name over the data below.
8. **Merge & Center** the **range A2:E2** to center the Monthly Customer Invoices subtitle.
9. Select the **range A4:A13** and choose **Home→Alignment→Increase Indent**.
10. Save the workbook.

Working with Numbers and Dates

Because Excel is often used to perform calculations, it's important to know how to enter numerical data properly. A number entered into Excel can be formatted in many ways—with a dollar sign, percent symbol, decimals, or no decimals—but the numerical entry in the cell does not change. Typically, to enter a numerical value into a cell, you simply type in the digits and adjust formatting after.

The default number format is General, which has no specific format. When a number format is applied to a cell, it remains with the cell even if the contents are changed or deleted. Here are some basic number format examples:

Number	Format	Result
2317.25	General	2317.25
2317.25	Comma Style	2,317.25
2317.25	Currency	$2,317.25
2317.25	Accounting	$ 2,317.25
0.25	Percent	25%

TIP! The differences between Currency and Accounting are the position of the $ sign and the indent from the right side of the cell.

The number format for the current cell is visible in the Number Format box on the Ribbon.

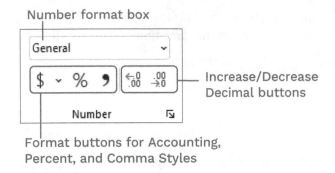

Number format box

General

$ ∨ % ,   ←0 .00 .00 →.0   Increase/Decrease Decimal buttons

Number

Format buttons for Accounting, Percent, and Comma Styles

Be aware that the numerical entry in the cell does not change when you increase or decrease the decimal (or when you change the number format). Doing so changes only the *appearance* of that number. Numbers with decimals can still have the decimals removed (decreased), but the number would then appear rounded up or rounded down from the actual entry, as shown in the following example. If the cell is used in a formula, the formula will use the actual numerical entry in the cell, *not the rounded number displayed on the screen.*

Number	Decimal Places	Result
23.64	3	23.640 (extra zero)
23.64	2	23.64 (no change)
23.64	1	23.6 (rounded down)
23.64	0	24 (rounded up)

Home→Number | Right-click→Format Cells→Number

Negative Numbers

Working with negative numbers is no different from working with other numbers, except that there are more options for displaying the negative values. Negative numbers have the currency, comma, and decimal options, but they can also be represented by a – (minus) symbol, red digits, parentheses, or both red digits and parentheses.

-12   12   (12)   (12)

Formatting examples for negative twelve

Date Entries

Date formatting is another kind of number formatting. After a cell has a date entered into it, you can change the display without changing the actual cell entry. Excel can also use dates to perform calculations in a formula.

A date can be entered many ways, though the best way is to enter it in the format MM/DD for the current year or MM/DD/YY for any other year. For example, 10/15 would be entered for October 15 of the current year, and 10/15/25 would be entered for October 15, 2025.

DEVELOP YOUR SKILLS: E1-D6

In this exercise, you will enter two new columns of information using currency and date formatting.

1. Save your workbook as: **E1-D6-Invoices**

2. In **cell F3**, enter the heading **Price Per Person** and tap Tab.

   Notice the font, fill, and wrap text formatting are copied from the previous headings, but the border style is not.

3. Enter the heading **Invoice Date** in **cell G3**.

4. Select the **range F3:G3** and apply **Thick Outside Borders**.

5. In **cell F4**, type the digits **899** and tap Tab.

6. In **cell G4**, type **9/8** and then click **Enter** ☑ on the Formula Bar.

   The digits 9/8 are automatically converted to display 8-Sep. In the Home→Number→Number Format box you can see the number format for cell G4 has changed to a Custom format.

7. Continue entering data in **columns F** and **G** as shown, starting in **cell F5**.

   The number format of the Invoice Date column is adjusted for you as you enter the data, as it was in cell G4. You will adjust the number format for the Price Per Person column after you have entered all the data.

	F	G
5	770	9/7
6	1200	9/1
7	950	9/9
8	875	9/8
9	800	9/8
10	560	9/5
11	870	9/8
12	650	9/6
13	900	9/9

8. Select the **range F4:F13** (the cells with the prices you just entered).

9. Choose **Home→Number→Accounting** (not the menu button ⌄) to apply the Accounting format to the selection.

   The prices now have a dollar sign, comma separator, and two decimal places. All the prices are even dollar amounts, so you can now eliminate the unnecessary decimals.

10. With the range F4:F13 still selected, choose **Home→Number→Decrease Decimal** twice.

11. Save the workbook.

Entering a Series Using AutoFill

When entering data into a worksheet, it is common to enter a series of data, which is a sequence of text, numbers, or dates. For example, you can enter a series of weekdays from Monday to Friday, a series of months from January to December, a series of numbers from 1 to 100, or a series of dates for the next two weeks.

Rather than type each item line by line, you only need to enter the first cell and then use AutoFill to quickly enter an entire column or row of data. To use AutoFill, you can drag the fill handle or double-click it (if there's adjacent data).

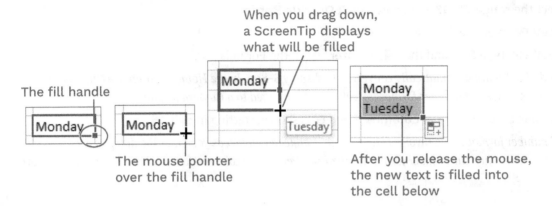

When you drag down, a ScreenTip displays what will be filled

The fill handle

The mouse pointer over the fill handle

After you release the mouse, the new text is filled into the cell below

Depending on the type of information in the selected cell(s), the fill handle performs different actions, such as copying, creating a series, or filling in a list. These figures show examples of series created with the AutoFill tool, which you can also try to create on your own in a blank Excel workbook.

Starting cell	Monday	Wed	March	Jan	Invoice 200	1st Day	10-Oct
AutoFill Results	Tuesday	Thu	April	Feb	Invoice 201	2nd Day	11-Oct
	Wednesday	Fri	May	Mar	Invoice 202	3rd Day	12-Oct
	Thursday	Sat	June	Apr	Invoice 203	4th Day	13-Oct
	Friday	Sun	July	May	Invoice 204	5th Day	14-Oct
	Saturday	Mon	August	Jun	Invoice 205	6th Day	15-Oct

When more than one cell is selected, the AutoFill tool will copy the pattern Excel finds in the selected data.

Starting cells	Monday	Jan		1	100	01-Jun
	Wednesday	Apr		2	120	01-Jul
AutoFill Results	Friday	Jul		3	140	01-Aug
	Sunday	Oct		4	160	01-Sep
	Tuesday	Jan		5	180	01-Oct
	Thursday	Apr		6	200	01-Nov
	Saturday	Jul		7	220	01-Dec

After you use AutoFill, the AutoFill Options ⊞ button appears below the filled cells. The AutoFill Options button allows you to modify the way the data was filled, and the options change depending on the type of data that was filled. For example, after filling in a series of dates, the option allows you to choose either days, weekdays, months, or years.

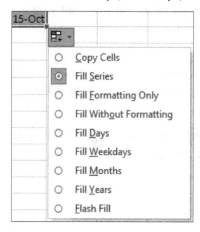

🌥 **View the video "Using AutoFill to Fill a Series."**

🌥 **View the video "Using AutoFill Options."**

DEVELOP YOUR SKILLS: E1-D7

In this exercise, you will enter invoice numbers for each customer using AutoFill.

1. Save your workbook as: **E1-D7-Invoices**
2. Type the column heading **Invoice #** in **cell H3** and tap ⌷Enter⌷.
3. In **cell H4**, type **#3982** and then click **Enter** on the Formula Bar so cell H4 remains active.

   The invoice number for Eric's trip is #3982. Invoice numbers will continue in sequence counting up by one, so the next invoice will be #3983 and so on.

4. Follow these steps to use AutoFill to enter the rest of the invoice numbers:

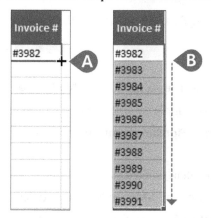

   A. In the active cell, place the mouse over the fill handle so the mouse pointer changes to the black cross.

   B. Drag down to **cell H13** to fill in the rest of the series.

   The invoice numbers have now been entered for all customers, ending with #3991 in cell H13.

5. Save the workbook.

Printing Worksheets

Now that you've entered all the required information into the worksheet, you may want to print your data. Although printing is becoming less common in the digital age, there may be times when you need a paper copy.

Printing a worksheet is simple, although sometimes adjustments need to be made so the cells, columns, and rows fit nicely on the page. To adjust the way your worksheet prints, you can use the Scale to Fit feature. This automatically resizes your content to print the desired number of pages.

Excel will not normally print the gridlines around the cells or the row and column headings, though you can change this setting in the Sheet Options group on the Page Layout tab of the Ribbon.

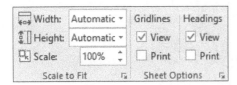

Because your workbook can contain multiple worksheets, there are three options for printing. In Backstage View you can choose from Print Active Sheets, which is the default option, Print Entire Workbook, which prints all worksheets in the workbook, or Print Selection, which will print only the currently selected cell(s).

> File→Print→Settings

> Page Layout→Scale to Fit

> Page Layout→Sheet Options

DEVELOP YOUR SKILLS: E1-D8

In this exercise, you will put the finishing touches on your worksheet. Then you will access the print preview and prepare your worksheet for printing.

1. Save your workbook as: **E1-D8-Invoices**
2. Select the **range A3:H3** and choose **Home→Font→Border menu button ⌄→No Border**.

   This removes all borders from the column headings so you can apply a border around all headings.

3. With the range A3:H3 still selected, choose **Home→Font→Border menu button ⌄→ Thick Outside Borders**.

   Now you need to center the titles over the data, including the newly added columns.

4. In **row 1** select the **range A1:H1** and choose **Home→Alignment→Merge & Center** twice.

   The first click of Merge & Center removes the merge formatting from the first five columns; the second click applies the merge formatting across all eight columns.

5. Select the **range A2:H2** and, again, choose **Home→Alignment→Merge & Center** twice.

   Both titles should now be centered over your data.

Change Print Options

6. Choose **File→Print** to access the print preview.

   Notice the document will print on one page, with the Invoice # column appearing at the right side of the page. If more columns of data were added they would print on a separate page. Also notice that the gridlines, which are the lines around the individual cells on the worksheet, do not print, nor do the row or column headings (A, B, C, 1, 2, 3, etc.).

7. Click **Back** ⊖ to return to your worksheet.

   You might see a dashed line between column H and column I, which indicates the print area for your worksheet. Next you will select an area of the sheet to print.

8. Select the **range A1:H8** (the titles, headings, and data for the first five customers) and then choose **File→Print** to access print preview again.

9. In the Settings section, choose **Print Active Sheets→Print Selection**.

   The print preview changes to show that the print area will include only the first five customers now.

10. In the Settings section, choose **Portrait Orientation→Landscape Orientation**.

    The printout will be much easier to read now, with the page turned to Landscape. Do not print at this time.

11. Save the workbook.

Zoom Tools

You may want to adjust the view to focus on one area of your worksheet, or you may want to get a broad view of the entire worksheet. The Zoom tools allow you to increase or decrease the magnification of your worksheet so you can see more or less of the worksheet at one time. Changing the view does not change how the worksheet will print. You can select a range of cells and click Zoom to Selection to focus on just that area of the worksheet, or you can jump back to 100% view to see your work in "real" size.

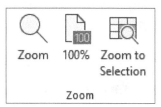

The Zoom tools on the View tab of the Ribbon allow you to customize magnification settings.

The Zoom slider on the status bar allows you to make quick adjustments by clicking + or –.

View→Zoom→Zoom

▎DEVELOP YOUR SKILLS: E1-D9

In this exercise, you will use the Zoom tools to focus on different areas of the worksheet.

1. Save your workbook as: **E1-D9-Invoices**

2. Select the customer invoice data in the **range A3:H13**.

3. Choose **View→Zoom→Zoom to Selection**.

   Your screen view will magnify so the range fills the entire screen; the exact zoom level will depend on your screen size.

4. Choose **View→Zoom→100%**.

   This returns the worksheet to its actual size.

5. Choose **View→Zoom→Zoom**.

6. In the Zoom dialog box, choose **Custom**, type **120** in the % box, and click **OK**.

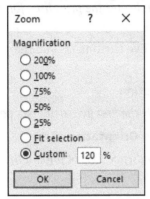

   Another option for quickly adjusting Zoom level is to use the Zoom slider on the status bar on the bottom-right side of the Excel window.

7. On the Zoom slider, click **Zoom Out** to reduce the magnification to 110%.

   When you save a file, it also saves the zoom settings so it will display the same the next time the file is opened.

8. Save the workbook.

Other Navigation Methods

Navigating a worksheet is simple using the mouse, scroll bar, and keyboard keys. However, as your workbook becomes larger and more complex, you may want other, faster methods of finding information.

Find

If you are looking for specific text or values, you can use the Find feature. Find searches within the worksheet to find the text or number provided, and the results show the exact cell location where the item is found. The results also show the entire cell value where the search string was found and can be used to navigate to that cell. Other options include searching for formatting; searching the entire workbook; and searching formulas, values, or comments.

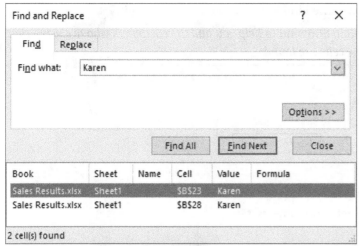

In this example, to find Karen's sales, searching for *Karen* shows two results in the Sales Results workbook on Sheet 1, in cells B23 and B28.

Home→Editing→Find & Select 🔍

DEVELOP YOUR SKILLS: E1-D10

In this exercise, you will use Find to search through the workbook.

1. Save your workbook as: **E1-D10-Invoices**
2. Choose **Home→Editing→Find & Select→Find**.
3. Type **David** in the Find What box and then click **Find All**.

   The result shows one cell found and the active cell jumps to cell A12, which contains David. *Now you will expand the search to the entire workbook.*

4. If the Within box is not showing on the Find tab of the Find and Replace dialog box, click **Options >>**.
5. In the Within menu, click **Sheet** to expand the options and select **Workbook**.

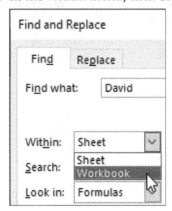

6. Click **Find All**.

   The result still shows just one cell found with David's name, since there are no other sheets in the workbook.

7. To start a new search, type **Sunwind** in the Find What box and click **Find All**.

The results now show all cells that contain Sunwind *to help you find the customers who are using that provider. For this search, five applicable cells are found.*

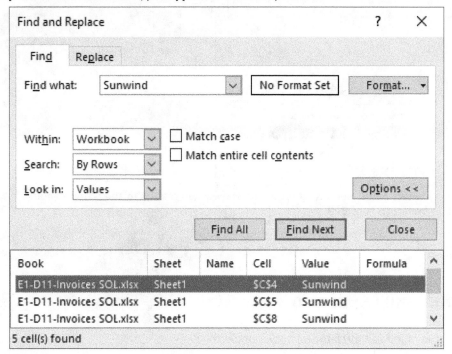

8. Scroll to the bottom of the results and click the last one; this takes you to **cell C13**, beside *Amanda Campbell*.

9. Close the Find and Replace dialog box.

10. Save the file.

Go To or the Name Box

The Go To command can be useful if you know the cell location you want to move to. Rather than scrolling, you can jump directly to that cell. The Go To dialog box will also show as many as four recently used cell locations should you need to go back to that spot again. If the workbook contains cells with defined names, you will see them listed in the Go To dialog box, which you can use to jump to that cell.

Here you can enter your desired cell location into the Reference box. Keep in mind cell references are not case-sensitive, so you can use either upper- or lowercase letters.

The Name box can also be used like the Go To command. Simply type the cell you want to jump to in the Name box and tap [Enter] to move to that cell.

DEVELOP YOUR SKILLS: E1-D11

In this exercise, you will use Go To to navigate the workbook.

1. Save your workbook as: **E1-D11-Invoices**
2. Choose **Home→Editing→Find & Select→Go To**.
3. In the Go To dialog box, type **a4** in the Reference box and click **OK**.

   The selected cell is now cell A4, where the customer data begins below the headings.

4. Choose **Home→Editing→Find & Select→Go To** again.
5. This time, below Reference type **as700** and then click **OK** or tap [Enter].

   Now you have the cell selected in column AS, row 700! As you can see, you can jump to any cell in the entire workbook, even cells that contain no data.

6. Choose **Home→Editing→Find & Select→Go To** once more.

   You will see a list including some of the recent cell locations you have searched for.

7. Click the cell reference **$A$4** in the Go To list and then click **OK**.
8. Save your work and close Excel.

Self-Assessment

Check your knowledge of this chapter's key concepts and skills using the online Self-Assessment Quiz.

Calculating Student Grades Using Formulas

In this chapter, you will use Excel to work with multiple worksheets created to record student grades. You will start by using formulas to calculate grade totals and grade percentages. You will also learn about managing and organizing worksheets to insert, delete, and even hide data, and also to make your data easier to find.

LEARNING OBJECTIVES

- Use formulas to perform calculations
- Rearrange data on a worksheet
- Manage multiple worksheets

CHAPTER TIMING

- Concepts & Practice: 01:10:00
- Self-Assessment: 00:15:00
- Total: 01:25:00

PROJECT: TRACKING STUDENT GRADES

LearnFast College is a school that provides fast-paced learning programs for college students. As an instructor there, you need to keep track of your students' grades for an Introduction to Business course. Excel will help you record marks and quickly calculate final grades for the course using a variety of formulas.

Learning Resources: **boostyourskills.lablearning.com**

Creating Formulas

Excel uses formulas to perform calculations, which are written as mathematical problems. To create a formula, you should always begin by typing the equals (=) sign in the cell. Then you list the numbers or cells to use in the formula, along with the operation to be performed.

The Formula Bar always displays the formula while the cell displays the results.

The formula =2*250 is entered in cell D2 and is displayed in the Formula Bar.

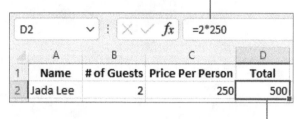

	A	B	C	D
1	Name	# of Guests	Price Per Person	Total
2	Jada Lee	2	250	500

The result of the formula, 500, is displayed in cell D2.

Mathematical Operators

Addition, subtraction, multiplication, and division are frequently used to perform calculations in Excel. Knowing the correct keystroke for each operation is important to ensure the correct result for your formulas.

KEYSTROKES FOR USING OPERATIONS IN FORMULAS			
Operation	**Keystroke**	**Example**	**Result**
Addition	+	=3+2	5
Subtraction	-	=3-2	1
Multiplication	*	=3*2	6
Division	/	=3/2	1.5
Exponent	^	=3^2	9

Cell References

Rather than typing numbers into your formulas, it is best to use cell references whenever possible. A cell reference takes the place of a number in a formula and makes it easier to copy formulas down a column or across a row. So, instead of =2*250, you could use =B2*C2 with the value *2* in cell B2, and the value *250* in cell C2.

View the video "Using Simple Formulas."

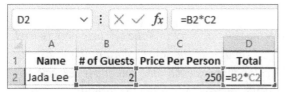

The formula in cell D2 references cells B2 and C2.

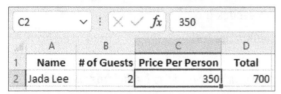

The formula result is 500.

Cell references can be typed using upper- or lowercase letters, or you can simply click with the mouse on the cell you want to use.

Another advantage of cell references is that Excel automatically recalculates the formula if the value in the cell reference changes. In the preceding example, if the value in cell C2 is changed to 350, the formula in cell D2 would automatically update to show the new result, 700, without any effort required.

C2		fx	350	
	A	B	C	D
1	Name	# of Guests	Price Per Person	Total
2	Jada Lee	2	350	700

The formula result in cell D2 is updated immediately when cell C2 is changed.

Order of Operations

When there is more than one operation in a formula, Excel must decide which operation to perform first. Excel follows the standard mathematical order of operations, commonly known by the acronym PEMDAS. That is, *Parentheses come first (also called brackets or round brackets), then Exponents, Multiplication, Division, Addition, and Subtraction.* PEMDAS is often remembered with the phrase "Please Excuse My Dear Aunt Sally."

☁ **View the video "Understanding Order of Operations."**

It's important to understand the order of operations because it can significantly change the outcome of your formula. The formula =2+3*5 would result in 17 because 3*5 is the first operation and then 2+15 is 17. The formula =(2+3)*5, on the other hand, results in 25, because (2+3) is the first operation and then 5*5 is 25.

DEVELOP YOUR SKILLS: E2-D1

In this exercise, you will create formulas to calculate the students' grades.

1. Start Excel, open **E2-D1-Grades** from your **Excel Chapter 2** folder, and save it as:
   E2-D1-NewGrades

   The Security Warning bar may display the first time you open this or another file. In this course, you can safely click Enable Content to continue opening the file.

2. Select **cell F6**, type **=D6+E6**, and then tap Enter .

    As you type each cell reference, Excel adds color to both the cell reference and the cell being referenced. The text D6 turns blue, and the cell has a border and light shading of the same color around it. As you continue typing the formula, the text E6 turns red. The color changes each time you add a new cell reference, which helps you visualize the cell references while entering or editing the formula.

    You entered a formula that added the two quiz scores, and cell F6 should now show the total of 172. Now you will enter the next formula using the mouse instead of typing the cell references.

3. Type **=** in **cell F7**, click **cell D7**, type **+** and click **cell E7**, and finally click **Enter** ✓ .

    The formula is similar, but this time the cell references refer to the information in row 7 and the result is 199. Notice that the formula is visible in the Formula Bar and the result is visible in the worksheet cell. Cell F6 uses cell references to cells D6 and E6, and cell F7 refers to cells D7 and E7, which means the relative position is the same and you can therefore use AutoFill to copy the formula down the column instead of manually entering it for each student.

4. Point to the fill handle in **cell F7** and drag down to **cell F17**.

    The quiz totals are calculated for all students. Now you will calculate project totals for the class.

5. Select **cell J6** and then type **=H6+I6** and click **Enter**.

6. Point to the fill handle in **cell J6** and, this time, double-click it.

    Double-clicking automatically fills the cells down the column according to the rows used in adjacent columns.

    Next you will create a formula to calculate the percentage grade for projects by dividing the project total by 200.

7. Select **cell K6**, type **=** and click **cell J6** to select it, and then type **/200** and click **Enter**.

    The mark has been calculated for the first student as 0.945, so next you will display it as a percentage. Then you will copy the formula down the column.

8. With cell K6 still selected, choose **Home→Number→Percent Style** % .

9. Point to the fill handle in **cell K6** and double-click it to fill the formula down **column K**.

10. Save the workbook.

Rearranging Data

When using a worksheet there may be times when you need to do more than simply enter data row by row. You may need to insert more information in the middle of existing data, remove chunks of data already entered, or move cells or entire sections of data around. You can also sort your data to put it into a more usable arrangement.

Insert and Delete Rows, Columns, and Cells

To add more data into your existing data, it might make sense to insert a new cell, column, or row. You can add one cell, row, or column, at a time, or several at once. Columns are inserted to the left of your selected column, and rows are inserted above your selected row. Inserting a cell or cells allows you to shift the existing data either right or down.

> Home→Cells→Insert 🔲 | Right-click column/row heading→Insert

> Home→Cells→Delete 🔳 | Right-click column/row heading→Delete

DEVELOP YOUR SKILLS: E2-D2

In this exercise, you will insert and delete both rows and columns, and insert cells to enter additional student data into the gradebook.

1. Save your workbook as: **E2-D2-NewGrades**

2. Select the cell with Sarah's name, **cell A16**, and choose **Home→Cells→Insert menu button** ∨→ **Insert Sheet Rows**.

   The data for rows 16:17 is shifted down to rows 17:18, and a blank row is inserted in row 16, the currently selected row.

3. Enter the following data for a new student in **row 16**:

First	Last	Student ID#	Quiz 1	Quiz 2	Quiz Total	Quiz %	Project 1	Project 2	Project Total	Project %
Robert	Moreira	53846	96	88	184		90	95	185	93%

   As you type in data, Excel automatically copies adjacent formulas. After entering the data for Quiz 1 and Quiz 2, the Quiz Total column should show 184 automatically; it's the result of the formula that adds the two quiz scores. After entering the two project marks, the total and percentage should also automatically calculate.

4. Select the cell with Todd's name, **cell A18**, and then choose **Home→Cells→Delete menu button** ∨→**Delete Sheet Rows**.

   All of Todd's information is removed from row 18. Now you need to add a third quiz score between columns E and F.

5. Follow these steps to insert a new column between **columns E** and **F**:

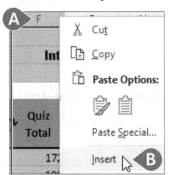

   A. Right-click the **column F** heading.

   B. Choose **Insert** from the menu.

   A new column is entered where column F was, and column F is shifted right to become column G.

6. Select the cell with the *Quiz 2* heading, **cell E5**, and use the **fill handle** to drag one cell to the right, inserting the heading name **Quiz 3** into **cell F5**.

   Because there are three quizzes now, the Quiz Total column formula needs to be updated to include the new quiz.

7. Select **cell G6**, which contains the total formula for Quiz 1 and Quiz 2.

8. To edit the formula, point to the Formula Bar and click to the right of the **cell E6** reference. Then type **+F6** and click **Enter**.

9. Point to the fill handle in **cell G6** and double-click to copy the new formula down **column G**.

    Even though the Quiz 3 grades in column F are blank, the formulas in column G will include those results once they are entered. Now you will insert a single cell for a new column heading.

10. Select the cell with the *Exam* heading, **cell M5**, and then choose **Home→Cells→Insert menu button ∨→Insert Cells.**

11. In the Insert dialog box, choose **Shift Cells Right** and click **OK**.

    The Exam *heading is shifted to the right into cell N5.*

12. With cell M5 still selected, type **Participation** as the new heading and then complete the entry.

13. Select the **range M5:O5** and adjust the column width to **11.5** so the headings fit properly.

14. Save the workbook.

Hide and Unhide Rows and Columns

Sometimes you may want to save data in your worksheet but have the information in certain rows or columns hidden from view. For example, a retailer might use an item's cost in one column to calculate the sale price in another. The cost column can be hidden from view to prevent customers from seeing how much profit the retailer is making, but the information is still saved and can still be used in a formula. Hidden rows and columns will not print, and a hidden row or column can easily be made visible using Unhide.

Hidden rows and columns can be identified by the gap in the column or row headings, as shown in the figure below:

	A	C
1		
3		

Row 2 and column B are hidden.

> **Home→Cells→Format→Hide & Unhide** | **Right-click column/row heading→Hide/Unhide**

Sort Data by Column

Excel can easily sort data in either alphabetic or numeric order, using any column of data. For example, you might want to sort by name, date, item number, or dollar amount. A sort keeps any adjacent data in the same row, so sorting by name, for example, means that data, such as addresses or phone numbers, stays with the correct name.

Sorting options depend on the type of data selected. For example, if numerical data is selected, the options are Smallest to Largest or Largest to Smallest. If text is selected, the options are either A to Z or Z to A.

> **Home→Editing→Sort & Filter** [↓]

In this exercise, you will hide and unhide a column and then sort the students first by grade and then by first name.

1. Save your workbook as: **E2-D3-NewGrades**

2. Point to the **column C** heading, right-click, and choose **Hide**.

   The Student ID# column is hidden from view, and now columns B and D are side by side.

3. Select **cell L6** and then choose **Home→Editing→Sort & Filter→Sort Largest to Smallest**.

   The students are now listed from highest to lowest according to the Project % column, so John is now the first student listed, Pamela is listed last, and all of the corresponding grades for each student are sorted along with the student names.

4. Select **cell A6** and choose **Home→Editing→Sort & Filter→Sort A to Z**.

   Ashley is now at the top of the list, and Sarah is at the bottom.

5. Point to the **column B** heading, press and hold the left mouse button, and then drag to the right to select **columns B–D**.

   To unhide columns or rows, you must select a continuous range surrounding the hidden column or row, so be sure to drag rather than selecting each column separately.

   After columns B–D are selected, there is no line separating the selected range.

6. Choose **Home→Cells→Format→Hide & Unhide→Unhide Columns**.

   Column C is once again displayed between columns B and D.

7. Save the workbook.

Managing Multiple Worksheets

By default, an Excel workbook contains one worksheet. You can, however, add multiple worksheets to be saved in the same workbook. This can make it easier to access different worksheets that are related to the same topic. You can also organize a workbook by deleting worksheets you don't need anymore, renaming the worksheets and changing the color of the sheet tab, and moving worksheets.

Insert and Delete Worksheets

Adding a new worksheet is as simple as clicking on the New Sheet button at the bottom of a workbook. When a workbook contains many worksheets, you may need to scroll through the worksheets using the left and right arrows located to the left of the sheet tabs at the bottom of the screen.

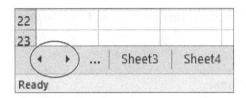

To delete a worksheet, you have to be more careful because, once deleted, you can't recover any of the data. Even the Undo button can't recover a deleted worksheet. For protection, Excel does ask you to confirm the action before you delete a worksheet.

Home→Cells→Insert ▦ menu button ⌄→Insert Sheet │ Right-click sheet tab→Insert...

Home→Cells→Delete ▣ menu button ⌄→Delete Sheet │ Right-click sheet tab→Delete

Rename Worksheets

The default names for worksheets don't really help someone understand what data is on the worksheet or what it is being used for. When you start adding more worksheets and need to quickly find the sheet with the information you need, it becomes important to name your sheets.

Names should be short and describe the purpose of the worksheet as clearly as possible. Certain characters, such as ? and /, are restricted, so it is best to stick to text and numbers. To rename a sheet, simply double-click the sheet tab and type the new name.

Examples of good worksheet names that are short, simple, and descriptive

Home→Cells→Format→Rename Sheet │ Double-click the sheet tab

DEVELOP YOUR SKILLS: E2-D4

In this exercise, you will insert a new sheet, delete a sheet, and rename a sheet.

1. Save your workbook as: **E2-D4-NewGrades**
2. Click the **New Sheet** button:

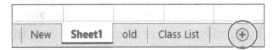

   Notice there is a new worksheet inserted to the right of the active sheet, New. *The default worksheet name is* Sheet *with a number, which increases each time you add a new sheet.*

3. Click the **old** worksheet tab to activate the sheet.
4. Choose **Home→Cells→Delete menu button ⌄→Delete Sheet** and click **Delete** or tap ⌷Enter⌷ when prompted in the dialog box.

   Because there is data on the old *worksheet, Excel asks you to confirm before it will delete and permanently remove the sheet. This step cannot be undone.*

5. To change the sheet name, double-click the **Sheet1** worksheet tab you just created; type **Participation** and tap [Enter].

6. Repeat step 5 to change the name of the **New** worksheet to: **Final Grades**

7. On the **Final Grades** worksheet, select the title in the merged **cell A2** and press [Ctrl]+[C] to copy the text *Introduction to Business*.

8. Click the **Participation** worksheet tab, ensure **cell A1** is the selected cell, and press [Ctrl]+[V] to paste the text.

9. In **cell A2**, below the class title, type **Participation Grades** and tap [Enter].

10. Select **cell A1**, choose **Home→Clipboard→Format Painter**, and then click **cell A2** to apply the formatting from cell A1.

    Clicking Format Painter once allows you to apply the formatting once, and then it is turned off. If you wanted to continue applying the same formatting to more cells or ranges, you would double-click the Format Painter instead.

    The range A2:O2 is merged and centered, and the text now has the same formatting as the title.

11. Save the workbook.

Move Worksheets

You may want to rearrange the order of the sheets at the bottom of the workbook. Excel doesn't have a feature for sorting worksheets, but you can drag worksheet tabs left or right to rearrange the order. You can also rearrange or duplicate the sheets using the Move or Copy dialog box.

Home→Cells→Format→Move or Copy Sheet | Right-click worksheet tab→Move or Copy

Change Worksheet Tab Colors

Finding the right worksheet can be a lot quicker if you use a system of colors for different worksheets. Colors could be assigned based on department, function, importance, or any method you choose. Adding a color to a worksheet tab can be done via the Ribbon or by right-clicking the tab.

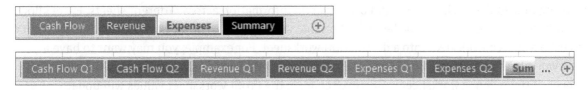

These are some examples of using tab colors to organize worksheets; notice the selected worksheet appears only lightly shaded.

Home→Cells→Format→Tab Color | Right-click worksheet tab→Tab Color

Hide Worksheets

Similar to hiding rows and columns, you may want to save a worksheet's information but have it hidden from view. Hiding a worksheet can also help organize your workbook if you have a lot of tabs or if the end-user will use only some of the worksheets. In this case, hiding the unused worksheets makes it a more user-friendly workbook. Once hidden, it is easy enough to unhide a worksheet when you need to use it again.

Home→Cells→Format→Hide & Unhide | Right-click worksheet tab→Hide/Unhide

In this exercise, you will reorganize and color the worksheet tabs.

1. Save your workbook as: **E2-D5-NewGrades**

2. Follow these steps to move the Final Grades worksheet and add a tab color:

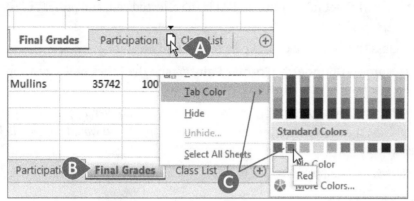

    A. Drag the **Final Grades** worksheet tab to the right side past the Participation sheet, as shown.

      Notice the small black arrow that follows your mouse pointer to indicate the new position of the sheet you are moving.

    B. Right-click the **Final Grades** worksheet tab.

    C. Choose **Tab Color→Standard Color Red**.

3. Change the color of the **Participation** sheet tab to **Standard Color Blue**.

    The Class List worksheet is not needed at this time, so you will hide it.

4. Right-click the **Class List** worksheet tab and choose **Hide**.

5. Save the workbook.

Create Cell References to Other Worksheets

When using multiple worksheets, you can use common information across different sheets. Excel allows you to link cells from different worksheets in the same workbook or in other workbooks. Linking inserts values from a source worksheet into a destination worksheet. For example, you may want to have a revenue worksheet and a profit worksheet; the profit worksheet can use the values from the revenue worksheet. If the revenue worksheet values ever change, the profit worksheet values will update automatically.

Referencing another worksheet requires the actual cell reference as well as the worksheet name and an exclamation point. Cell references to other workbooks require the workbook name, sheet name, and cell reference. Cell references to other worksheets or workbooks can be used to simply link the data or can be used in a formula.

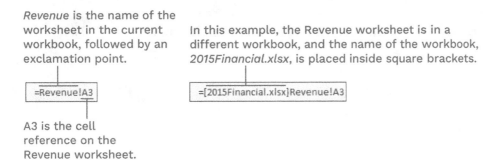

Revenue is the name of the worksheet in the current workbook, followed by an exclamation point.

In this example, the Revenue worksheet is in a different workbook, and the name of the workbook, *2015Financial.xlsx*, is placed inside square brackets.

=Revenue!A3

=[2015Financial.xlsx]Revenue!A3

A3 is the cell reference on the Revenue worksheet.

It is possible to manually type a cell reference to another worksheet or workbook; however, it is simpler and much more accurate to use the point-and-click method. If you point and click, Excel inserts all the necessary formatting, such as brackets and exclamation points.

DEVELOP YOUR SKILLS: E2-D6

In this exercise, you will use linking formulas to add student names to a worksheet.

1. Save your workbook as: **E2-D6-NewGrades**
2. Click the **Participation** worksheet tab to activate that worksheet, and then select **cell A4**.
3. Enter the heading **First** in **cell A4**, tap Tab, enter the heading **Last** in **cell B4**, and tap Enter.
4. In **cell A5**, type **=** and then click the **Final Grades** worksheet tab.

   You are now looking at the Final Grades worksheet but notice that the Formula Bar shows the beginning of the formula you are entering on the Participation worksheet, including the Final Grades worksheet name.

   Excel adds single quotes around any worksheet name that contains a space.

5. Select **cell A6** and then click **Enter** on the Formula Bar.

   WARNING! Completing the entry this way and not clicking the Participation worksheet tab is very important, because doing so would change your formula. Completing the entry instantly brings you back to the Participation worksheet. You will now see the name Ashley in cell A5 and the formula ='Final Grades'!A6 in the Formula Bar.

6. With cell A5 still selected, use the **fill handle** to drag one cell to the right, inserting the last name for Ashley into **cell B5**.
7. With the range A5:B5 still selected, drag the **fill handle** down to **row 16**.

   The names for all twelve students are now added to the Participation worksheet, and if the names are edited on the Final Grades worksheet, changes will automatically be updated on the Participation worksheet. Felecia has informed the school the correct spelling of her name is "Felicia," so you will update this now.

8. Go to the **Final Grades** sheet and select **Felecia** in **cell A10**.

9. Edit the name by double-clicking, deleting the second *e*, and typing an **i**, and then complete the entry.

10. Go back to the **Participation** worksheet and notice Felicia's name has now been updated in **cell A9**.

4	First	Last
5	Ashley	Ronayne
6	Atif	Khalil
7	Austin	Farrell
8	Crystal	Robinson
9	Felicia	Murray
10	Jessica	McInnis

11. Save the workbook.

Create a Copy of a Worksheet

Rather than starting with a new, blank worksheet, you can save a lot of time by using an existing worksheet that already has some of the information you need or has the structure and formatting you want. Creating a copy of a worksheet does not affect the original worksheet. The new worksheet will have the same name but with *(2)* added to the end to indicate it is a second version.

Home→Cells→Format→Move or Copy Sheet | Right-click worksheet tab→Move or Copy

Edit Multiple Sheets at One Time

It is also possible to select several worksheets at the same time. With multiple sheets selected you can modify all of the selected sheets simultaneously by making changes on just one sheet. When you edit one, the others update automatically. You can enter text or formulas, or change cell format in the same cell in all of the selected sheets simultaneously. You need to be very careful with this feature, however, to ensure you are not replacing existing data in one of the worksheets you can't see!

Multiple sheets can be selected (or grouped) by holding the Ctrl key while clicking additional sheet tabs. For consecutive sheets, you can also hold the Shift key and click the last sheet you wish to select. To deselect (or ungroup) the multiple worksheets, either select a different sheet or right-click one of the sheet tabs and choose Ungroup Sheets.

DEVELOP YOUR SKILLS: E2-D7

In this exercise, you will create a new worksheet by copying the Participation sheet and make changes to both at once.

1. Save your workbook as: **E2-D7-NewGrades**

2. Right-click the **Participation** worksheet tab and choose **Move or Copy.**

3. Follow these steps to copy the sheet and position it at the end of the workbook:

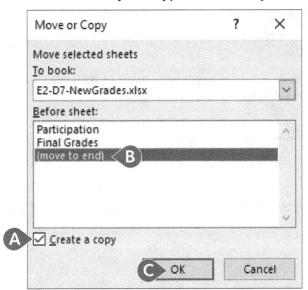

A. Click the checkbox to select **Create a Copy**.

B. In the Before Sheet box choose **(move to end)**.

C. Click **OK**.

The new worksheet is created to the right of the Final Grades sheet; it is identical to Participation and named Participation (2).

4. Right-click the **Participation** sheet tab again and choose **Move or Copy**.

5. This time *do not* click the Create a Copy box. In the Before Sheet box choose **Participation (2)** and **OK**.

The original Participation sheet is now positioned to the right of the Final Grades sheet and before the Participation (2) sheet.

6. Double-click the **Participation (2)** sheet tab; rename it **Exam** and tap Enter.

Your sheet tabs should now look like this:

7. With the Exam sheet still active, select the merged **cell A2** and double-click the word **Participation** in the Formula Bar.

This method of editing cell contents allows you to replace part of the cell without retyping the whole thing.

8. Type **Exam** and complete the entry, so the subtitle in **cell A2** now reads *Exam Grades*.

Edit Multiple Sheets at Once

Now you will select both the Participation and Exam worksheets to edit them both at once because you want the same changes applied to both.

9. With the Exam worksheet still active, press and hold the Ctrl key and click the **Participation** worksheet tab.

Both worksheets are now selected, their names are both bold, and there is a thick line below both sheet tabs. The Final Grades worksheet is not selected.

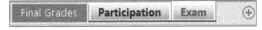

10. With both sheets selected, select the **range A4:B4**.

11. Apply bold formatting, increase the font size to 12 points, and center-align the content.

12. Add a **Thick Bottom Border** and the fill color **Green, Accent 6, Lighter 40%** (last column, fourth row).

13. Click the **Participation** worksheet tab to confirm your changes were made to both sheets and then click the **Final Grades** worksheet tab to deselect the other two sheets.

14. Save the workbook and close Excel.

Self-Assessment

 Check your knowledge of this chapter's key concepts and skills using the online Self-Assessment Quiz.

Performing Calculations Using Functions

3

In this chapter, you will begin using functions in your formulas to make complex calculations quicker and easier. You will also learn about the difference between a relative and an absolute reference and practice using both in your formulas.

LEARNING OBJECTIVES

- Create formulas with functions
- Use AutoSum
- Use relative and absolute cell references in formulas
- Define names for cells and ranges
- Use names in formulas

CHAPTER TIMING

- Concepts & Practice: 01:10:00
- Self-Assessment: 00:15:00
- Total: 01:25:00

PROJECT: TRACKING PROGRESS

As an instructor at LearnFast College, you have already recorded the student grades for your Introduction to Business course. Now you will use functions to perform a variety of calculations that will help you analyze the students' performance.

Learning Resources: **boostyourskills.lablearning.com**

Using Functions in Formulas

Functions are an important part of Excel. They allow you to do much more than simple mathematical operations. For example, adding two or three cells together is not a problem; however, if you needed to add up hundreds or even thousands of cells, it would be quite the tedious task! You would need a formula such as: =A1+A2+A3+A4... and so on.

The SUM function, in this case, is easier because it allows you to specify a range instead of individual cells. The function then tells Excel what operation to perform on the range, in this case addition. This is one of the reasons Excel is much more efficient than using a calculator!

Formulas with functions are inserted into a cell starting with the equals (=) sign, just like other formulas. This is followed by the function name and one or more arguments inside parentheses. An argument is the name for the numbers, cells, or ranges used in the function.

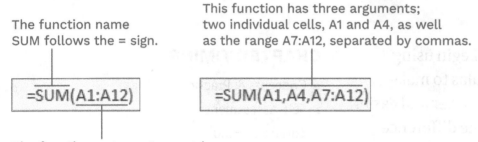

The function name SUM follows the = sign.

This function has three arguments; two individual cells, A1 and A4, as well as the range A7:A12, separated by commas.

=SUM(A1:A12)

=SUM(A1,A4,A7:A12)

The function arguments must be placed inside parentheses. The argument is the range A1:A12, so Excel will add all of the values contained in that range.

Functions can be typed directly into a cell, if you know the name of the function you wish to use, or inserted a number of other ways. Functions are available from the Formulas tab on the Ribbon, by using AutoSum, or by using the Insert Function button on the Formula Bar. The most common functions can be inserted quickly and easily from the AutoSum drop-down menu on the Home tab of the Ribbon.

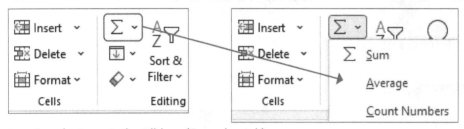

AutoSum button on the Ribbon (Formulas tab)

Insert Function button on the Formula Bar

When you insert a function by typing, Excel will suggest names for functions as you type. For example, typing =s will generate a list of functions that start with the letter *S*; you can ignore the prompt and type the full function name or double-click one of the suggestions that appears.

In this exercise, you will create a formula using the SUM function to calculate the final grade for each student.

1. Start Excel; open **E3-D1-SummerGrades** from your **Excel Chapter 3** folder and save it as: **E3-D1-FallGrades**

2. On the **Final Grades** worksheet, select **cell G6** and then type **=SUM(C6:F6)** and click **Enter** ☑.

   The formula in the Formula Bar shows the SUM function, and the total of cells C6:F6 is displayed in cell G6. The final grade for the first student, Ashley, is 37%.

   Currently there are only two grades being added (28% and 9%). The other grades will be added to the total once they are calculated on the Quizzes and Exam worksheets.

3. In **cell G7**, type **=SUM(** and use the mouse to select the **range C7:F7**; then click **Enter**.

   It's good practice to type the closing parenthesis after the function arguments, but notice in the Formula Bar that Excel automatically inserts it for you. The sum for the second student, Atif, now shows 36%.

4. Point to the fill handle in **cell G7** and double-click to fill the formula down **column G**.

5. Save the workbook.

The AutoSum Feature

The AutoSum feature not only makes it easy to find some of the simplest functions, it also helps identify and enter the range of cells you are most likely to use in your function. Often when you have a column of numbers, you want to add a total at the bottom of the column. In a row, the total would be placed on the right side of the row.

AutoSum will automatically search for adjacent data, either directly above or to the left of the selected cell. Therefore, selecting the cell at the bottom of a column or the right side of a row and clicking AutoSum will very quickly enter the SUM function, as well as the range of cells necessary to add all the numbers in that column or row. If necessary, you can alter the range Excel selects by dragging to select the desired cells before completing the entry.

Another option is to select the data in the row or column first and then click AutoSum.

SUM, AVERAGE, COUNT, MAX, and MIN

The SUM function is just one of the AutoSum options; other frequently used functions can be found via the AutoSum drop-down menu. These functions take a set of numbers identified in the arguments and can be used to find the average, count how many numbers are in the set, or locate the highest or lowest value. Similar to AutoSum, these functions automatically search for adjacent data, either directly above or to the left of the selected cell.

AUTOSUM FUNCTIONS	
Function Name	**Description**
SUM	Adds the values in the cells
AVERAGE	Calculates the average of the values in the cells
COUNT	Counts the number of cells that contain numerical values; cells containing text and blank cells are ignored
MAX	Returns the highest value
MIN	Returns the lowest value

Home→Editing→AutoSum Σ menu button ∨

Insert Function

For more complex functions, the Insert Function button opens a dialog box that allows you to search for functions and enter function arguments. In the Insert Function dialog box you can search for your desired function by keyword or browse by category. After choosing the function, the Function Arguments dialog box opens, from which you enter the numbers, cell references, or criteria to use in the function.

☁ **View the video "Entering a Formula Using Insert Function."**

▌ DEVELOP YOUR SKILLS: E3-D2

In this exercise, you will use AutoSum to calculate the total each student earned on their quizzes, as well as to calculate the class average for each quiz.

1. Save your workbook as: **E3-D2-FallGrades**
2. Click the **Quizzes** worksheet tab and select the empty cell under *Quiz Total* for Ashley, **cell H6.**
3. Choose **Home→Editing→AutoSum.**

   The SUM function is entered into cell H6 with the range C6:G6. Excel finds five adjacent cells to the left of cell H6 containing numerical data, so the range C6:G6 is automatically entered into the function arguments within parentheses.

Quiz 1	Quiz 2	Quiz 3	Quiz 4	Quiz 5	Quiz Total	Quiz %
91	81	88	84	60	=SUM(C6:G6)	
100	99	67	55	85	SUM(**number1**, [number2], ...)	

4. Click **Enter** to finish the entry and show the result of the formula, 404, in **cell H6.**
5. Use the **fill handle** to copy the formula in **cell H6** down the column for the rest of the students.

   Next you will calculate the class average for each quiz.

6. In **cell A18**, enter: `Class Average`

7. Format **cell A18** with bold and italic formatting, and then merge and center **cells A18** and **B18**.

8. Select **cell C18** and choose **Home→Editing→AutoSum menu button ⌄→Average**.

9. Complete the entry in **cell C18** and then use the **fill handle** to copy the average formula from **cell C18** to the right, into the **range D18:G18** below all five quizzes.

10. Decrease the decimal in the range of selected cells so only one decimal place is displayed and then apply bold formatting and a top cell border.

    Now you want to find the average for each student.

11. Insert a new column to the left of **column I**.

12. Enter `Student Average` into **cell I4**.

13. Select **cell I6** and choose **Home→Editing→AutoSum menu button ⌄→Average** but do not complete the entry.

    This time AutoSum selects the range C6:H6, which is incorrect because the average for the five quizzes should not include the total. Now you will select the correct range.

14. Use the mouse to drag and select the correct **range C6:G6** and then complete the entry.

15. Use the **fill handle** in **cell I6** to copy the formula down the column for the rest of the students.

    Next you need to calculate the exam grades for each student.

16. Click the **Exam** worksheet tab and select the empty cell under *Exam Total* for Ashley, **cell H6**.

17. Use AutoSum to add the Section 1 to Section 5 exam marks for Ashley, and then copy the formula down **column H** for the other students.

18. Save your work.

Using Relative and Absolute Cell References

Cell references make it easier to copy formulas when you want to perform the same calculation with new numbers each time. Without cell references, each calculation would need to be typed individually, like with a calculator—slowly and tediously. A *relative* cell reference, which is the default in Excel, is one in which the location of the cell remains relative to the cell that contains the formula. This makes repeating the same calculation many times quick and easy!

For example, if the formula =A3-B3 is in cell C3, the relative position of A3 is two cells to the left of C3, and B3 is one cell to the left of C3. When you copy the formula to another cell, the cell references change to be in the same relative position. So, if you copy the formula =A3-B3 from cell C3 down to cell C4, the formula there will be =A4-B4. Excel updates the new cell references to be in the same relative position to cell C4; that is, two cells to the left and one cell to the left.

| **TIP!** Remember that a relative cell reference changes when it is copied.

C3	▾	:	✕	✓	*fx*	=A3-B3

◢	A	B	C
3	64	21	43
4	68	32	

C4	▾	:	✕	✓	*fx*	=A4-B4

◢	A	B	C
3	64	21	43
4	68	32	36

The original formula is seen in the Formula Bar, with relative references to both cells A3 and B3.

The copied formula is displayed with the new cell references A4 and B4.

Absolute Cell References

In some situations, you do not want the cell reference to change when you move or copy the formula. To ensure the cell reference does not change, use an *absolute* cell reference. You can think of an absolute cell reference as being locked in place; that is, the cell reference will not change when copied to other cells.

To make a cell reference absolute, start with a relative cell reference such as A1 and add a dollar sign in front of the column and row components, like this: $A$1.

There are two ways to create an absolute cell reference:

1. Type the cell reference and include dollar signs in front of the column and row references.
2. Use the mouse pointer to select the cell and then tap F4 on the keyboard, which inserts both dollar signs into the cell reference at once.

Example: If the formula =$A$3-B3 is entered in cell C3 and then copied to cell C4, the formula in cell C4 would be =$A$3-B4. $A$3 is an absolute reference, so it does not change; B3 is a relative reference, so it changes to B4.

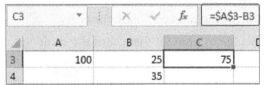
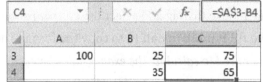

The original formula shows in the Formula Bar and contains an absolute reference to cell $A$3.

After the formula is copied, the absolute reference $A$3 does not change.

 View the Video "Relative and Absolute Cell References."

Mixed Cell References

It's also possible to create a mix between a relative and an absolute reference in a cell reference. For example, $A3 is a reference to cell A3 where the column reference is absolute (column A will not change when copied) and the row reference is relative (row 3 will change when copied). This can be useful when copying a formula both across a row and down a column.

After you have tapped the F4 key once, tapping it a second time changes the absolute reference to a mixed reference with only a dollar $ sign in front of the row reference. A third tap of F4 places the dollar $ sign in front of only the column reference, and a fourth tap removes all dollar $ signs so it is once again a relative cell reference.

Display and Print Formulas

To see a formula you have entered, you must first select the cell and then check the Formula Bar because it is the result of the formula that is displayed in the worksheet cell. This means that to check your formulas, you have to click each cell and review them one at a time. When you have many cells with formulas, this is very hard and time-consuming to do.

An easier way is to display all formulas within their cells. The Show Formulas button is a toggle that can be turned on and off as necessary.

> **TIP!** You can still edit the formulas and print the worksheet while Show Formulas is turned on.

When Show Formulas is turned on, Excel automatically widens columns to show more of the cell contents.

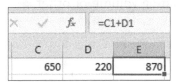

Normally the cell must be selected for you to see the formula.

C	D	E
650	220	=C3+D3
480	195	=C4+D4
300	217	=C5+D5

After turning on Show Formulas, the formulas display in the worksheet without selecting the cell (but you can't see the results).

> Formulas→Formula Auditing→Show Formulas

DEVELOP YOUR SKILLS: E3-D3

In this exercise, you will use formulas with absolute references to find the percentage grades for the class's exams and quizzes.

1. Save your workbook as: **E3-D3-FallGrades**

2. On the **Exam** worksheet, enter **150** in **cell H5** and **40%** in **cell I5**.

   To get a grade out of 40% for each student, you need to divide their exam score by 150 then multiply by 40%. You will use the values in cells H5 and I5 to do this.

3. In **cell I6**, type **=H6/H5** but do not complete the entry.

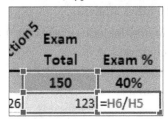

   Cell H6 shows Ashley's total exam grade. This will change for each student when we copy the formula. Cell H5 is the number of total points the exam is worth, in this case 150, which should not change for each student; therefore, cell H5 needs to be an absolute reference.

   While using F4 *to edit a formula as we will, the insertion point must be immediately before or after the reference to cell H5 or the correct cell reference won't be converted.*

4. While still in edit mode in **cell I6**, tap F4 on the keyboard to make the reference for **cell H5** absolute (dollar $ signs are placed in front of the column and row).

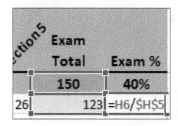

The last step is to multiply each mark by 40%, which also does not change for each student.

5. Continuing in edit mode in **cell I6**, type ***I5** and tap [F4], and then click **Enter**.

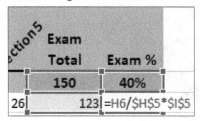

Cell I5 is now an absolute cell reference. Ashley's total exam grade is calculated as 33%.

6. Copy the formula down **column I** for the other students.

7. Select **cell I7** and ensure the formula copied correctly. The formula should be =H7/$H$5*$I$5 and the result for Atif is 32%.

   Now you will use absolute cell references to calculate the students' quiz grades.

8. Click the **Quizzes** worksheet tab and enter **500** in **cell H5** and **20%** in **cell J5**.

9. Enter this formula in **cell J6** to calculate the quiz percentage: **=H6/$H$5*$J$5**

   You can decide for yourself if you would prefer to type in the dollar signs individually or use the [F4] key!

10. Copy the formula down **column J** to calculate the grades for the other students.

11. Click the **Final Grades** worksheet tab and notice the Final Grade now includes grades for the quizzes and exams, along with the grades for projects and participation.

12. Save your work.

Creating Names for Cells and Ranges

When you need to refer to the same cell or range of cells repeatedly in your formulas, consider creating a name for that cell or range. It's easier to remember a name than to scroll or click around your workbook looking for the cells you want to use. This is especially true if you are using a cell or range from another worksheet or even another workbook.

NOTE! Cell names *cannot* contain spaces.

You can create names directly in the Name Box or via the Formulas tab on the Ribbon. You can also create, edit, or delete cell names using the Name Manager. Name references are automatically absolute cell references; that is, the reference will not change when moved or copied.

The cell name in the Name Box, *TaxRate* (does not contain a space), refers to cell B2.

The default name for the selected cell, A1, is displayed in the Name Box.

Formulas→Defined Names

Using Cell Names in Formulas

You use a cell name in a formula just as you would any other cell reference. The cell name can be typed, or the cell can be selected with the mouse. You can also begin to type the first few letters of the name and then double-click the name from the AutoComplete list that appears.

Typing the beginning of the cell name will bring up suggested names.

The formula, after the cell name has been inserted, highlights the cell named *TaxRate*.

The formula's result is displayed; 100 multiplied by 18% is *18*.

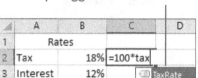
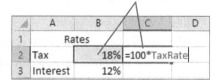
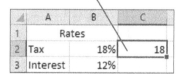

DEVELOP YOUR SKILLS: E3-D4

In this exercise, you will define names for ranges and cells, and then enter formulas to analyze and update the grades using those names for the cell references.

1. Save your workbook as: **E3-D4-FallGrades**

2. On the **Final Grades** worksheet, select the **range G6:G17**.

3. Click inside the **Name Box**, which currently displays *G6*, and then type **Final** and tap ⌷Enter⌷.

   Final *is now the name that refers to the range G6:G17. The name* Final *can now be used in formulas to analyze the grades.*

   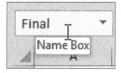

4. Beginning in **cell I5**, enter the following:

	I
5	Grade Analysis
6	Highest
7	Lowest
8	Average

5. Add bold and italic formatting to the **range I5:I8** and AutoFit the column width to fit the text you just entered.

6. In **cell J6**, type the formula **=MAX(Final)** and tap Enter.

7. In **cell J7**, type **=MIN(** and then use the mouse to select the **range G6:G17**.

   Excel automatically uses the name Final *inside the formula for the range you just selected.*

8. Type **)** to complete the formula and then tap Enter.

9. Now type **=AVERAGE(Fi** in **cell J8** and then use the mouse to double-click the name **Final** from the suggested list.

Average	=AVERAGE(Fi	
	AVERAGE(number1, [numbe	
	_fx_ FILTERXML	
	Final	
	_fx_ FIND	

10. Type **)** to complete the formula and then tap Enter.

11. Apply bold formatting and the **Percent Style** number format to the **range J6:J8**.

    The highest, lowest, and average grades for the class are now displayed.

    Next you will create names for the values of each part of the students' grades. This way, if the values change later you can easily update the grade formulas with the new values.

12. Enter this data in the **range A21:B25**:

	A	B
21	Values	
22	Quizzes	20%
23	Projects	30%
24	Participation	10%
25	Exam	40%

13. AutoFit the width of **column A** to fit the word *Participation* in **cell A24**.

14. Select **cell B22** and choose **Formulas→Defined Names→Define Name**.

    Excel adds the name Quizzes *into the Name field based on the adjacent cell.*

15. Ensure that *Quizzes* is inserted in the Name field and click **OK**.

16. Repeat step 14 but select **cell B23** and use the proposed cell name *Projects*.

17. Repeat for **cell B24** and **cell B25**, using the proposed cell names *Participation* and *Exam*, respectively.

18. Choose **Formulas→Defined Names→Name Manager** and make sure all four names, as well as the name *Final* (five total names) have been added to the list, and then close the Name Manager.

19. Click the **Quizzes** worksheet tab, select **cell J5**, and enter: `=Quizzes`

    The formula enters the value from the cell named Quizzes (20%) in cell J5. If the value needs to be changed, it can be updated on the Final Grades sheet, and then the Quizzes sheet and all necessary formulas will instantly update, too.

20. Click the **Exam** worksheet tab, select **cell I5**, and enter: `=Exam`

21. Switch back to the **Final Grades** sheet and change the values in **cell B22** and **cell B25** to **10%** and **50%**, respectively.

    The quiz grades now reflect a grade out of 10 in column C, and the exam grades reflect a grade out of 50 in column E. Review the Quizzes and Exam sheets to see the changes there.

22. Save the workbook and close Excel.

Self-Assessment

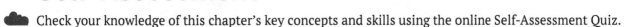 Check your knowledge of this chapter's key concepts and skills using the online Self-Assessment Quiz.

Data Visualization and Images

In this chapter, you will use a variety of ways to create visually interesting worksheets. You will learn when to create charts, which chart types to use for different situations, and how charts are particularly useful in understanding relationships among numbers in a worksheet. In this chapter, you will also learn about formatting data based on desired conditions and inserting pictures and shapes.

LEARNING OBJECTIVES

- Insert charts
- Use chart tools to modify charts
- Move and size charts
- Edit chart data
- Add images to a worksheet
- Apply conditional formatting

CHAPTER TIMING

- Concepts & Practice: 01:10:00
- Self-Assessment: 00:15:00
- Total: 01:25:00

PROJECT: REPORTING COMPANY SALES DATA

Airspace Travel has gathered data from six months of sales, and you need to create charts that will help visualize trends in the data. You have to decide what data to use to create the charts, and the chart types that will best help the company understand how it is performing. You want to show sales comparisons month by month, illustrate the contributions of each travel agent to compare them side by side, and highlight the top and bottom performers throughout the year.

Learning Resources: **boostyourskills.lablearning.com**

Create Charts to Compare Data

There are many situations in which we are presented with numerical data, and it would be easier to interpret the data if we could visualize it in chart form. Charts are created from worksheet data. Similar to a formula, the data is linked so that if the data changes, the chart changes as well. Creating a chart is as easy as selecting the data and chart type. Excel does the rest! After the chart is created, you can add or modify chart elements to change the way your chart looks.

Chart Types

Excel has more than a dozen different types of charts to choose from, with variations of each chart type as well. However, it is important to remember that the purpose of a chart is to simplify data, not to make it more complicated. The most common options to use are a column or bar chart, a line chart, or a pie chart.

Column Charts and Bar Charts

A column chart displays data in columns across the horizontal axis. A bar chart displays data in bars across the vertical axis. They are basically the same, except one is vertical and the other is horizontal. Column charts and bar charts are useful to compare data across several categories.

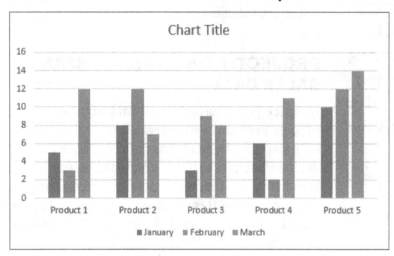

Line Charts

A line chart displays a series of data in a line or several lines and is useful for showing trends in data over time, such as days, months, or years. Line charts are best for a large amount of data and when the order of data—for example, chronological—is important. Line charts are very similar to column charts and have most of the same features.

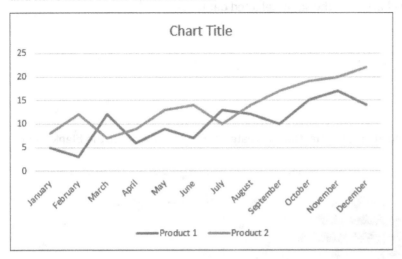

Pie Charts

A pie chart shows a comparison of data as parts of the whole. Pie charts are best for a small amount of data; too many pieces will be hard to see in a pie chart. Pie charts can contain only one series of data, and they do not have a horizontal or vertical axis like column and line charts.

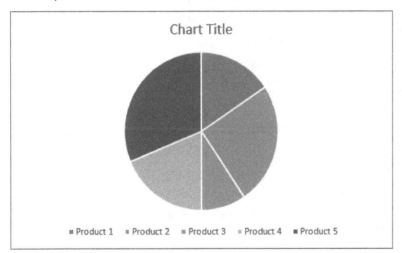

Excel also has a Recommended Charts option that will list the top chart options for you based on the data you have selected. The Insert Chart window shows a preview of what your chart will look like before you decide which one to use.

Insert→Charts

Insert→Charts→Recommended Charts

Selecting Chart Data

Choosing the right data is very important to make sure Excel can create the chart correctly. The best method is to select the data and include the appropriate row and column headings. Select an equal number of cells in each row of data, even if some of those cells are empty.

You can create a column, bar, or line chart from the same selected data.

Q1 Revenue			
	January	February	March
Product 1	1200	1123	1150
Product 2	1301	1235	1260
Product 3	1080	1100	1120
Product 4	1250	1300	1275

The data, including row and column headings, is selected to create your chart. Note that the blank cell in the top-left corner is also included.

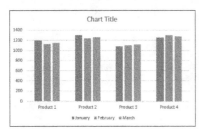 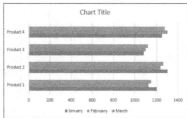 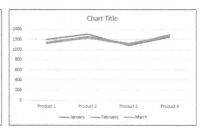

These three charts result from the same selection of data.

To create a pie chart, you can only select one data series.

Q1 Revenue			
	January	February	March
Product 1	1200	1123	1150
Product 2	1301	1235	1260
Product 3	1080	1100	1120
Product 4	1250	1300	1275

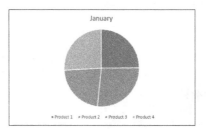

Only the January data series is selected to create this pie chart.

If you want to create charts showing only some of the data, use the ⌈Ctrl⌉ key to select the desired data.

Q1 Revenue			
	January	February	March
Product 1	1200	1123	1150
Product 2	1301	1235	1260
Product 3	1080	1100	1120
Product 4	1250	1300	1275

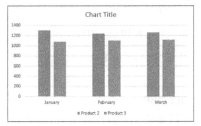

For a column, bar, or line chart showing only Products 2 and 3, you would select the three rows of data, including the blank cell.

Chart Elements

A chart is made up of different elements that can be added, removed, or modified. These elements can help others understand the information on the chart, or accentuate certain aspects of the data. There is a wide range of options for changing the look and style of your chart with each of the chart elements.

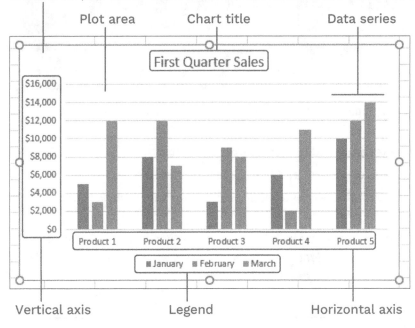

In this exercise, you will select data and use it to create a chart.

1. Start Excel; open **E4-D1-Sales** from the **Excel Chapter 4** folder and save it as:
   E4-D1-SalesCharts

2. Follow these steps to insert a column chart:

   A. Select the **range A3:D8** to compare the results for all agents for the first three months of the year.

   B. Choose **Insert→Charts→Recommended Charts** from the Ribbon.

   C. Excel recommends a clustered column chart. Click **OK** to insert the suggested chart.

   Your chart will be inserted into your worksheet as a floating object, meaning it can be moved easily by dragging.

   After creating your chart, notice that resting the mouse pointer over a chart element displays a ScreenTip with the name of that element and that pointing to your data will tell you the data series, point, and value.

3. Save the workbook.

Chart Tools

There are countless ways of formatting a chart; your chart can be as simple or as creative as you like. The way you format it will likely depend on your purpose and how much time you want to spend working on it. The chart tools are found on contextual tabs, meaning they are only available while a chart is selected. You can also use the Format pane on the right side of the screen to format chart elements. The formatting options change for each chart element.

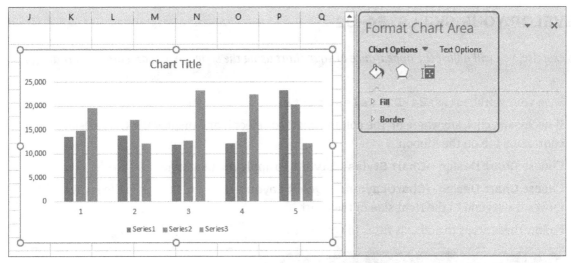

The formatting pane title and menu options change depending on what is selected in the worksheet. In this case, the chart area is selected so the Format Chart Area pane shows.

Chart Design

You can use design tools to quickly and easily change the way your chart looks, using features like Chart Styles and Quick Layout. Styles modify the colors, shading, and layout of the various chart elements in one easy step. To change the appearance of a chart, there are many other design options, including changing the chart type, changing colors, or adding and removing various chart elements like chart titles, axis titles, data labels, and more.

☁ **View the Video "Using the Chart Design Tools."**

The Chart Formatting Buttons

The chart formatting buttons can add elements to your chart, change the style, or filter the data visible on the chart.

One of the great features of Excel charts is the ability to filter data without changing the data selection or creating a new chart. You can simply filter the data to focus on the sets of data you want to compare and then add or remove the other series or categories as desired.

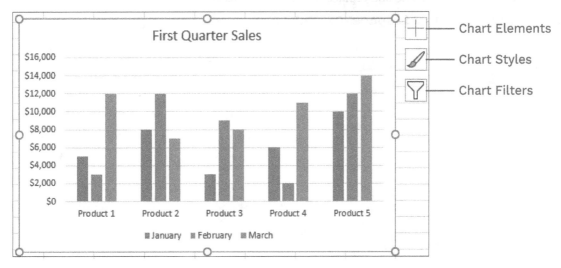

DEVELOP YOUR SKILLS: E4-D2

In this exercise, you will adjust the appearance of your chart using the style, layout, and other chart design tools.

1. Save your workbook as: **E4-D2-SalesCharts**

2. If necessary, click anywhere on the column chart to select it and display the Chart Design contextual tab on the Ribbon.

3. Choose **Chart Design→Chart Styles→Style 8** to apply the new style.

4. Choose **Chart Design→Chart Layouts→Quick Layout→Layout 1** to apply the layout, which moves the legend to the right side of the chart.

5. Follow these steps to add axis titles to your chart:

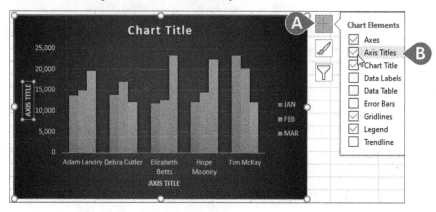

   A. Click the **Chart Elements** button.

   B. Click the checkbox beside **Axis Titles**.

6. Point to the title on the vertical axis, which you just added, and triple-click to select the entire text.

7. Type **Monthly Sales** for the axis title.

   After entering an axis title, or a chart title, do not press Enter. *Simply deselect the object or continue with the next task.*

8. Select the horizontal axis title and replace the text with: **Agent**

9. Change the chart title to: **Airspace Q1 Sales**

10. Follow these steps to change the chart type:

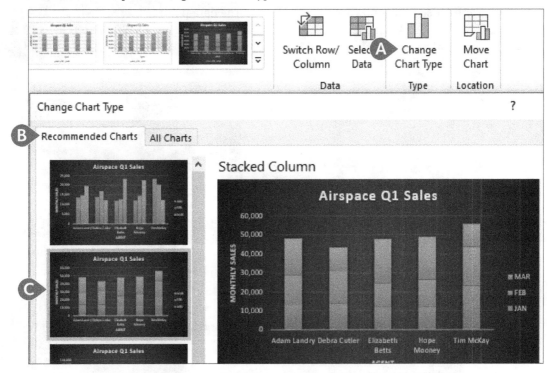

A. Click the **Change Chart Type** button on the Ribbon to open the dialog box.

B. Click the **Recommended Charts** tab.

C. Choose the second option, **Stacked Column**, and click **OK**.

This chart more clearly shows a comparison of the total for each agent during the three months, as well as the sales for each individual month.

11. Save the workbook.

Chart Format

Beyond changing the basic style of a chart, you may want to choose your own colors for the chart area, plot area, or data series. This can be done by modifying the fill or outline of a specific chart element. The fill can be a color, gradient, texture, or even a picture. Other possibilities include adding shapes or WordArt to a chart.

Axis Options

Adjusting the axes can focus the chart on significant differences in the data, or simply change the appearance of the axes using number formatting, such as to display numbers as currency. One of the axis options is the minimum and maximum value displayed on the axis. For example, if the data you are charting all falls between 1,000 and 1,300, you can set your minimum to 1,000. This highlights the differences, because the first 1,000 units are the same for all the data points.

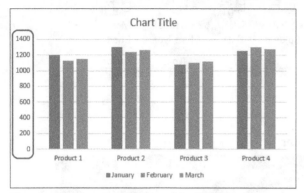

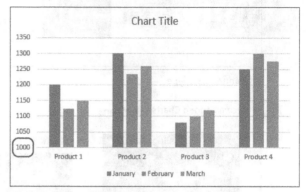

The data looks very similar with the axis values ranging from 0 to 1400.

The product differences are much easier to see with the axis values starting at 1000.

Format→Current Selection→Format Selection | Right-click axis→Format Axis

DEVELOP YOUR SKILLS: E4-D3

In this exercise, you will adjust the chart colors and axis numbering.

1. Save your workbook as: **E4-D3-SalesCharts**

2. Continuing with the Airspace Q1 Sales column chart, follow these steps to adjust the color of the FEB series:

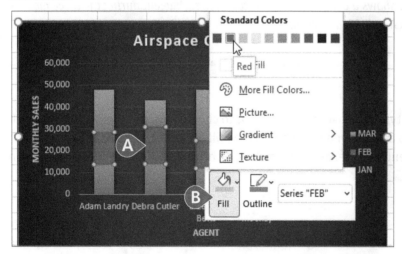

A. Click once on any orange block to select the FEB data series.

It's important to click only once. One click selects the whole series; clicking a second time would select only one data point from the series to modify.

NOTE! You can see what's selected by the four corner circles. If only one data point is selected, deselect the series by clicking anywhere else, and try again to select all five orange columns.

B. Right-click any of the selected orange data points, click **Fill** in the shortcut menu, and choose **Red** from the Standard Colors section.

3. Repeat step 2 to adjust the fill color for the MAR series to **Purple** (under Standard Colors).

4. Follow these steps to adjust the vertical axis:

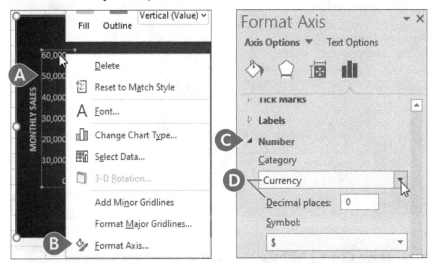

A. Point to a number on the vertical axis and then right-click to display the shortcut menu.

It is important to point to a number to get the right menu; if you are between the numbers, the Chart Area shortcut menu will appear, which has different options. Ensure the shortcut menu displays Format Axis at the bottom. If not, keep trying until you get it.

B. Choose the **Format Axis** command.

C. Scroll to the bottom of the Format Axis pane and click **Number** to expand the menu. (Depending on the size of your display, you may need to scroll down again to see the Number options.)

D. Choose **Currency** from the Category list using the menu button ⌄ and, if necessary, change the decimal places to **0**.

The number format is changed for the vertical axis. You can either leave the Format Axis pane open or close it by clicking the "X" in the top-right corner.

5. Save the workbook.

Move and Size Charts

Charts can be moved around on a worksheet or moved to a different worksheet. A chart can be moved on the same sheet by simply dragging. Be sure, however, to click the chart area and not another chart element or you will only move that element and not the whole chart.

Because charts take up a lot of space, and you may want more than one chart in your workbook, it's often a good idea to move a chart onto a new, separate sheet. Charts that are moved onto their own sheet are referred to as chart sheets because they don't contain any rows, columns, or cells—just the chart itself. After moving a chart to a chart sheet, you can continue to work on the chart just like before.

To resize a chart, the chart must first be selected. Then you can drag any of the sizing handles to resize appropriately. You can also resize a chart from the Ribbon to specify the exact height and width. Charts on a chart sheet, however, can't be resized.

The mouse pointer over the chart area displays the four-pointed arrow; drag to move the chart.

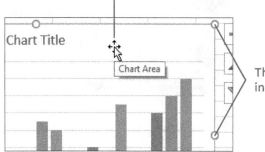

The sizing handles can be used to increase or decrease the chart size.

Chart Design→Location→Move Chart | Right-click chart area→Move Chart

Format→Size

DEVELOP YOUR SKILLS: E4-D4

In this exercise, you will move the existing chart and then create another chart and resize it.

1. Save your workbook as: **E4-D4-SalesCharts**

2. With the Airspace Q1 Sales chart selected, choose **Chart Design→Location→Move Chart** to open the Move Chart dialog box.

   Remember, the chart must be selected to display the Chart Tools contextual tabs on the Ribbon.

3. Choose **New Sheet**, type **Q1 Sales** for the name of the worksheet, and click **OK**.

   This moves the chart to a chart sheet, which has no cells, and resizes the chart to fit your screen.

4. Click the **Sales** worksheet tab to create a new chart.

5. Select the **range A3:G6**, which contains the data for Adam, Debra, and Elizabeth.

6. Choose **Insert→Charts→Insert Line or Area Chart menu button ⌄→Line** (the first option in the 2-D Line group).

7. Drag the chart so it is directly below the data.

8. Replace the chart title with the name: **Semiannual Sales**

9. Save the workbook.

Edit Chart Data

After a chart has been created, the data is linked, so if you change the data in the worksheet source, the chart is automatically updated. You can also add or remove data from the chart or filter the chart to change the data displayed. The easiest way to change the chart data is to reselect the entire range to be used, but you can also add or remove individual data series, points, or labels.

Rather than adding and removing data, sometimes a better option is to keep all existing data in the chart and use a filter to display only the data you want to see. The Chart Filters feature allows you to quickly filter specific series and category values and then remove the filter later to display all the data again.

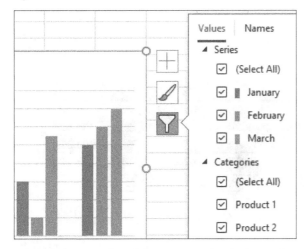

With the Chart Filter feature, you check the series and categories to display and uncheck the ones to hide.

Another way to rearrange your chart data is by swapping the Horizontal Axis and the Legend categories using the Switch Row/Column button. This allows different comparisons to be made, such as switching from comparing months side by side to product categories side by side, with one click.

> Chart Design→Data→Select Data

> Chart Design→Data→Switch Row/Column

❚ DEVELOP YOUR SKILLS: E4-D5

In this exercise, you will edit the chart to include all five sales agents and then filter the data in the chart.

1. Save your workbook as: **E4-D5-SalesCharts**
2. Ensure the **Semiannual Sales** chart is still selected on the Sales worksheet.

3. Right-click anywhere in the chart and choose **Select Data** from the shortcut menu.

The Select Data Source dialog box appears. The current data range is selected and the corresponding cells on the worksheet are surrounded by an animated border.

3	Agent	JAN	FEB	MAR	APR	MAY	JUN	Total
4	Adam Landry	13,629	14,841	19,611	19,737	15,325	16,248	$99,391
5	Debra Cutler	13,904	17,040	12,207	9,044	18,848	13,322	$84,365
6	Elizabeth Betts	11,907	12,685	23,329	15,208	20,050	17,030	$100,209
7	Hope Mooney	12,083	14,490	22,446	12,670	16,211	15,581	$93,481
8	Tim McKay	23,272	20,287	12,161	21,237	16,247	11,548	$104,752

Select Data Source — ? ✕

Chart data range: =Sales!$A$3:$G$6

4. Drag across the worksheet **range A3:G8** to select the new data and click **OK**.

3	Agent	JAN	FEB	MAR	APR	MAY	JUN	Total
4	Adam Landry	13,629	14,841	19,611	19,737	15,325	16,248	$99,391
5	Debra Cutler	13,904	17,040	12,207	9,044	18,848	13,322	$84,365
6	Elizabeth Betts	11,907	12,685	23,329	15,208	20,050	17,030	$100,209
7	Hope Mooney	12,083	14,490	22,446	12,670	16,211	15,581	$93,481
8	Tim McKay	23,272	20,287	12,161	21,237	16,247	11,548	$104,752

Select Data Source — ? ✕

Chart data range: =Sales!$A$3:$G$8

The new data displays five lines in the chart, one for each of the five agents.

5. Click the **Chart Filters** 🔽 button next to the chart and click the checkboxes next to **Adam**, **Elizabeth**, and **Tim** to remove the checks and filter out their data; then click **Apply**.

You should now see only Debra's and Hope's data on the chart and only their names in the legend.

6. Change the number format for the vertical axis to display the **Currency** number format with no decimals.

7. Save the workbook.

Adding Images

For the most part, Excel is used for text and numerical data; however, you can also add pictures and shapes to your worksheets. Pictures might be used to display a company logo, add information, or simply bring a little excitement to an otherwise plain set of data. You can add pictures saved on your device or search for pictures online. There are a variety of shapes and icons to choose from that can also be used for visual effect. Text boxes can be added for easier formatting and positioning of graphical text on a worksheet.

Pictures and shapes have their own sets of tools on the Ribbon, found on the Picture Format and Shape Format tabs, respectively. Both of these contextual tabs give you a great number of options for changing the style, shape, color, and size of the object and for modifying many other aspects.

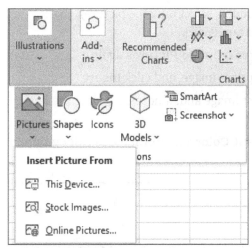

Depending on the size of your display, you may need to expand the Illustrations menu to find the options for pictures and various graphical tools.

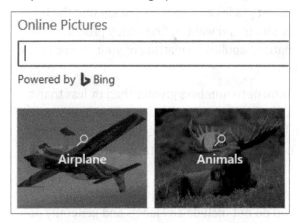

Rather than use a picture saved to your device, you can browse for a picture by clicking a category in the Online Pictures gallery or entering a search term.

When searching online you may find pictures that are protected by copyright. It is important to respect copyright laws. By default, the online picture search in Excel displays only pictures licensed under Creative Commons, meaning you can use these pictures freely.

> Insert→Illustrations→Pictures *or* Shapes

> Insert→Text→Text Box

DEVELOP YOUR SKILLS: E4-D6

In this exercise, you will add a picture to the worksheet and make some modifications to the picture.

1. Save your workbook as: **E4-D6-SalesCharts**
2. On the Sales sheet, click **cell J1** and then choose **Insert→Illustrations→Pictures→Online Pictures** to open the dialog box.
3. Click **Airplane** in the gallery and then choose a suitable image (perhaps a cartoon plane with no background) and click **Insert**.

   Because this is an online search, the results will change frequently, and you may not see the same images from one search to the next. Some online images are also inserted with licensing information, which refers to the Creative Commons license to use the image.

4. With the image selected (if licensing information is included, select only the picture), go to **Picture Format→Size→Height**, type **1** in the box, and tap Enter.

5. Click **cell I1** and choose **Insert→Illustrations→Pictures→Online Pictures** again.

6. Enter **spaceship** in the search box, choose an appropriate image, and click **Insert**.

7. Resize the image to be **1** inch in height to match the first image and, if necessary, drag the images to reposition them so they do not overlap.

8. Choose **Picture Format→Adjust→Color→Blue, Accent Color 1 Light** (in the Recolor group).

9. Save the workbook.

Conditional Formatting

Another way to better visualize your data is to use conditional formatting. Conditional formatting takes a set of data, applies a rule or rules, and modifies the formatting of the cells that match the rule. For example, you may have a large set of data containing student grades and want to quickly find the top three marks. Or you may have sales data for a group of products and want to find which product sells the most and which one sells the least. Conditional formatting applies formatting of your choice to the cells that meet these criteria so you can quickly find them.

Rules can be created to draw attention to the top or bottom, or to numbers greater than or less than a specific number. You can also highlight a cell with a number equal to a specific amount or a cell that contains certain text. Other conditional formatting can be applied to all the selected cells, including data bars, color scales, and icon sets, which are useful for visualizing a set of data as a group. There are so many options!

To apply conditional formatting, the first step is always to select the entire range of data to apply the rule to. For conditional formatting, unlike with charts, you do not include any labels and generally don't include any totals unless you set up a separate rule for total rows or columns. Different rule options are available from the Conditional Formatting drop-down menu, but the criteria and formatting can also be modified to suit your needs. After a rule has been created, you can delete the rule using Clear Rules. Select Manage Rules to see all of the existing rules for either the current selection or the entire worksheet.

	A	B	C	D
1		January	February	March
2	Product 1	5	3	12
3	Product 2	8	12	7
4	Product 3	3	9	8
5	Product 4	6	2	11
6	Product 5	10	12	14

The worksheet before creating conditional formatting, with the range selected

	A	B	C	D
1		January	February	March
2	Product 1	5	3	12
3	Product 2	8	12	7
4	Product 3	3	9	8
5	Product 4	6	2	11
6	Product 5	10	12	14

The worksheet after the conditional formatting rule is applied to the range, showing the top five items with a light red fill and dark red text

NOTE! When a conditional formatting rule is created for the top five items, if two or more items are tied for fifth highest, six or more items could be included in the conditional formatting.

 View the video "Highlighting Data with Conditional Formatting."

After a conditional formatting rule is created, the formatting is automatically updated to reflect the new data if it changes.

Home→Styles→Conditional Formatting ▦

DEVELOP YOUR SKILLS: E4-D7

In this exercise, you will alter the appearance of the data using conditional formatting to show some of the top and bottom sales numbers for the agents.

1. Save your workbook as: **E4-D7-SalesCharts**
2. Select the **range B4:G8** and choose **Home→Styles→Conditional Formatting→ Highlight Cells Rules→Greater Than...**.
3. In the Greater Than dialog box, type **20000** in the first box (that's 20,000 with no comma).

   The preview shows which data this will apply to, with the default format.

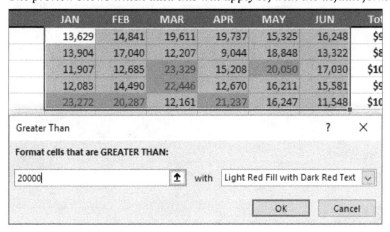

4. Click **OK** to apply the default format and close the dialog box.

   For the six-month total, you want to see the top and bottom agents, so you will apply two new rules to the data in column H under Total.

5. Select the **range H4:H8** and choose **Home→Styles→Conditional Formatting→ Top/Bottom Rules→Top 10 Items...**.
6. In the dialog box change the *10* to **1** and set the format to **Green Fill with Dark Green Text**; click **OK**.
7. With the **range H4:H8** still selected, choose **Home→Styles→Conditional Formatting→ Top/Bottom Rules→Bottom 10 Items...**.
8. Change the *10* to **1** and select the **Yellow Fill with Dark Yellow Text** format; then click **OK**.

   Now the data needs to be updated. A sale was missed for Debra in March, so the number should be higher.

9. Select **cell D5** and increase the number *12,207* by entering: **22207**

   The formatting for cell D7 changes to red fill and red text because it is greater than 20,000. The formatting in the Total column also changes because Debra no longer has the lowest total, and your Semiannual Sales chart below the data updates as well.

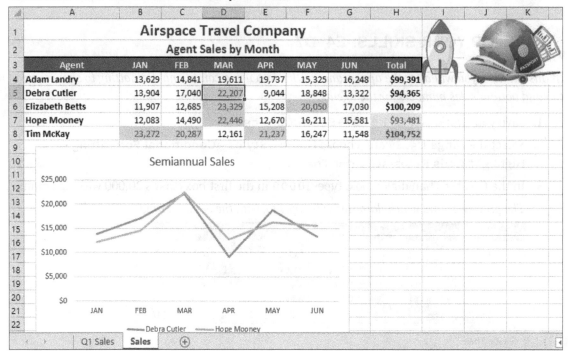

10. Save the workbook and close Excel.

Self-Assessment

Check your knowledge of this chapter's key concepts and skills using the online Self-Assessment Quiz.

Organizing Large Worksheets

In this chapter, you will learn how to effectively manage worksheets containing large amounts of data. You will use some exciting Excel tools to organize and view data, perform calculations, and restrict data entry.

LEARNING OBJECTIVES

- Create a template
- Start a workbook from a template
- Change worksheet view options
- Sort and filter data
- Create IF functions
- Apply data validation rules
- Use the Scale to Fit printing options
- Create and modify tables

CHAPTER TIMING

- Concepts & Practice: 01:10:00
- Self-Assessment: 00:15:00
- Total: 01:25:00

PROJECT: PREPARING COMPANY PAYROLL DATA

Every two weeks, Airspace Travel goes through the process of compiling the data from hours worked and commissions earned to calculate employee paychecks. You have been asked to manage this process, which means taking the data and importing it into a template and then inserting the required formulas into the sheet that will calculate gross pay. You will also need to organize the data so it is presentable, easy to read, and easy to print, if necessary.

Learning Resources: **boostyourskills.lablearning.com**

Starting with a Template

Using templates in Excel is a way to save yourself a lot of work. Templates allow you to use a preexisting workbook, which usually has the formatting, headings, and formulas already created for you, when creating many similar documents. For example, templates are useful when creating invoices, where the structure and format are the same and only information such as names, dates, and amounts needs to be changed for each new file. Excel offers a large collection of online templates you can search through to find something suitable for your purpose.

Another option is to create your own template. Creating your own template means creating a workbook as usual, inserting text and formulas, and formatting as you desire, but not filling in any actual data. To create the template, you change the type of file to Excel Template when you go to save the workbook.

The default file type when saving your work is Excel Workbook; when creating your own template, change the file type to Excel Template.

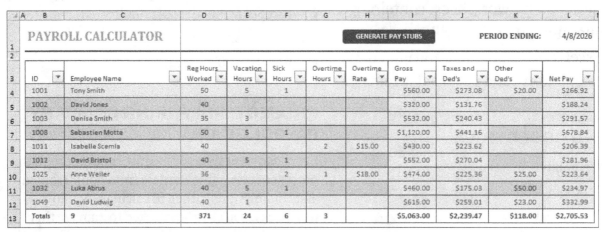

ID	Employee Name	Reg Hours Worked	Vacation Hours	Sick Hours	Overtime Hours	Overtime Rate	Gross Pay	Taxes and Ded's	Other Ded's	Net Pay
1001	Tony Smith	50	5	1			$560.00	$273.08	$20.00	$266.92
1002	David Jones	40					$320.00	$131.76		$188.24
1003	Denise Smith	35	3				$532.00	$240.43		$291.57
1008	Sebastien Motte	50	5	1			$1,120.00	$441.16		$678.84
1011	Isabelle Scemla	40			2	$15.00	$430.00	$223.62		$206.39
1012	David Bristol	40	5	1			$552.00	$270.04		$281.96
1025	Anne Weiler	36		2	1	$18.00	$474.00	$225.36	$25.00	$223.64
1032	Luka Abrus	40	5	1			$460.00	$175.03	$50.00	$234.97
1049	David Ludwig	40	1				$615.00	$259.01	$23.00	$332.99
Totals	9	371	24	6	3		$5,063.00	$2,239.47	$118.00	$2,705.53

This template is designed for payroll calculations and already has the structure, formatting, and formulas in place.

| NOTE! Be aware that some templates require users to have advanced Excel knowledge!

When you open a template, Excel creates a *copy* of the template file; changes do not affect the template itself, and the default file type reverts to Excel Workbook when you go to save the file.

DEVELOP YOUR SKILLS: E5-D1

In this exercise, you will browse templates, create your own template, and start a new workbook using your template.

1. Start Excel and click **New** on the left side of the screen.

   A list of templates displays. The first is Blank Workbook, and then there are several Excel feature tours, followed by a list of template options you can scroll down and browse through. There are many options, including templates to create schedules, calendars, budgets, and more.

2. Click in the **Search for Online Templates** box at the top of the screen, type **Payroll**, and tap Enter .

Excel searches through thousands of online templates and shows a list of templates related to your search. If you like, you can click an option to preview it, or open a template to look at it.

Now you will create a template to be used for Airspace Travel.

3. If necessary, close any open files, then open **E5-D1-PayrollBlank** from your **Excel Chapter 5** folder.

This is the file you want to start with every two weeks when you are creating the payroll.

4. Choose **File→Save As→Browse**.

5. In the Save As dialog box, type **E5-D1-PayrollTemplate** in the File Name box, then click the **Save as Type** menu and select **Excel Template**.

File name:	E5-D1-PayrollTemplate
Save as type:	Excel Workbook
Authors:	Excel Workbook
	Excel Macro-Enabled Workbook
	Excel Binary Workbook
	Excel 97-2003 Workbook
	CSV UTF-8 (Comma delimited)
	XML Data
⌃ Hide Folders	Single File Web Page
	Web Page
	Excel Template
	Excel Macro-Enabled Template

You are choosing the type of file first because, by default, saving as a template will save the file to a custom Office template directory created by Microsoft. However, you can navigate back to your file storage location and save the template there instead.

6. Navigate to the **Excel Chapter 5** folder in your file storage location and click **Save**.

Now that the file is saved as a template, you don't want to make any more changes to it, so you need to close it and then open a copy of the template using File Explorer.

NOTE! If you want to edit the template itself, use File→Open from within Excel to open the template file; to open a *copy* of the template, you can either use File→New to find templates saved in your custom Office template directory or simply open the template from inside File Explorer.

7. Close Excel; then use File Explorer to open **E5-D1-PayrollTemplate** from your **Excel Chapter 5** folder.

NOTE! Notice that a 1 has been added to the end of the filename in the title bar, similar to when you create a new blank workbook and the default name is Book1. Changing this file will not affect the template; it is a new and separate file.

8. Use **Save As** to save the workbook as: **E5-D1-PayrollP17**

Now that it has been saved, this is just a regular Excel file for you to work on, and the template remains unchanged for future use.

Adjusting View Options

When you have large amounts of data, it can be difficult to see it all and do what you need to do. For example, when you scroll down the worksheet, you will no longer see your headings, so you might lose track of what information is in each column. Or, you might want to see different parts of a spreadsheet at the same time for comparison. Using different view options makes it easier to work with these large worksheets.

Freeze Panes

To keep the headings in your worksheet visible while you scroll through your data, you can use the Freeze Panes feature. You can freeze rows or columns, or both at the same time. You can unfreeze the panes again at any time.

If cell B5 is selected, this option would freeze column A *and* rows 1:4, so the Inventory ID and all column headings would always remain visible.

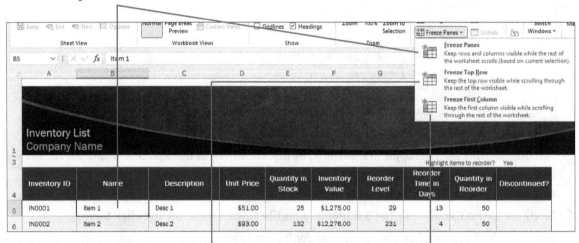

This option freezes row 1 only.

This freezes column A only; you cannot use Freeze Top Row and Freeze First Column at the same time.

View→Window→Freeze Panes

Split a Window

Another option is to split the Excel window, either into two halves or four quadrants. This allows you to scroll through different areas of your worksheet in the different split views, which is useful if you need to refer back and forth to data from different sections of your worksheet. Similar to Freeze Panes, the location of the split is based on the current active cell. To divide your worksheet in two halves, simply choose a cell in column A before creating the split. You can remove the split at any time.

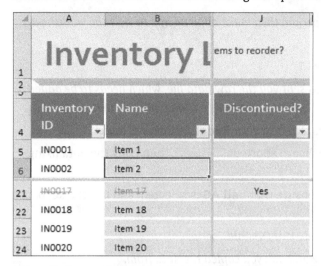

The split lines shown here divide the worksheet into four quadrants, and each can be scrolled through separately to view four different areas of the worksheet.

View→Window→Split ⊟

Change the Workbook View

Another issue with large worksheets is understanding how your worksheet will look when it is printed. To see how your worksheet will look when printed, or to see where page breaks will occur, you can use the Page Layout view or Page Break Preview.

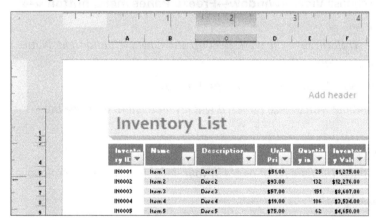

Page Layout view shows the ruler and allows you to view and edit the margins and header and footer sections.

View→Workbook Views

In this exercise, you will copy the data for the payroll period, then make adjustments to view the worksheet several different ways.

1. Save your workbook as: **E5-D2-PayrollP17**

    A coworker from the accounting department has sent you the raw data file, which needs to be added to the payroll file for pay period 17. You will insert the data by simply copying and pasting.

2. Open **E5-D2-PayrollPeriod17data**, which is saved in your **Excel Chapter 5** folder.

3. Select all data in the worksheet using the keyboard shortcut Ctrl+A, then copy the data using the keyboard shortcut Ctrl+C.

4. Return to the **E5-D2-PayrollP17** workbook, ensure that **cell A6** is selected, and use the keyboard shortcut Ctrl+V to paste the data.

5. Autofit **column E** so the department names are fully visible.

    Now that you have the data, you can close the workbook you copied the data from.

6. Switch back to and close **E5-D2-PayrollPeriod17data**.

    When closing the file, you may see a dialog box asking you to either save or delete the data on the Clipboard; if so, click No to delete it.

7. Select **cell C6** and choose **View→Window→Split**.

    Use the scroll bars or mouse wheel to scroll through the worksheet in each of the four quadrants.

8. Turn off the split by choosing **View→Window→Split** a second time.

9. Scroll back to the top-left portion of your worksheet if you are not already there.

10. Select **cell C6** again, and this time choose **View→Window→Freeze Panes menu button ⌄→ Freeze Panes**.

    Use the scroll bars or mouse wheel to scroll through the worksheet up and down, left and right. Notice that the headings and employee names remain visible.

11. Change the view by choosing **View→Workbook Views→Page Layout**.

    Because Page Layout View isn't compatible with Freeze Panes, it will prompt you to unfreeze the panes.

12. Click **OK** to unfreeze and continue.

    The status bar at the bottom now displays the number of pages in your document. You can scroll down to view the second page.

13. Switch back to the **Normal** view.

14. Save the workbook.

Organizing Data with Sorts and Filters

When you have large amounts of data, you need tools to help you make sense of it. Sorting gives you the ability to rearrange your data in the way that makes the most sense for your purpose. Filtering then allows you to narrow down your data to focus on certain parts of it.

Custom Sorts

Sorting can be performed on any column, using text values, numerical values, or even cell color or font color. Values can be sorted in either ascending or descending order, depending on the type of data being sorted: text, numbers, or perhaps dates.

In addition to a simple one-step sort, you can add multiple levels to your sorting for even better organization; for example, you might have an employee database with information like departments, job titles, office locations, sales performance data, and how long employees have been with the company, and you might decide to sort the data based on department first and then by length of time with the company.

To sort by a single column, you can use Ribbon commands or a shortcut menu. For more advanced sorting and to use multiple sort levels, use the Custom Sort dialog box.

Filters

Filtering allows you to choose what data to include (show) and what data to filter out (hide). You can also filter by text or numbers. For text you can create many filters to find data. This can help you find text that begins with or ends with a specific letter or that contains a certain string of text. For numeric values there are also numerous different ways to create rules to find values that are greater than, less than, equal to, and so on. Using the same company example, you could filter the list multiple ways to view only employees in the sales department, with five or more years of experience, and with less than $10,000 in sales last month.

A customer list with no sort or filter applied

Customers	Country
Carol Gregory	USA
Natasha Dyas	Canada
James Norman	Mexico
Joshua Garcia	USA
Sarah Mckinnon	USA
Shannon Miller	Mexico
Katrina Kormylo	Canada
Susan Colley	USA
William Emerson	Canada
Eugene Fink	USA

A customer list sorted by Country and then by Customers

Customers	Country
Katrina Kormylo	Canada
Natasha Dyas	Canada
William Emerson	Canada
James Norman	Mexico
Shannon Miller	Mexico
Carol Gregory	USA
Eugene Fink	USA
Joshua Garcia	USA
Sarah Mckinnon	USA
Susan Colley	USA

A customer list filtered to show only customers in the USA

Customers	Country
Carol Gregory	USA
Eugene Fink	USA
Joshua Garcia	USA
Sarah Mckinnon	USA
Susan Colley	USA

View the video "Using Sort and Filter."

Data→Sort & Filter→Sort 🔢 | Home→Editing→Sort & Filter ↕️→Custom Sort... | Right-click data→Sort→Custom Sort...

Data→Sort & Filter→Filter 🔽

DEVELOP YOUR SKILLS: E5-D3

In this exercise, you will use Sort & Filter to organize the employee data and edit the pay rate for some of the employees.

1. Save your workbook as: **E5-D3-PayrollP17**
2. Select one cell that contains data within the **range A6:H63**.
3. Choose **Data→Sort & Filter→Sort**.

   Excel automatically selects the entire range of adjacent data to sort, which is easier than trying to select the entire range yourself, especially if there are hundreds or even thousands of rows of data.

4. Follow these steps to sort the data with multiple levels:

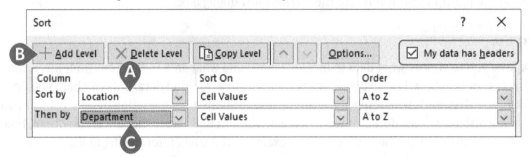

   A. Choose to sort first by **Location**.

   Excel recognizes that your data has headers in the top row, so you can select the name of the column you wish to sort by from the drop-down menu; without headers, the menu would show only Column A, Column B, etc.

   B. Click **Add Level** to perform an additional sort.

   C. Choose **Department** for the second sort level and click **OK**.

   Your data is now sorted, with Los Angeles employees listed at the top and Vancouver employees listed at the bottom. Within each location the employees are sorted by department.

First Name	Last Name	Employee ID#	Location	Department
Jasmin	Newton	13651	Los Angeles	Administration
Tim	Parker	17232	Los Angeles	Administration
Carol	Gregory	16688	Los Angeles	Management
Kobe	Curry	20303	Los Angeles	Sales
Tracy	Bryant	14917	Los Angeles	Sales
Cam	Owens	22404	Los Angeles	Sales
Ashley	Bradford	17571	Miami	Administration
Deborah	Secrett	16735	Miami	Administration
Adel	Kahlmeier	13089	Miami	Administration
Brett	Aberle	22113	Miami	Administration
Tony	Duncan	12743	Miami	Administration
James	Norman	13733	Miami	Management
Melissa	Coelho	21635	Miami	Management
Sophia	Maria	13365	Miami	Management
Steven	Samuel	15563	Miami	Sales

   Now you can filter your data to narrow it down.

5. Ensure that you still have a cell selected within the sorted list.

   Remember, you need only a single cell selected anywhere within the range of data you wish to sort or filter; Excel will automatically detect the correct range.

6. Choose **Data→Sort & Filter→Filter**.

   Notice the menu buttons that appear beside all of your column headings.

7. Follow these steps to filter your data:

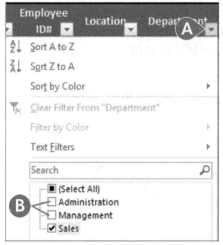
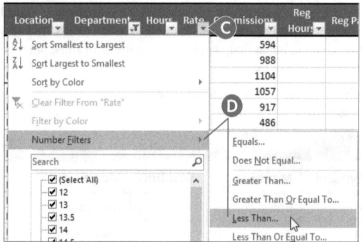
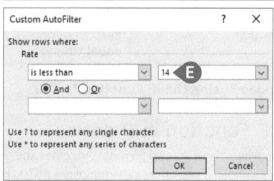

A. Click the **Department menu** button ∨.

B. Filter the Department column to include only Sales employees by removing the checks next to **Administration** and **Management**; click **OK**.

C. Click the **Rate menu** button ∨.

D. Choose **Number Filters→Less Than** to open the dialog box.

E. Type **14** to the right of *Show rows where rate is less than* and click **OK**.

   Your worksheet now displays only the six employees in the Sales department who have a rate below $14. Notice the Filter symbol beside the two columns with filters applied to them, Department and Rate.

8. The company has decided to increase all Sales employees to a minimum wage of $14 per hour, so adjust the rate for the six employees listed to: **14**

TIP!   After typing the value in the first cell, you can use the fill handle to copy the number 14; it won't affect the rows hidden by the filter.

9. Choose **Data→Sort & Filter→Filter** to turn off filters, which will remove all filters and redisplay all data.

10. Save the workbook.

The IF Function

There are many functions available in the Excel Function Library, but most of us use only a handful of these on a regular basis. Once you understand simple functions like SUM and AVERAGE, you can start exploring additional, more advanced functions. As you learn more about functions, it becomes easier to understand which functions to use and how to insert the function with the correct arguments.

The IF function is used quite frequently because it is helpful in many situations. It allows you to determine the value to enter in a cell based on the outcome of a logical test. The IF function also provides the basis for many other statistical functions, such as COUNTIF and SUMIF. Although the IF function seems rather challenging at first, it gets easier to use with some practice and is almost like creating a sentence in the form of a question.

Logical tests for IF functions include comparison operators, and it's important to understand the symbols used.

COMPARISON OPERATORS			
Symbol	**Meaning**	**Symbol**	**Meaning**
=	Equal to	<>	Not equal to
>	Greater than	>=	Greater than or equal to
<	Less than	<=	Less than or equal to

Greater	>	Than
2	>	1

The arrow points to the smaller number. If you can remember 2 is greater than 1, the less than symbol is the opposite.

☁ **View the video "Using the IF Function."**

Example: IF Function in Practice

Use the IF function where there are two possible outcomes and there are defined criteria to determine each outcome. For example, if you offer sales employees a $100 bonus if they achieve $5,000 in sales for the month, you can use an IF function to determine which employees qualify. In this case, the condition is that sales must be greater than or equal to $5,000, which needs to be written as a logical test.

THE IF FUNCTION		
Arguments	**Description**	**Examples**
Logical Test	This is a question or criterion that must be a yes/no or true/false question, using a comparison operator, that usually includes at least one cell reference.	D2>5000 D2>=A1
There are two possible outcomes for any logical test, so you need to enter two values:		
Value if true	If the answer is true, this determines what result is placed in the cell after completing the formula. The result can be text, numbers, cell references, or even another formula.	100 "Yes" D2*10%
Value if false	If the answer is not true, it must be false, so what will the result be? Again, the result can be text, numbers, cell references, or a formula.	0 "No" D2*2%

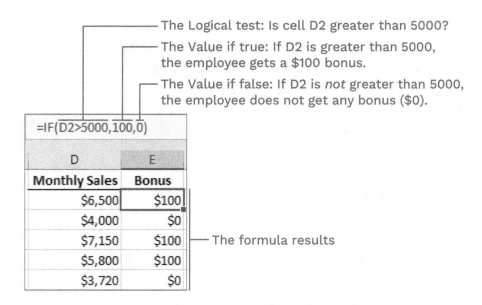

The Logical test: Is cell D2 greater than 5000?

The Value if true: If D2 is greater than 5000, the employee gets a $100 bonus.

The Value if false: If D2 is *not* greater than 5000, the employee does not get any bonus ($0).

=IF(D2>5000,100,0)

D	E
Monthly Sales	**Bonus**
$6,500	$100
$4,000	$0
$7,150	$100
$5,800	$100
$3,720	$0

The formula results

DEVELOP YOUR SKILLS: E5-D4

In this exercise, you will create several formulas using the IF function to calculate the number of regular hours and overtime hours each employee worked. You will then calculate total Gross Pay.

1. Save your workbook as: **E5-D4-PayrollP17**
2. Select **cell I6** and click **Insert Function** fx on the Formula Bar.
3. Choose the **IF** function (usually displayed by default under Most Recently Used; if not, select the **Logical** category first) and click **OK**.
4. Follow these steps to create a formula using the IF function to calculate the number of regular hours for employees:

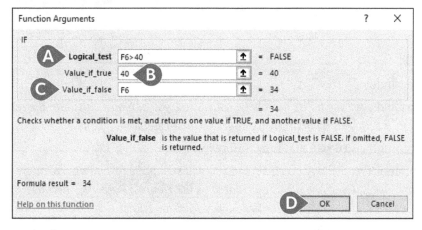

   A. In the Logical_Test box enter **F6>40** to determine whether the employee worked more than 40 hours.

   B. In the Value_If_True box enter **40** because if the employee did work more than 40 hours, that person would receive regular pay for 40 hours and the rest would be considered overtime.

   C. In the Value_If_False box enter **F6** because if the employee worked 40 hours or fewer, all hours worked would be considered regular hours.

   D. Click **OK**.

The result of the formula is 34; Jasmin worked 34 hours total, so her regular hours equal 34.

5. Select **cell K6** and enter this formula: `=IF(F6>40,F6-40,0)`

   The function arguments are typed within parentheses and separated by commas. The result of the formula is zero; Jasmin only worked 34 hours, so there are no overtime hours to be paid.

   To edit or to simply double-check the formula, you can click Insert Function at any time to open the Function Arguments dialog box.

6. If necessary, select **cell K6** again, and then click **Insert Function** and compare your screen to the following:

   The Logical_test box has the same logical test, *F6>40*, which determines whether the employee worked more than 40 hours.

   The Value_if_true box contains *F6-40*, because if the employee did in fact work more than 40 hours, that employee would receive overtime pay for the total number of hours less 40, the first 40 of which would be paid at the regular rate.

   The Value_if_false box says *0*, because if the employee worked 40 hours or less, that employee does not receive any overtime pay.

Function Arguments		? ✕
IF		
Logical_test	`F6>40` ⬆	= FALSE
Value_if_true	`F6-40` ⬆	= -6
Value_if_false	`0` ⬆	= 0
		= 0

   Checks whether a condition is met, and returns one value if TRUE, and another value if FALSE.

   Logical_test is any value or expression that can be evaluated to TRUE or FALSE.

   Formula result = 0

   Help on this function | OK | Cancel

7. Click **OK** to close the window.

   Since the regular hours and overtime hours have been calculated, you can now calculate the regular pay and overtime pay for employees by multiplying hours by their rate.

8. In **cell J6**, enter the formula `=I6*G6` and tap ⊞Tab twice.

   We know that Jasmin doesn't receive any overtime, but you will set up the formula to calculate overtime pay for all employees. Overtime pay is calculated as OT Hours x Rate x 1.5 because employees get time-and-a-half for overtime (100% + 50% = 150% or 1.5).

9. In **cell L6**, enter the formula `=K6*G6*1.5` and tap ⊞Tab.

   Total gross pay includes regular pay, as well as any overtime pay and commissions.

10. Enter the formula to calculate gross pay, which is: `=J6+L6+H6`

11. Apply bold formatting and **Currency** number formatting to **cell M6**.

12. Select the **range I6:M6** and double-click the **fill handle** to fill down the formulas for all employees.

Double-clicking is much easier in this case than dragging the fill handle all the way down to row 63, and all five columns can be filled at once rather than one at a time.

Gross pay is now calculated for all employees. You can double-check your formulas visually by checking a few examples of employees who worked overtime and a few who didn't. For example, you can quickly see that Cam Owens (row 11) worked 47 hours and received 7 hours of overtime pay.

13. Save the workbook.

Controlling Data Entry with Data Validation

When entering values into an Excel worksheet, it is important to be consistent and accurate. However, mistakes can be made, especially if you ask someone else to do the data entry for you. To ensure accuracy and consistency, you can use data validation to create criteria for cells that limit the possible entries into those cells.

Normally, you set up data validation rules before entering the values. You also need to select the entire range where you intend to enter the data, so you are creating the rule for that full range. This is important because creating criteria for a cell that already contains data won't tell you if that data was correctly entered—unless you use the Circle Invalid Data option from the Data Validation menu.

The criteria you choose can restrict the type of data as well as the range of acceptable values. For example, you could restrict data entry to whole numbers between 0 and 100, or you could restrict data entry to a text list. You can also create a custom input message to assist the user in entering the acceptable data and an error alert if they enter an unacceptable value.

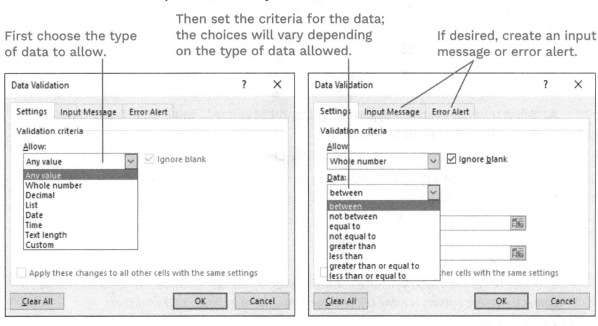

Data→Data Tools→Data Validation

In this exercise, you will create data validation criteria to choose the Department for each employee from a list and to restrict the number of hours that can be entered.

1. Save your workbook as: **E5-D5-PayrollP17**

   To begin, you will remove the data in the Department and Hours columns for the first six employees so you can create data validation rules that change how data is entered.

2. Select the **range E6:F11** and delete the data.

   Now you will use data validation rules to ensure the Department column is correctly populated using one of three choices from a list.

3. Follow these steps to create the data validation rule:

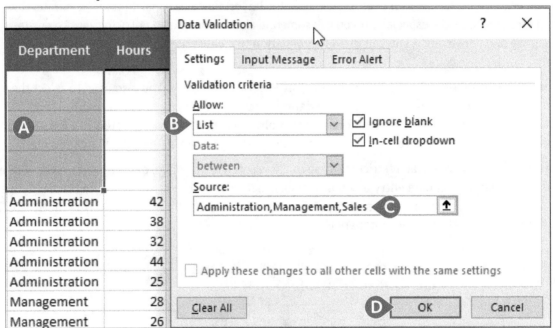

   A. Select the cells where the department data will be entered (**range E6:E11**) and choose **Data→Data Tools→Data Validation**.

   B. Click the **Allow menu** button ⌄ and choose **List**.

      Allowing the List data type means only values you specify can be entered into the cells, which the user chooses from a list.

   C. In the Source box, type **Administration,Management,Sales** and ensure each word is separated by a comma but *no space*.

   D. Click **OK**.

   The three items typed into the Source box will appear for the user to choose from; an alternative to typing the source options is using cell references to a list of items on your worksheet.

4. Select **cell E6**.

5. Type **Mgmt** and then tap ⎙Enter⎙.

   A window will pop up telling you the value you entered doesn't match the data validation restrictions for the cell.

6. Click **Cancel**.

7. Now type **Ad** and tap Enter.

   This time typing just a few letters enters the entire department name from the list.

   You can also use the mouse to select a name from the drop-down menu button ⌄ to the right of the cell, which displays the options you typed for the source of the list.

8. Use the **menu** button ⌄ to select **Administration** from the list of Departments for Tim in **cell E7**.

9. Using whichever method you prefer, enter the departments for the other four employees:

   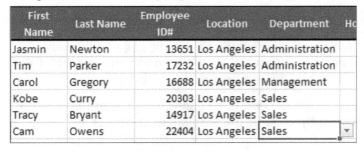

First Name	Last Name	Employee ID#	Location	Department	H
Jasmin	Newton	13651	Los Angeles	Administration	
Tim	Parker	17232	Los Angeles	Administration	
Carol	Gregory	16688	Los Angeles	Management	
Kobe	Curry	20303	Los Angeles	Sales	
Tracy	Bryant	14917	Los Angeles	Sales	
Cam	Owens	22404	Los Angeles	Sales	

10. Select the **range F6:F11** to create data validation criteria for the hours to be entered.

11. Choose **Data→Data Tools→Data Validation** and set the criteria to allow only a **Whole Number** between **0** (minimum) and **60** (maximum).

12. Click the **Input Message** tab and enter the following into the Input Message field:

    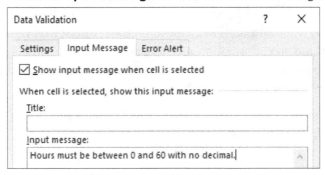

13. Click **OK** to complete the settings and then select **cell F6**.

    A ScreenTip appears with the message you entered.

14. To test the data validation rule, type **61** in **cell F6** and tap Enter. Read the message and then click **Retry**. Test again by typing **40.5** and tapping Enter; click **Cancel** to stop editing the cell.

    If you need someone else to enter the data, you can be confident no data will be entered that doesn't meet your criteria. For example, you won't end up accidentally paying someone for 400 hours instead of 40!

15. Enter these hours for the six employees in Los Angeles, starting with Jasmin in **cell F6**: **34, 27, 40, 36, 30, 47**

16. Save the workbook.

Printing Options

To print large worksheets in a professional, presentable format, you may need to make some adjustments. For example, you may want to ensure that column headings are visible on all pages, you may want to choose how your data is divided across several pages, or you may want to add additional information that isn't part of the worksheet itself to the top or bottom of each printed page.

PRINTING OPTIONS	
Feature	**Description**
Print Titles	Print the same headings on all pages by repeating the same rows or the same columns on all pages.
Print Area	Print only a specific area of your worksheet rather than the whole thing.
Breaks	Determine where one page ends and the next page begins when printing. Page breaks in Excel are both horizontal and vertical. Existing page breaks can be moved and new ones can be inserted.
Scale to Fit	Force data onto a desired number of pages, using width and height, by scaling or shrinking the size of the worksheet contents.

☁ **View the video "Printing a Large Worksheet."**

Page Layout→Page Setup

Headers and Footers

When you are printing a worksheet, you may want information included on the printout that doesn't need to be shown on the screen. This might include information such as a title, company name, your own name, the page number, or perhaps the current date. There are tools in Excel for automatically entering some of this information, or you can manually type the information you want to appear.

In Excel, both the Header and Footer areas have three distinct sections. These are not part of the worksheet, so they do not have a cell address like the worksheet cells.

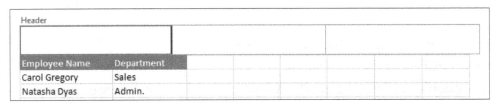

TIP! Navigating to the Footer section can be tricky, but there's a button on the Ribbon that makes it much easier than scrolling down: Header & Footer Tools Design→Navigation→Go to Footer.

Insert→Text→Header & Footer 🗎

View→Workbook Views→Page Layout 🗎

DEVELOP YOUR SKILLS: E5-D6

In this exercise, you will set up the print area, repeat the column headings on every page, and adjust other print settings.

1. Save your workbook as: **E5-D6-PayrollP17**

2. Choose **File→Print** to see the print preview.

   Notice that the worksheet prints on four pages, and the OT Hours, OT Pay, and Gross Pay columns appear on pages three and four. The first adjustment to be made is to adjust the worksheet width to one page.

3. Use the **Back** button to return to your worksheet.

4. Choose **Page Layout→Scale to Fit→Width→1 page**.

5. Go back to the preview and see that the worksheet now prints on two pages—one page wide and two pages long.

6. Use the **Back** button to return to your worksheet.

Print Repeating Headings

7. Choose **Page Layout→Page Setup→Print Titles**.

8. Follow these steps to print repeating headings:

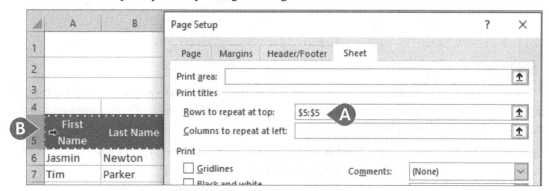

A. Select the box next to **Rows to Repeat at Top**.

B. Click anywhere in **row 5**.

When you click to select the row, Excel adds the correct formatting to the row reference.

9. Click **OK**.

   You won't notice anything different in the current view, but you can check the print preview to see the repeating row on page two.

10. Choose **File→Print** and below the preview use the **right-pointing arrow** to advance to page two.

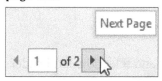

   Now you can see the same headings with the blue background on page two that are printed on page one.

11. Use the **Back** button to return to your worksheet.

Set the Print Area

12. Select the **range A5:M11**.

You must select the desired range before setting the print area.

13. Choose **Page Layout→Page Setup→Print Area→Set Print Area**.

Only the selected range will print, which means the Los Angeles employees and the headings in row 5.

14. Go to the print preview to view the change and then return to your worksheet.

15. Choose **Page Layout→Page Setup→Print Area→Clear Print Area**.

Now the whole worksheet will print once again because the specified print area has been cleared.

Set Page Breaks

For editing some of the page layout settings, it is best to be in Page Layout view. However, for adding/ adjusting page breaks, it is best to be in Page Break Preview.

16. Choose **View→Workbook Views→Page Break Preview**.

There are two pages in the print area, and the page break falls between Natasha Dyas *and* Joshua Garcia.

36	Terrence	King
37	Lorraine	Martine
38	Natasha	Dyas
39	Joshua	Garcia
40	Karen	Ablitt
41	Megan	Dorfling

17. Place the mouse pointer over the page break line to display the two-way arrow and then drag the page break up and place it below **row 11**, where the data for Los Angeles employees ends and the data for Miami employees begins.

Because the area below the page break is now too big to fit on one page, Excel automatically adds a new page break, so your worksheet will now print on three pages.

18. Drag the new page break up below **row 28**, where the data for Miami employees ends.

Because the rest of the data does fit on page three, you have to manually insert two more page breaks to print New York, Toronto, and Vancouver on separate pages.

19. Select **cell A38**, below the row where the data for New York employees ends, and choose **Page Layout→Page Setup→Breaks→Insert Page Break**.

20. Insert another page break above the Vancouver employees.

21. Change the workbook view back to **Normal** and then go to the print preview.

The data will print on five pages, one for each location, with the column headings repeated at the top of each page.

Insert Header

22. Return to your worksheet and then switch to **Page Layout** view and select the left header section.

You will see the Header & Footer Tools Design tab appear on the Ribbon, which allows you to insert formatted elements like page numbers and the current date.

23. Choose **Header & Footer Tools→Design→Header & Footer Elements→File Name**.

    Notice the code that is inserted; the code will display and print the filename when you click outside of the left header box. Also, if the filename ever changes, the text in the header will update automatically.

24. Select the center header section and insert the **Page Number**.

25. Insert the **Current Date** in the right header section.

26. Deselect the header area, switch back to **Normal** view, and then go to the print preview one last time.

    Excel won't let you change the workbook view while you are editing the header, so be sure to click a cell on the worksheet before changing the view.

27. Save the workbook.

Excel Tables

Tables allow you to more easily organize and analyze related data. Tables simplify the process of performing sorts, filtering your data, calculating totals, and even modifying the format of your data. The process of taking existing data and inserting a table is very simple, and you can convert a table back to a normal range of cells at any time without losing any data.

The header row makes sorting and filtering easy using the menu buttons ▼ in the header cells. ────

Banded rows (alternating colors) can be added or removed, and you can use Table Styles to modify the colors.

Employee Name	Department	Salary
Carol Gregory	Sales	$40,000
Natasha Dyas	Admin.	$34,500
James Norman	Management	$68,000
Joshua Garcia	Sales	$46,000
Sarah Mckinnon	Sales	$42,750
Shannon Miller	Management	$52,000
Katrina Kormylo	Admin.	$48,000
Susan Colley	Sales	$44,800
William Emerson	Admin.	$41,000
Eugene Fink	Sales	$37,000

Employee Name ▼	Department ▼	Salary ▼
Carol Gregory	Sales	$40,000
Natasha Dyas	Admin.	$34,500
James Norman	Management	$68,000
Joshua Garcia	Sales	$46,000
Sarah Mckinnon	Sales	$42,750
Shannon Miller	Management	$52,000
Katrina Kormylo	Admin.	$48,000
Susan Colley	Sales	$44,800
William Emerson	Admin.	$41,000
Eugene Fink	Sales	$37,000
Total		10 $454,050

Use the Total row to add functions ──── like Count (Department) and Sum (Salary) via the cell menu button ▼.

The same data, before and after a table is inserted

As you add more data to the bottom or right of the table, the table area expands to include the new adjacent rows or columns. Another nice feature is that entering a formula in one table cell will automatically copy the formula to all cells in that table column.

Insert→Tables→Table ⊞

Table Design→Tools→Convert to Range 🖫

DEVELOP YOUR SKILLS: E5-D7

In this exercise, you will create a table and perform tasks such as filtering, sorting, and calculating totals.

1. Save your file as: **E5-D7-PayrollP17**
2. Select **cell J6** and choose **Insert→Tables→Table**.

   Excel looks for the adjacent range of data and suggests the range A5:M63, which includes the table headers.

3. Click **OK** to accept the suggested table area.

   You may see a warning suggesting there are external data ranges. If so, choose to convert the selection to a table and remove all external connections.

4. Click the **Department menu** button ⌄.

   Notice the sort and filtering options available.

5. Uncheck the filter boxes for **Administration** and **Sales** and click **OK**.

   Only employees in the Management department are now visible in the list.

6. Use the **Rate menu** button ⌄ to sort the **Management** department employees by rate, from largest to smallest.

7. Choose **Table Design→Table Style Options→Total Row**.

   Notice that in column M there is a total automatically calculated for the Management department, which shows the sum of the department's gross pay.

8. Select **cell F64**, click the **menu** button ⌄, and select **Sum**.

   The total hours for Management employees are calculated, showing 416 hours.

9. Change the Table Style to **White, Table Style Medium 1**.

10. Use the **Department** filter to hide the Management data and display the Sales department only.

11. Use the **Location menu** button ⌄ to re-sort the data by Location from A to Z.

    Locations should be listed in order from A to Z, and the Total row at the bottom of the table should recalculate the total hours and gross pay.

First Name ▼	Hours ▼	Gross Pay ▼
Total	1152	$40,921.50

12. Save the workbook and close Excel.

Self-Assessment

 Check your knowledge of this chapter's key concepts and skills using the online Self-Assessment Quiz.

MICROSOFT EXCEL 2021/365

Advanced Workbook Formatting

In this chapter, you will work with various tools useful for customizing your workbooks to suit your own, specific needs. For example, an invoice workbook you send to your customers at work might look quite different from a rough workbook you are using for your personal budget at home. You will learn ways to set up and adjust your worksheet to look consistent, professional, and presentable, as well as how to track information about the document.

LEARNING OBJECTIVES

- Apply and customize themes
- Create and use cell styles
- Apply cell borders and fill
- Create custom number formats
- Customize the page setup
- Edit document properties

CHAPTER TIMING

- Concepts & Practice: 01:20:00
- Self-Assessment: 00:15:00
- Total: 01:35:00

PROJECT: PREPARING COMPANY DOCUMENTS

In addition to being an instructor at LearnFast College, you serve on different committees and work with various teams on special projects. LearnFast is currently preparing its annual performance review in which it reports to employees, management, and investors on how well the college did last year. You have volunteered to review the Excel file and use your skills to add appropriate formatting before the report is distributed and presented at the annual meeting.

Learning Resources: **boostyourskills.lablearning.com**

Formatting with Themes

Themes are an easy way to personalize a workbook with a unique set of colors, fonts, and effects. You can apply a different theme to an existing workbook or choose the desired theme when you first begin working on a new workbook. The theme is applied to the whole workbook, so all worksheets will have a consistent look.

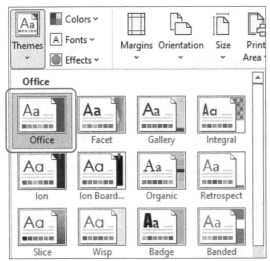

All Office applications have a standard set of themes, and you can scroll through, preview, and select a theme from the gallery; the current theme is highlighted in gray.

The theme controls the default font used in the workbook. This may affect the default column width and row height in the workbook as well, depending on the chosen theme.

The default/theme fonts for the Office theme (left) and the Slice theme (right)

The theme also changes the color palette for formatting options such as fill color, font color, and border color. If your existing workbook uses theme colors for formatting and you change the theme, the formatting in the workbook will change to match the new theme colors. However, if your existing workbook uses standard colors for fill, font, and/or border formatting, those colors will always stay the same regardless of the theme.

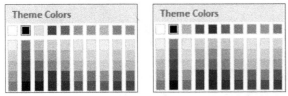

The color palettes for the Office theme (left) and the Slice theme (right)

Customizing Themes

You can modify an existing theme by changing each of the three elements individually: the colors, fonts, or effects. For example, to modify the colors, you can choose from the list of color combinations available or customize even further by choosing each individual color to be used in the theme.

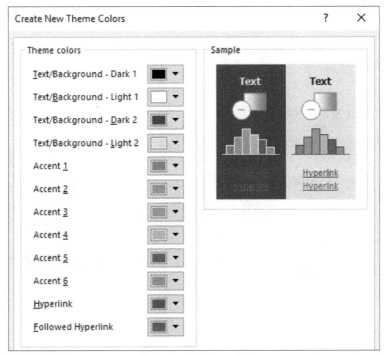

The Create New Theme Colors window allows you to choose four theme colors for text/background and six accent colors, in addition to the colors used for hyperlinks and followed hyperlinks.

To modify the theme fonts, you can also choose from the gallery of options or choose your own custom heading font and body font.

> **TIP!** After you have modified any part of a theme, you can save your theme to use again in other documents.

Page Layout→Themes [Aa]

Page Layout→Themes→Themes→Save Current Theme

DEVELOP YOUR SKILLS: E6-D1

In this exercise, you will modify the workbook's theme and theme colors to match the LearnFast College school colors.

1. Start Excel, open **E6-D1-PerformanceData** from your **Excel Chapter 6** folder, and save it as: **E6-D1-PerformanceReport**

   To begin, you will choose a different theme for the document, which will change the font, font color, and fill color in both worksheets.

2. Choose **Page Layout→Themes→Themes**.

   As you place the mouse over the different themes, you can see a preview of the changes on the worksheet. Modifying the theme means any existing content that is formatted using a theme font or a theme color will change to match the new theme.

3. Choose the **Slice** theme.

4. Choose **Home→Font→Fill Color ⌄ menu button**.

   The theme colors showing in the Fill Color menu have changed, but do NOT select any of the colors at this time. You will adjust two of the colors in the next steps.

5. Choose **Page Layout→Themes→Colors→Customize Colors…**.

6. Follow these steps to set the colors for Accent 4 and Accent 5:

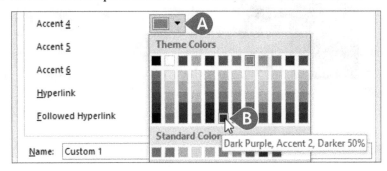

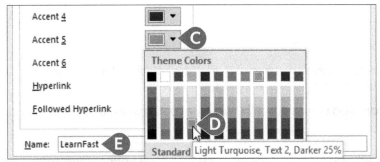

   A. Click the **color menu** button ▼ beside Accent 4.

   B. Choose **Dark Purple, Accent 2, Darker 50%**.

   C. Click the **color menu** button ▼ beside Accent 5.

   D. Choose **Light Turquoise, Text 2, Darker 25%**.

   E. Type **LearnFast** in the Name box for the new theme colors and click **Save**.

   The new colors for Accent 4 and 5 are seen in the headings at the top of the worksheet. These colors are now saved for use in other workbooks.

7. Save the file.

| **NOTE!** Always leave your file open at the end of an exercise unless instructed to close it.

Cell Styles

You can use Excel's built-in cell styles to give your worksheet a quick, uniform design. The Cell Styles option combines formatting such as font, color, fill, and alignment. There are numerous options, including cell styles for data such as input and output styles, cell styles for formatting your titles and headings, and themed styles that change depending on the theme.

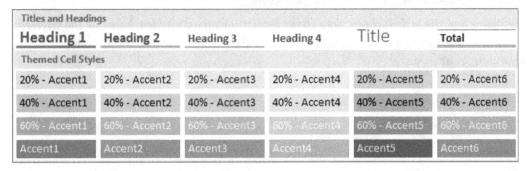

You can also create new cell styles or modify existing cell styles; however, these changes apply only to the current workbook (unless you merge the cell styles from one workbook to another). The simplest way to create a new style is to format one cell the way you wish the style to appear, and then create a new style based on the selected cell. Excel refers to this as creating a new style "by example."

To modify a cell style, you can right-click any style in the gallery and choose the Modify option. This opens the Style dialog box, from where you can make your modifications.

Home→Styles→Cell Styles 📝

DEVELOP YOUR SKILLS: E6-D2

In this exercise, you will create and apply cell styles to the worksheet to ensure consistent formatting.

1. Save your file as: **E6-D2-PerformanceReport**

   First you will apply the Total cell style to the totals for each of the four data categories.

2. Go to the **2026** sheet, if necessary, and select the totals for the student enrollments in the **range A11:C11**.

3. Choose **Home→Styles→Cell Styles** to open the cell style gallery, if necessary.

   Depending on your monitor size, you may already see the gallery; if so, click the More button to expand it.

4. In the Titles and Headings group, select the **Total** style.

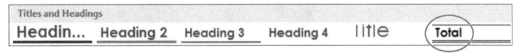

5. Apply the **Total** style to the totals for the three other data categories in the **ranges E11:G11, I11:K11**, and **M11:O11**.

| TIP! Use the Format Painter for quick work.

6. Locate the headings below *Student Enrollments* and select the **range A6:C6**, taking care to include the blank cell, **cell A6**.

7. Apply the **Heading 3** style to the selected range.

8. Apply the same style, **Heading 3**, to the **ranges E6:G6**, **I6:K6**, and **M6:O6**.

Next you will create a new cell style based on the title near the top of the worksheet and apply it to the headings.

9. Select **cell A2**, which contains the text *Annual Performance Review*.

10. Choose **Home→Styles→Cell Styles→New Cell Style...**.

In the Style dialog box, the Style Includes area shows formatting already added, based on the selected cell; if desired, you could modify the formatting by clicking the Format button. For this exercise, you will keep the settings as they are.

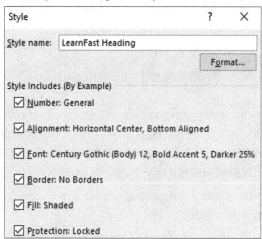

11. Enter **LearnFast Heading** for the new style's name and click **OK** to accept all other settings.

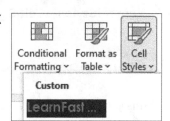

Your new cell style is now available in the Cell Styles gallery in the Custom group.

12. Apply the **LearnFast Heading** style to **cells A5**, **E5**, **I5**, and **M5**.

13. Save the file.

Using the Format Cells Dialog Box

Excel has many formatting and other features available right from the Ribbon, and there are even more cell formatting options in the Format Cells dialog box. The Format Cells dialog box is useful when you have a cell or range that requires specific formatting adjustments.

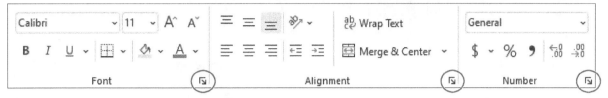

The dialog box launchers on the Home tab offer quick, alternative ways to open the Format Cells dialog box.

The Format Cells dialog box has six tabs with additional options for formatting; the active tab depends on which method you use to open the dialog box.

Home→Cells→Format 🔲→Format Cells

Cell Borders and Fill

The borders options available on the Ribbon are very plain, unless you use the Draw Borders features. Another option is to select the desired cells and open the Format Cells dialog box. From there you can choose from a gallery of line styles, choose a color, and apply the border to the desired area of the selected cell or range. You can also see a preview of all these options before applying them to the worksheet.

Likewise, if you want a cell formatted with a fill other than a solid color, you can open the Format Cells dialog box to access fill options, such as gradients and patterns.

DEVELOP YOUR SKILLS: E6-D3

In this exercise, you will use the Format Cells dialog box to create customized border and fill formatting.

1. Save your file as: **E6-D3-PerformanceReport**
2. Select **cell A1**, which contains the title *LearnFast College*.
3. Choose **Home→Cells→Format→Format Cells**.

4. Follow these steps to create a unique border:

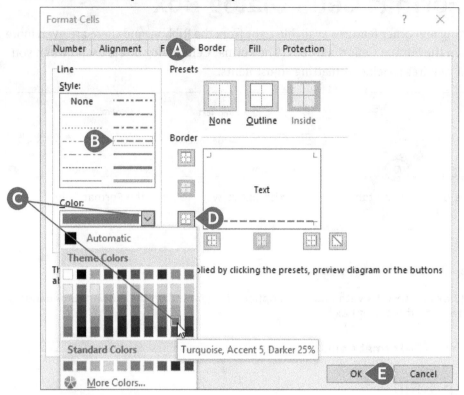

A. Click the **Border** tab.

B. Select the thick dashed line style, the fourth option in the second column.

C. Click the **Color menu** button ⌄ and select **Turquoise, Accent 5, Darker 25%**.

D. Click the **Bottom Border** button to add a border at the bottom of the selected cell.

   Hint: You can also click near the bottom of the preview below the word Text to apply a border to the bottom.

E. Click **OK**.

   Remember, you can't see the border while the cell is still selected.

5. Click **cell A5** to select that cell and deselect **cell A1**, which allows you to see the border you just created.

6. Select the **range A4:O4**, the blank row between the titles and headings.

7. Reopen the Format Cells dialog box by clicking the **Font Settings** dialog box launcher.

8. Follow these steps to create a pattern fill:

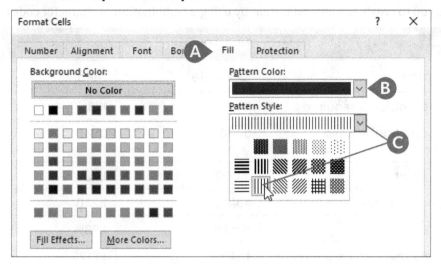

A. Click the **Fill** tab.

B. Click the **Pattern Color menu** button ⌄ and select **Dark Purple, Accent 4**.

C. Click the **Pattern Style menu** button ⌄ and select **Thin Vertical Stripe**.

9. Click **OK**.

The purple pattern is inserted into the range, creating an interesting visual effect.

10. Save the file.

Creating Custom Number Formats

Although Excel has many number formats to choose from, there may be times you need to modify the number formatting for your own purposes. For example, you may want to add text or symbols to the number formatting, such as *99USD*, or you may want to display a number with preceding zeroes, such as *000395*.

You create custom formatting in the Format Cells dialog box. The Number tab includes the Custom category, which allows you to create the desired format by using a combination of character codes.

CUSTOM NUMBER FORMATTING			
Code	**Description**	**Example**	**Display**
#	Digit placeholder, if required	###	123
0	Digit placeholder, always displayed	0000	0123
.	Decimal point	#.000	1.230
,	Thousands separator	#,###	1,230
%	Percentage	#.##%	1.23%
$ - + / ( )	Characters that can be added to the displayed number	+$###	+$123
"abc"	Displays the text inside the double quotes	###"USD"	123USD
[Red]	Displays values in the color specified	[Red]#,###	1,230

You can also specify a different format for each of the different types of values: positive values, negative values, zero values, and text. Each format must be created in that specific order and separated by semicolons. For example, you could format positive numbers in blue, negative values in red, zero values in black, and all text values in green using this code: [Blue]General;[Red]General;[Black]General;[Green] General

 View the video "Custom Number Formatting."

International Formatting

Excel includes formatting options for creating dates and currency according to international standards. For example, if you are sending a worksheet to users in Ireland or Japan, you may want to include the Euro or Yen currency format, respectively. Similarly, if you're sending a worksheet to users in Greece, you may want to adjust the date format according to that country's standard. These additional options are available from the Currency and Date categories on the Number tab in the Format Cells dialog box.

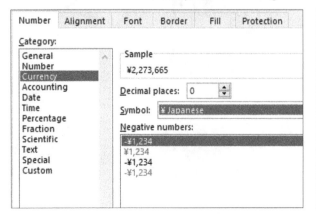
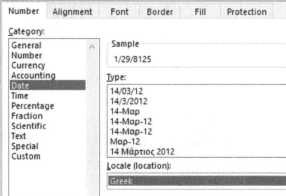

DEVELOP YOUR SKILLS: E6-D4

In this exercise, you will create custom number formatting to enhance the data display.

1. Save your file as: **E6-D4-PerformanceReport**
2. Select the **range C7:C11**, which shows the change from the previous year to the current year.

   Right now, it's difficult to read the values in this column, so you will add custom number formatting to make the data easier to understand.

3. Open the Format Cells dialog box by clicking the **Number Format** dialog box launcher.

4. Choose **Custom** from the bottom of the Category list.
5. Click in the **Type** box, delete **General**, and enter: **+0.00%; [Red] -0.00%**

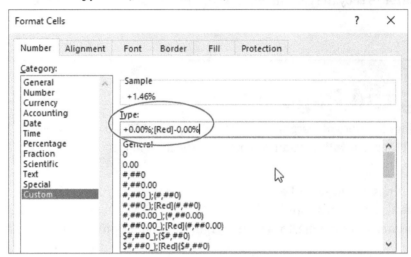

The first group of characters represents positive numbers, the second represents negative numbers, and the semicolon separates the two. Positive numbers will display the plus sign and percent sign with two decimal places; negative numbers will have the percent sign and two decimals, but they will show a negative sign and display in red.

6. Click **OK** to apply the new number formatting.

Student Enrollments		
	Current Year	Change
Q1	1248	+1.46%
Q2	1213	+5.48%
Q3	1377	-1.64%
Q4	1385	+0.87%
Total	5223	+1.36%

7. Use the **Format Painter** to apply the same number format to the other columns below the *Change* heading in the **ranges G7:G11, K7:K11,** and **O7:O11**.
8. Select the current year revenue data in the **range J7:J11** and then reopen the Format Cells dialog box.

9. On the Number tab, select the **Custom** category, type `$#,###,"K"` in the Type box, and click **OK**.

This code inserts the dollar sign and abbreviates the digits by rounding to the nearest thousand (because there is no digit placeholder following the second thousand separator) and adds the letter K at the end to represent the word thousand.

Revenue		
	Current Year	**Change**
Q1	$2,274K	-1.05%
Q2	$2,173K	+10.14%
Q3	$2,221K	+13.75%
Q4	$2,457K	-8.38%
Total	**$9,125K**	**+2.47%**

10. Use the **Format Painter** to copy the current year revenue format to the current year expenses in the **range N7:N11**.

11. Save the file.

Customizing the Page Setup

The default workbook settings are Normal margins (0.7" left and right, 0.75" top and bottom) on ordinary letter-size (8.5" x 11") paper with portrait orientation. The margin is the white space around the edge of your printed file.

You can customize these settings as necessary. For example, you can create narrower margins to fit more data on one sheet. These page settings are not fully visible from the Normal view; to see how your document will look when printed (for example, to see the margins or orientation), go to Page Layout view or the Print Preview.

Adding a Worksheet Background Image

If your worksheet is meant for display on the screen only, a worksheet background can add some visual interest and personality. The background will not print, so if you plan to print the worksheet, keep this in mind. The background picture can be inserted from your computer files, from an online image search using Bing, or from your OneDrive account.

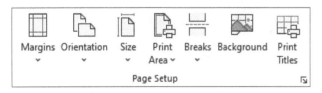

Page Layout→Page Setup

In this exercise, you will modify the page setup to fit the data on one page and insert a background picture.

1. Save your file as: **E6-D5-PerformanceReport**
2. Choose **View→Workbook Views→Page Layout**.

   When modifying page layout settings, it's a good idea to switch to Page Layout view so you can see the changes being made. Currently the data is split on two pages, and the margins are visible at the top and sides of the worksheet.
3. Choose **Page Layout→Page Setup→Margins→Narrow**.

   Now more of the data fits on the first page but some data is still on page 2.
4. Choose **Page Layout→Page Setup→Orientation→Landscape**.

   Again, more data is visible on page 1, but there are still two pages, so one more change is needed.
5. Choose **Page Layout→Page Setup→Size→Legal**.

   Now all the data will fit on one sheet of paper.
6. Change the view back to **Normal**.
7. Insert a background by choosing **Page Layout→Page Setup→Background**.
8. In the From a File section, click **Browse** to insert a file saved on your computer.
9. Navigate to your **Excel Chapter 6** folder, select the **Graduate.jpg** picture, and click **Insert**.

   The picture of the graduation cap and diploma is now displayed in the background, behind the data. You may notice the picture is tiled—that is, it repeats over and over again horizontally and vertically. There is no way to change this setting in Excel for background images.
10. Save the file.

Editing Document Properties

The Excel file's document properties can tell you, or anyone else who accesses the file, important information about it. The document properties already include information such as the date the file was created, the date it was last modified, the author (creator), and file size. Other information can also be added to the document properties, such as a title, subject, tags (keywords), or comments.

File→Info

In this exercise, you will modify the document properties to include a title, tags, category, and subject.

1. Save your file as: **E6-D6-PerformanceReport**
2. Choose **File** to go to Backstage view, and then select the **Info** button from the left side menu.

   Notice the Protect Workbook, Inspect Workbook, and other options on the left side and the Properties section on the right side of the screen.
3. Click in the **Add a Title** box and enter this text, tapping Tab when finished: **Final Performance Report**

4. Enter the remaining document properties as shown:

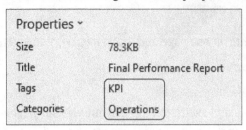

5. Click **Show All Properties** at the bottom of the Properties list to expand the list.

6. Click the **Specify the Subject** box and type: `2025 and 2026 Performance`

7. Use the **Back** button to return to your worksheet.

8. Save your workbook and close Excel.

Self-Assessment

 Check your knowledge of this chapter's key concepts and skills using the online Self-Assessment Quiz.

Date Functions and Conditional Formatting

7

In this chapter, you will use a variety of methods to work with an important type of data in Excel: date and time information. Dates provide useful information for all kinds of data, such as when customer invoices are due and when payments were made, or recording company expenses, schedules, and reports. You will also explore creating and customizing conditional formatting rules to gain valuable insight into the data in your worksheet.

LEARNING OBJECTIVES

- Identify date serial numbers
- Apply custom date formatting
- Enter times
- Create functions using dates
- Perform date and time calculations
- Create customized conditional formatting rules
- Edit rules using the Conditional Formatting Rules Manager

CHAPTER TIMING

- Concepts & Practice: 01:20:00
- Self-Assessment: 00:15:00
- Total: 01:35:00

PROJECT: UPDATING COMPANY DOCUMENTS

Airspace Travel, which provides travel packages to tropical destinations, prides itself on providing top-notch customer service. As part of its service plan, the company carefully tracks its customers' travel dates and flight times, as well as the frequency of their trips. You have been lending your Excel expertise to the company, and now Airspace has given you the task of reviewing and updating their travel information.

Learning Resources: **boostyourskills.lablearning.com**

Date Serial Numbers

In Excel, dates are stored as sequential serial numbers. To understand dates in Excel, you must also know that Excel dates start with January 1, 1900. The serial number for January 1, 1900, is *1*, and the serial numbers increase by one for each day after that date. For example, the serial number *501* represents *May 15, 1901*, which is exactly 500 days after January 1, 1900.

Using serial numbers for dates is helpful because it means that they can be used in calculations and functions. For example, you can use a formula to find the days until a payment is due by starting with the due date and subtracting today's date.

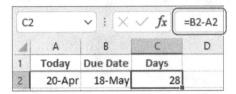

The formula in cell C2, *=B2-A2*, subtracts today's date in cell A2 from the due date in cell B2.

Applying Custom Date Formatting

There are many ways to enter a date into a cell, and depending on how you do so, Excel will apply one of the default date formats—usually either *4/17/2026* or *17-Apr*. After entering a date, you have the option of adjusting the date formatting using the Number Format drop-down menu or applying custom date formatting. The Number Format menu gives you two options, Short Date and Long Date; for example, *4/17/2026* and *Friday, April 17, 2026*, respectively.

Additional date formatting options are available from the Format Cells dialog box, either in the Date or the Custom category. Both categories have many options to choose from under Type.

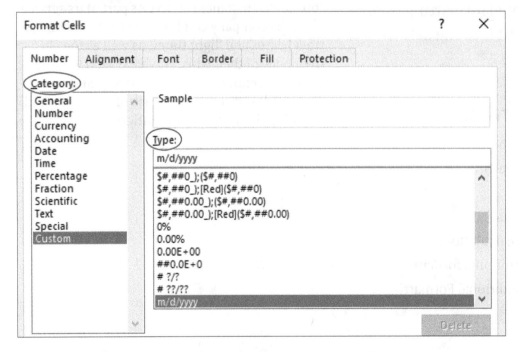

In Custom format, *d* represents the day, *m* represents the month, and *y* represents the year. You can also create your own date formats by using the codes *d, m,* and *y* in different combinations, similar to creating other custom number formats.

CUSTOM DATE FORMATTING			
Category	**Format Type**	**Description**	**Display for April 17, 2026**
Date	3/14	Month/Day	4/17
	3/14/12	Month/Day/Year	4/17/26
	March-12	Month-Year	April-26
	March 14, 2012	Month Day, Year	April 17, 2026
Custom	d-mmm	Day-Month	17-Apr
	d-mmmm	Day-Month	17-April
	d-mmm-yy	Day-Month-Year	17-Apr-26
	dddd mmmm "the" d	Day of the Week Month "the" Day	Friday April the 17

☁ **View the video "Custom Date Formatting."**

DEVELOP YOUR SKILLS: E7-D1

In this exercise, you will enter dates and then use those dates in a simple calculation. You will also apply different formatting to the dates.

1. Start Excel; open a new, blank workbook and save it to your **Excel Chapter 7** folder as: **E7-D1-DaysOld**

2. In **cell A1**, enter today's date in the format *mm/dd* and tap ⏎Enter.

   When only the month and day are entered, Excel automatically assigns the current year to the date (even though the year does not display in the worksheet, it is stored in the Formula Bar).

3. In **cell A2**, enter your birth date, including the year, and tap ⏎Enter.

4. In **cell A3**, enter the formula: **=A1-A2**

   To find the difference between two dates, always subtract the lower date from the higher date (remember each day counts up by one), and the result is the number of days between the two. The result in cell A3 shows how old you are, calculated in the number of days! Notice that the number format in cell A3 is General.

   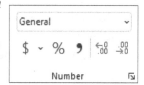

5. Select the two dates in the **range A1:A2** and choose **Home→Number→Number Format menu button ⌄→General**.

   The format for the two dates is converted to General, which means the serial number for those dates is now displayed.

6. With the same range selected, choose **Home→Number→Number Format menu button ⌄→ Long Date**.

   The Long Date format displays the day of the week, so you can see the day of the week on which you were born (in case you don't remember!).

7. In **cell B3**, type **days old** and tap ⏎Enter.

8. Save the file and close it.

Now you will apply various formatting to the dates in the Airspace customer invoices file.

9. Open **E7-D1-Invoices** from your **Excel Chapter 7** folder and save it as: **E7-D1-Clients**

10. Select the invoice dates in the **range G4:G13**.

11. Open the Format Cells dialog box by clicking the **Number Format** dialog box launcher.

Because you opened the dialog box from the Number group on the Ribbon, the active tab is Number.

12. If necessary, choose **Custom** from the Category list.

13. Clear the existing text in the Type box and then enter the code **mmm-d** and click **OK**.

The date display is now reversed, showing the short-form text for the month and then the day.

14. Select the travel dates in the **range J4:J13**.

Invoice Date
Sep-8
Sep-7
Sep-1

15. Open the Format Cells dialog box from the Number group again and ensure the **Custom** category is selected.

The day of the week is important to know for travel information, so you will add the day of the week using a custom date format.

16. In the Type box, enter the code **ddd mmm-d** and click **OK**.

The day of the week now precedes the month for the dates in the Travel Date column.

Travel Date
Mon Oct-12
Wed Sep-30
Sun Oct-4

17. Save the workbook.

Entering Time Information

Much like you do with dates, you can enter times exactly as you want them to appear in the workbook. For example, if you type *6:00* into a cell, Excel will recognize this as a time entry and display it in the cell as *6:00*. Just like dates and numbers, times are right-aligned by default.

6:00
20-Jun
500

Also similar to dates, each time has a serial number attached to it. Because each day is 1, each hour is 1/24 (or 0.041667 if written as a decimal). Therefore, if you enter *6:00*, Excel displays the time as *6:00* but stores the information as 0.25 (six hours is one-quarter of the day). Combining the date and time would mean that 12:00 noon on July 1, 2010, is stored with the serial number 40360.5; the date serial number is 40360 and the time is 0.5, halfway through the day.

Most of the time, you won't have to worry about the serial number. As long as the time is entered correctly, Excel will apply the correct custom number formatting.

You can also add an AM/PM designation, if you prefer, rather than using a 24-hour clock, but you must enter a space between the time and either AM/PM. You can enter *6:00 AM* for the morning or *6:00 PM* for the evening (note the space before *AM* and *PM*). If no designation is entered, Excel assumes you are using the 24-hour system, so 6:00 is stored as 6:00 AM. You can also use number formatting to customize the way the time displays on the worksheet.

TIME ENTRIES		
Entry	**Display**	**Time Stored As**
6:00	6:00	6:00:00 AM or 0.25
9:00 AM	9:00 AM	9:00:00 AM or 0.375
12:00	12:00	12:00:00 PM or 0.5
13:30	13:30	1:30:00 PM or 0.5625
6:00 PM	6:00 PM	6:00:00 PM or 0.75

DEVELOP YOUR SKILLS: E7-D2

In this exercise, you will enter the flight times for Airspace's clients into the worksheet.

1. Save your file as: **E7-D2-Clients**

   The first time in cell M4 displays the AM designation, while the rest of the times are displayed in the 24-hour system (for example, 20:00).

2. Select the flight times in the **range M5:M10** and choose **Home→Number→Number Format menu button ⌄→General**.

   The serial numbers for the flight times are displayed.

   Now you will adjust the number formatting to display the correct time format.

3. With the flight times in the range M5:M10 still selected, click the **Number Format** launcher in the Number group on the Ribbon.

4. Choose **Time** from the Category list, and then choose the third option, which will display hours:minutes AM/PM, from the Type list and click **OK**.

5. Enter the remaining clients' flight times into the **range M11:M13** as shown.

   Be sure to type hour:minutes AM/PM and include the space to display the correct designation for AM or PM.

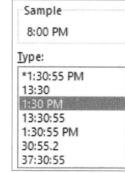

⬜	A	B	M
11	Karynn	Alida	5:30 PM
12	David	Monton	7:20 AM
13	Amanda	Campbell	9:00 AM

6. Save the file.

Using Date Functions

Excel has many date functions available in the Function Library. Dates are commonly found in Excel worksheets because they provide useful information about when an event or a transaction took place. Date information becomes even more useful when you can use it in formulas and functions. For example, you can use date functions to insert the current date or to extract information from a date, such as the month or year.

You enter date functions just like you do other functions, such as SUM. For example, you can use the TODAY function to enter today's date like this: =TODAY(). For this function, no arguments are entered inside the parentheses.

DATE FUNCTIONS		
Function	**Description**	**Example**
TODAY()	Displays the current date based on today's serial number; the date automatically updates when the worksheet is recalculated or reopened; no arguments are included in the parentheses	Formula: =TODAY() *Result:* 2/21/2026
NOW()	Like TODAY but also displays the time (based on the computer's clock); no arguments are included in the parentheses	Formula: =NOW() *Result:* 2/21/2026 11:09
DATE (year,month,day)	Returns a specific date based on the arguments entered	Formula: =DATE(2026,12,20) *Result:* 12/20/2026
YEAR(date)	Returns the year of the specified date as either a serial number or a cell reference to a cell containing a date	Cell B23: 12/20/2026 Formula: =YEAR(B23) *Result:* 2026
WEEKDAY()	Returns the number of the corresponding day for the date provided, entered either as a serial number or a cell reference, from 1 to 7; Sunday is 1	Formula: =WEEKDAY(B23) *Result:* 1
WORKDAY()	Used for adding workdays (Monday to Friday) to a start date, such as adding 10 business days to the date of an invoice; holidays can be skipped if listed somewhere in the workbook	Cell G1: 12/25/2026 Formula: =WORKDAY(B23,5,G1) *Result:* 12/28/2026

DEVELOP YOUR SKILLS: E7-D3

In this exercise, you will use date functions to enter date-related information into your worksheets.

1. Save your file as: **E7-D3-Clients**
2. Insert a new row above the column headings in **row 3** of the worksheet.
3. In **cell D3**, type **Month:** and tap [Tab].
4. In **cell E3**, enter the formula **=G5** and complete the entry.

   You wish to display the month of the listed invoices, so you will edit the number format to display only the month of the first invoice listed.

5. With cell E3 selected, open the Format Cells dialog box from the Number group on the Ribbon.
6. Ensure the Custom category is chosen; in the Type box, edit the code to display **mmmm** only and click **OK**.

   The code mmmm displays the full month name, whereas the code mmm displays the three-letter abbreviation, and no day or year information. Cell E3 now displays September.

7. Merge and center the **range E3:F3**.
8. In **cell H3**, enter **Year:** and tap [Tab].

9. In **cell I3**, enter the formula `=YEAR(G5)` and complete the entry.

   The formula argument is simply looking for a serial number, which is provided by entering a cell reference to a cell that contains a date. The result of the formula is the year from the date of the first listed invoice in cell G5, which is 2026.

10. Merge and center the **range I3:J3**.

11. Go to the **Client History** worksheet and insert a new row above the column headings in **row 3**.

12. In **cell A3**, enter `As Of:` and then merge and center the **range A3:B3**.

13. In **cell C3**, enter the formula `=TODAY()` and then merge and center the **range C3:F3**.

14. Apply the **Long Date** number format to **cell C3**.

15. Save the file.

Calculations Using Date and Time

When you understand the basic principles of dates and time in Excel, there are many valuable ways to use this information. You can perform mathematical operations such as addition and subtraction to find the difference between two dates or add a number of days to a particular date. Likewise, you can take two times and find the time difference or add and subtract hours and even minutes.

You can combine these mathematical operations with the date functions for even more applications. For example, you can use the TODAY function to insert today's date in one cell and enter a future date such as next Christmas in another cell, and then use a formula to subtract today from Christmas to determine the number of days remaining until the holiday. Any time you open the file, the TODAY function updates to the current date, so the formula calculation updates the number of days until Christmas. Of course, in business, there are much more practical applications.

DEVELOP YOUR SKILLS: E7-D4

In this exercise, you will use date functions to enter date-related information in your worksheets.

1. Save your file as: `E7-D4-Clients`

2. Go to the **Sept** worksheet.

   Airspace Travel allows customers to take up to three months after their travel date to pay for their trip, so you will enter a formula to calculate the due date.

3. In **cell L5** of the Balance Due Date column, enter this formula: `=EDATE(J5,3)`

   The EDATE function takes two arguments: the start date, which is the travel date in cell J5, and the number of months to add to the date, which is three. The result of the formula for the first client is January 12, three months after October 12.

4. Copy the formula down the column for the remaining clients.

   You instruct your clients to arrive at the airport three hours before their flight time, so now you will enter a formula to calculate their planned arrival times.

5. In **cell N5**, enter the formula: `=M5-(1/24*3)`

   This formula takes the time saved in cell M5 and subtracts three hours (one hour is 1/24). The result of the formula for the first client is 8:00 AM.

6. Copy the formula down the column for all clients.

7. Go to the **Client History** sheet and insert a column to the left of **column F**.

8. In **cell F4**, enter the heading: `Days Since Travelled`

9. In **cell F5**, enter the formula: `=$C$3-E5`

   Because cell C3 contains the TODAY function and cell E5 contains the last travel date, the formula result will update to show the new number of days since that customer has travelled each time you open the file. However, you must first change the number format so it does not show a date.

10. Apply the **General** number format to **cell F5**.

    Now you can see how many days since the first customer, Eric, took his last trip. This information could be used to reach out to customers who haven't travelled in a long time. Of course, this number will depend on the day on which you complete this exercise.

11. Copy the formula down the column for the remaining clients.

    Because the formula uses an absolute reference to cell C3, that cell reference stays the same for each customer.

12. Insert a column to the left of **column E**.

13. In **cell E4**, enter the heading: `Years of Loyalty`

    Now you want to enter a formula to find the number of years since each customer first became a client. The YEARFRAC function will find the difference between the dates and will return a whole number for complete years and then convert excess days into a fraction of a year. For example, 1 year and six months would display as 1.5.

14. In **cell E5**, insert the formula: `=YEARFRAC(D5,$C$3)`

    Again, you must convert the number format for the result to make sense.

15. Choose **Home→Number→Comma Style** to apply that number format to **cell E5**.

16. Choose **Home→Number→Decrease Decimal** to reduce the number of decimal places showing to one.

17. Copy the formula in **cell E5** down the rest of the column.

    The results of the formula will again depend on the day the exercise is completed and will update each day the file is opened.

18. Save the file.

Conditional Formatting Using Graphics and Custom Rules

Conditional formatting applies formatting to cells that meet your desired criteria. For example, there are preset conditional formatting options for the top or bottom numbers in the selected range, or cells that are greater than, less than, or equal to a number of your choice. You can create multiple rules for the same set of data, and the rules are applied in the order that you choose. Conditional formatting is always updated whenever the data changes.

If none of the options in the Conditional Formatting menu has your desired criteria, you can create a new conditional formatting rule. New rules can be created using the same basic principles as the preset rules; however, you can customize the specific way the rules are applied. You can also create conditional formatting rules based on the outcome of a formula.

Conditional Formatting with Graphics

Another option for conditional formatting is to use data bars, color scales, and icon sets to visualize your data by breaking it into three equal parts: values that are above average, average, and below average in the selected range. There are many quick options to choose from in the Conditional Formatting menu, or you can create a custom rule. Another option is to modify the graphics so the three ranges are not three equal parts; for example, the top 10%, middle 80%, and bottom 10% instead.

Expenses	Actual	Budget	Difference
Bank Fees	7,200	7,300 ✓	100
Insurance	18,230	17,000 ✗	-1,230
Rent	25000	25000 ✓	0

This data uses conditional formatting with data bars, a color scale, and an icon set to highlight trends and important information.

The Conditional Formatting Rules Manager

Use the Conditional Formatting Rules Manager to create, edit, and delete rules or to rearrange the order in which they are applied. To see which rules have been created, you can choose to show the formatting rules for the current selection or the full worksheet.

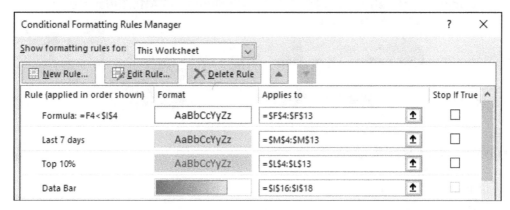

In this example, you see the four rules on the current worksheet and the ranges to which the rules apply.

Conditional Formatting Using Formulas

Creating a custom rule that uses a formula is another way of expanding the possibilities of conditional formatting. Instead of comparing the cells in the selected range to the other cells within that range, a rule allows any cell to be compared to a number or any other cell; if the formula is true, the formatting is applied.

To determine which employees are due for their annual wage review, you could highlight their names if one year has passed since their last review. The conditional formatting rule will compare their last review date in column C plus 365 (one year) to see if it's less than today's date, entered in cell B13. The formula for the conditional formatting applied to the names in column A would be: =C2+365<$B$13

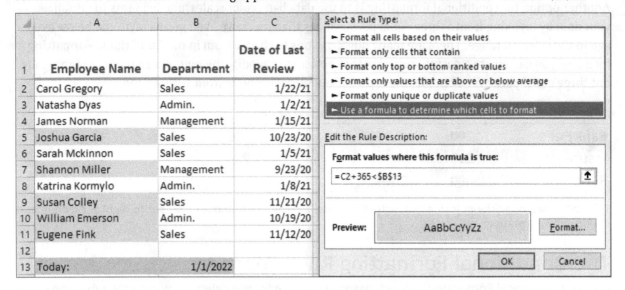

TIP! C2 is a relative reference and $B$13 is an absolute reference. In conditional formatting, the rule is written for the first cell in the range (cell A2 here) and automatically adjusts cell references for each row/column (A3:A11). Today's date is a constant, so an absolute cell reference is required.

Home→Styles→Conditional Formatting→New Rule

Home→Styles→Conditional Formatting→Manage Rules

DEVELOP YOUR SKILLS: E7-D5

In this exercise, you will create and modify conditional formatting rules to highlight important information about your clients.

1. Save your file as: **E7-D5-Clients**

2. If necessary, select the data under *Years of Loyalty* in the **range E5:E14** (Client History sheet).

3. Choose **Home→Styles→Conditional Formatting→Icon Sets→3 Stars** (in the Ratings group).

   The icons give an indication of the newest and oldest customers, but you have a loyalty program that you want to use instead.

4. In **cell A17**, enter **Loyalty Program** and then merge and center the **range A17:B17** and apply a thick bottom border.

5. Enter the qualifications for Silver and Gold status in the **range A18:B19**:

	A	B
17	**Loyalty Program**	
18	Silver	3
19	Gold	5

Edit an Existing Rule

6. Choose **Home→Styles→Conditional Formatting→Manage Rules**.

7. Follow these steps to edit the rule:

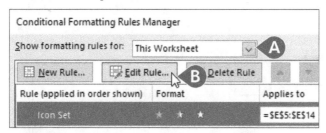

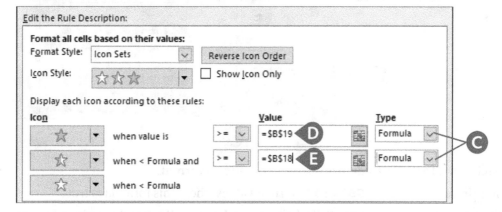

A. Select **This Worksheet** to show all rules on the worksheet.

B. Click **Edit Rule…**.

C. In the Edit Formatting Rule dialog box, change the type for each value to **Formula**.

D. Click the box for the first value and then click **cell B19** on the worksheet.

E. Click the box for the second value and then click **cell B18** on the worksheet.

8. Click **OK** to finish editing the rule; click **OK** again to close the Rules Manager.

The full star icon is applied to Gold clients, a half star is applied to Silver clients, and the rest have an empty star.

Create a New Rule Using a Formula

9. Go to the **Sept** worksheet and select the invoice dates in the **range G5:G14**.

You want to know which customers booked their trips less than 30 days in advance, so you will create a rule to highlight these customers.

10. Choose **Home→Styles→Conditional Formatting→New Rule**.

11. Follow these steps to create the new rule:

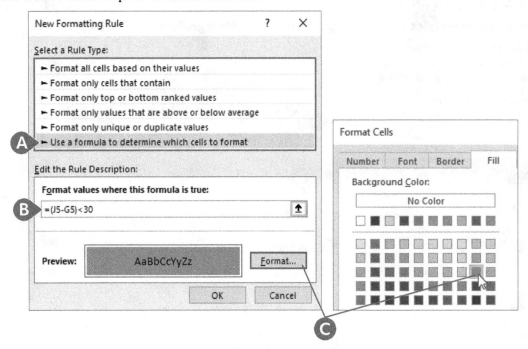

A. Select **Use a formula to determine which cells to format**.

B. Enter the formula **= (J5-G5) <30** to format values where this formula is true.

C. Click **Format...**; in the Format Cells dialog box, click the **Fill** tab and choose any light blue color.

12. Click **OK** twice, once to close the Format Cells dialog box and again to create and apply the new rule.

The rule takes the difference between the travel date in column J and the invoice date in column G, and then applies the blue fill if the difference is less than 30 days. The rule applies to four out of the ten customers.

First Name	Last Name	Provider	Destination	# of Guests	Price Per Person	Invoice Date
Eric	Snow	Sunwind	Jamaica	2	$ 899	Sep-8
Alison	Lobosco	Sunwind	Mexico	2	$ 770	Sep-7
Lacy	Henrich	TrueBlue	Dominican Republic	4	$ 1,200	Sep-1
Will	Johns	Eastjet	Cuba	3	$ 950	Sep-9
Nicki	Hollinger	Sunwind	Mexico	1	$ 875	Sep-8
Lennard	Williams	TrueBlue	Brazil	6	$ 800	Sep-8
Kerri	Knechtel	TrueBlue	Columbia	4	$ 560	Sep-5
Karynn	Alida	Sunwind	Bahamas	2	$ 870	Sep-8
David	Monton	Eastjet	Dominican Republic	2	$ 650	Sep-6
Amanda	Campbell	Sunwind	Jamaica	7	$ 900	Sep-9

13. Save and close the file.

Self-Assessment

Check your knowledge of this chapter's key concepts and skills using the online Self-Assessment Quiz.

MICROSOFT EXCEL 2021/365

Financial Functions and What-If Analysis

In this chapter, you will learn about some of the financial functions frequently used in Excel. You will use these functions to analyze potentially changing circumstances with the What-If Analysis tools. What-if analyses allow you to see how the results of formulas change by altering the input values, such as the interest rate used in financial functions.

LEARNING OBJECTIVES

- Create financial functions
- Create one-variable and two-variable data tables
- Use the What-If Analysis tools to create scenarios
- Adjust input values using Goal Seek

CHAPTER TIMING

- Concepts & Practice: 01:20:00
- Self-Assessment: 00:15:00
- Total: 01:35:00

PROJECT: MAKING FINANCIAL DECISIONS

Airspace Travel has a number of big financial decisions to make. The company is currently seeing rapid growth in its business, but it is running out of office space and needs to expand. The owners have asked you to help them prepare for and analyze the potential impact of several decisions, including the purchase of a new office building, an investment opportunity, and an equipment purchase. You will use the tools in Excel, including various financial functions and What-If Analysis tools, to help them make the best choices.

Learning Resources: **boostyourskills.lablearning.com**

Creating Financial Functions

Completing financial calculations is an important part of using Excel, and there is a whole category of financial functions to use. These types of calculations might include calculating your monthly payment on a loan or mortgage, finding out how much an investment will be worth in the future, or determining how long it will take to pay off a debt. Financial functions can be useful because they provide valuable information for decision-making, analysis, and forecasting. These functions can also provide the basis for more in-depth analysis tools in Excel.

Input Values for Financial Functions

When creating financial functions, it's good practice to avoid inserting constant values in your function arguments. A better way is to store the constant values, or inputs, on the worksheet so they are always visible and can be quickly changed and updated in all formulas.

For example, to calculate a payment, you could insert the interest rate directly into the PMT function arguments. If you need to change the interest rate, you would have to go into the formula and manually change it. But if the interest rate is stored in a cell and properly labeled, changing the interest rate in that cell will automatically update any formula that refers to that interest rate.

This might not make a big difference if you have only one formula, but for large, complex worksheets you might have many different formulas all using the same input, such as the interest rate!

> Formulas→Function Library→Financial

Financial Function Arguments

The arguments for many financial functions are similar, and Excel will help you build the correct formula to achieve the desired result. As with other functions, you can enter the arguments in the Insert Function dialog box or type them directly into the cell. With more complex functions, it can be easier to visualize your arguments using the dialog box.

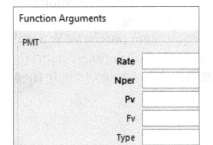
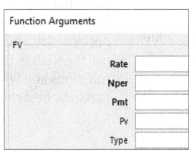
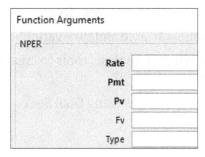

The field names for required arguments are shown in bold in the dialog box; the others are optional arguments.

FINANCIAL FUNCTION ARGUMENTS	
Argument	**Description**
Rate	Interest rate per payment period; so if the annual interest rate is 5%, the interest rate per period for a monthly payment would be 5% / 12
Nper	Number of payment periods over the life of the loan or investment, often monthly; so a five-year loan with monthly payments would have 5 x 12 = 60 payment periods
Pmt	Payment made on the loan or amount invested each period, which is a constant value (cannot change) over the life of the loan or investment
Pv	Loan amount or initial amount invested (Present Value)
Fv	Ending balance; for loans it's usually zero (or omitted) to pay off the loan, and for investments it's the desired amount at the end of the term (Future Value)
Type	Indicates whether payments are due at the beginning or end of each period

When financial functions are used in Excel, payments are considered negative values. For example, a $50,000 loan with 5% annual interest over 60 months would be paid back in installments payments of –$943.56.

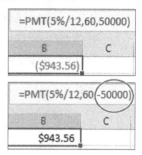

If you want the payment to appear as a positive number, you can reverse this by entering a negative number for the Pv argument (the loan amount) and think of that as a negative number, which represents a "debt."

PMT Function

The PMT, or Payment, function is used to calculate the amount of each payment required to pay off a loan, where the payments and interest remain constant over the life of the loan. This is also called a *term loan* because there is a predetermined time period, or number of payments, to pay off the loan. The PMT function can also be used to determine how much you must save (the payment) each month to reach some future value amount. Again, this assumes the interest and payments are consistent and the length of time is known.

For example, you may want to know the payments required to pay off a $50,000 loan in five years at 5% annual interest or how much you have to save each month to have $50,000 saved after five years at the same interest rate. The Pv in the figure on the left below is the $50,000 loan, and the Fv on the right is the future value of $50,000 saved.

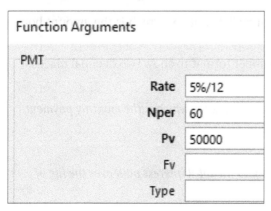
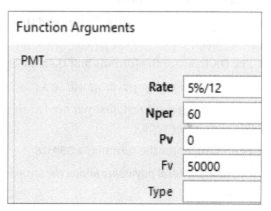

DEVELOP YOUR SKILLS: E8-D1

The Airspace owners are currently looking at buying a property for $650,000 with a $100,000 down payment for a thirty-year mortgage at 2.75% APR. In this exercise, you will find the amount of the monthly mortgage payment for the new office space and total interest over the life of the loan.

1. Start Excel, open **E8-D1-ATC** from your **Excel Chapter 8** folder, and save it as:
   E8-D1-ATCFinancials

2. Ensure the **Mortgage** sheet is active and **cell C8** is selected.

   The first step is to calculate the amount of the loan by starting with the purchase price and subtracting the down payment.

3. In **cell C8**, enter the formula: **=C4-C5**

   The loan amount will be $550,000. Now you can calculate the monthly payment based on the loan amount, interest rate, and term.

4. Select **cell C9** and choose **Formulas→Function Library→Financial→PMT** to insert the PMT function (you will need to scroll down through the list).

   As with other functions, you can either type or point and click to insert cell references. The point-and-click method can improve reliability and help ensure you select the correct cell.

5. Follow these steps to insert the PMT function arguments:

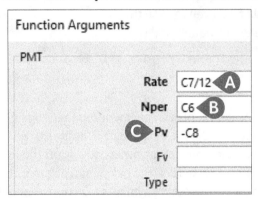

   A. Click **cell C7** and type **/12** to divide the annual percentage rate (APR) by 12, which returns the interest rate per month.

   If necessary, move the dialog box out of the way so you can click the cell in the worksheet.

   B. Tap ⌷Tab⌷ to move to the Nper box and then click **cell C6** for the number of payments (length of the term in months).

   C. Tap ⌷Tab⌷ to move to the Pv box and then type **–** and click **cell C8**, which is the amount borrowed.

6. Click **OK** to enter the formula and then adjust the number format to show two decimal places.

   The monthly mortgage payment will be $2,245.33.

   To calculate total interest, first you need to calculate total payments, which is the monthly payment multiplied by the term.

7. In **cell C10**, enter the formula: **=C9*C6**

   Next, take the total payments minus the loan amount to find the total interest paid over the life of the loan.

8. In **cell C11**, enter the formula: `=C10-C8`

   The total interest cost of the mortgage will be $258,318.

9. Save the file.

FV Function

The FV, or Future Value, function calculates the future value of an investment when you specify the interest rate, length of the investment, and amount of each payment. Like the PMT function, the interest rate and payments must be constant throughout the term. For example, if you know you can invest $200 each month for 10 years into an account that earns 7% interest per year, the FV function will tell you how much you will have saved up at the end. You can include the Pv argument if the starting investment in the account is more than zero.

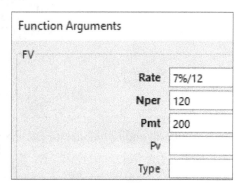

DEVELOP YOUR SKILLS: E8-D2

In this exercise, you will use the FV function to find out how much you would have after 10 years if Airspace were to invest $100,000 instead of purchasing the new office space.

1. Save your file as: **E8-D2-ATCFinancials**
2. Go to the **Investment** sheet and ensure **cell C7** is active.
3. Choose **Formulas→Function Library→Financial→FV** to insert the FV function.
4. Follow these steps to insert the FV function arguments:

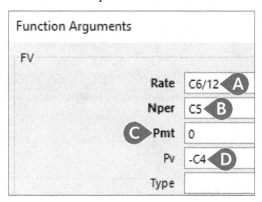

   A. Click **cell C6** and then type **/12** to get the interest rate per month.

   B. Tap Tab and click **cell C5** (length of the term in months).

   C. Tap Tab and enter **0** for the payment amount.

   D. Tap Tab then type – and click **cell C4** (amount you are investing up front).

   E. Click **OK**.

   With the compounding monthly interest, you would have $191,218 in 10 years. Now you will find out how much you would have if you were to invest an additional $200 each month.

5. Enter **200** in **cell C8**.

6. In **cell C9**, enter an FV function with the same arguments as step 4, except this time for the **Pmt** argument, type – and select **cell C8**.

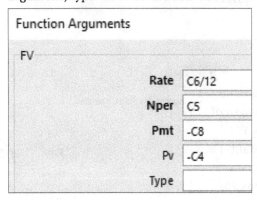

With an additional investment of $200 per month, you would have $224,899 after 10 years.

7. Save the file.

NPER Function

The NPER function is similar to the PMT and FV functions, but for this function the missing information is the number of periods, or the length of the term, required to reach the financial goal. Again, this could be reaching some investment amount or paying off some amount of debt where the interest rate remains constant. For example, if you want to pay off a $15,000 loan at 6% interest per year, you can find out how long it will take if you pay $400 per month.

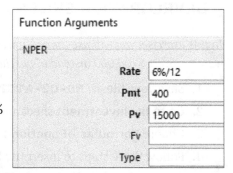

DEVELOP YOUR SKILLS: E8-D3

In this exercise, you will use the NPER function to determine how long it will take to pay for a new printer that costs $12,000 if Airspace opens a line of credit and pays $250 consistently each month.

1. Save your file as: **E8-D3-ATCFinancials**
2. Go to the **Printer** worksheet and ensure **cell C7** is selected.
3. Choose **Formulas→Function Library→Financial→NPER**.
4. Follow these steps to insert the NPER function arguments:

   A. Click **cell C6** and then type **/12** to determine the interest rate per month.

   B. Tap ⟨Tab⟩ and click **cell C5** for the payment amount for each month.

   C. Tap ⟨Tab⟩ and then type – and click **cell C4** (amount being borrowed up front to cover the purchase).

   D. Click **OK**.

   The loan would take just over 51 months to be paid off.

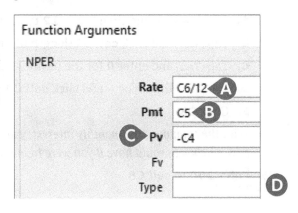

5. Remove all of the decimals from the number format of **cell C7**.

6. Save the file.

Using What-If Analysis Tools

To understand the basics of using the What-If Analysis tools, you should recognize that it is just that: asking the question, what if? *What if the interest rate increases on my loan? What if I invest $200 per month instead of $150?*

To answer these questions, you could create your formula and then go through and systematically change the values of the arguments to see the different results. However, the What-If Analysis tools provide better ways to examine different possibilities and try out alternate values in your formulas via the Scenario Manager, Goal Seek, and data tables. What-if analyses work best with complex formulas, such as the financial functions PMT, FV, and NPER, because there are several input values that can potentially change.

Data Tables

A data table is *not* a table and it *does not* allow you to sort or filter or insert a total row. Data tables are quite different! A data table allows you to insert multiple input values to replace an argument in your formula and see the results for all of them at the same time.

One-Variable Data Tables

To create a one-variable data table, you must first set up the table. The table requires *either* a row or column of input cells to replace one of the formula arguments, as well as the cell that contains the formula itself. To use a column input cell, the formula must be at the top of the column; to use a row input cell, the formula must be the first cell at the left of the row.

> **NOTE!** For a one-variable table, you enter only one input cell to change, hence either a row or a column (not both).

For example, you might want to use the Future Value function to determine how much you would have after 10 years (120 months) based on different monthly investment amounts. If you know you can invest at a constant rate of 3.75% interest per year, you could use the following table. As your monthly investment amount grows, so does the amount you have at the end (the future value).

Cell D7 contains the formula *=FV(C2/12,C4,–C3)*. The result is zero because cell C3 is blank, meaning the payment is zero. The formula also refers to the 3.75% rate in cell C2 and the number of periods (*120*) in cell C4.

Cell C3 is the payment amount, the argument that replaces zero with the new input values.

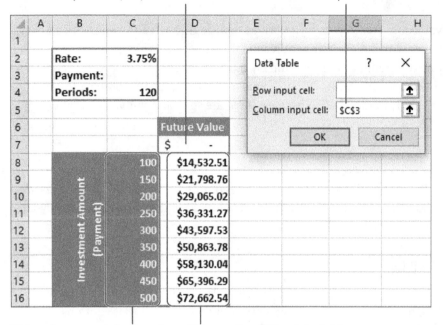

This column contains input values to be used in the formula instead of the existing payment value.

The results of the data table display below the formula.

You can also create a larger table that has multiple what-if formulas but still only one *variable* input for each of the formulas.

Two-Variable Data Tables

A two-variable data table is similar to a one-variable table, except that there is both a row and a column of input values to replace *two* different arguments in the formula. The formula for a two-variable table *must be in the upper-left cell* of the table.

In the following example, the period is still 10 years and the investment varies from 100 to 500, but now the interest rate also varies from 3.5% to 4.25%.

Cell C7 contains the formula =FV(C2/12,C4,-C3). The result is zero because cells C2 and C3 are blank. The formula also refers to the periods (120) in cell C4.

This row contains input values to use in the formula instead of the existing rate value.

Cell C2 is the rate and cell C3 is the payment amount. These are the two arguments to be replaced by the payment (column) and rate (row) input values.

	A	B	C	D	E	F	G	H	I	J
1										
2		Rate:						Data Table	?	✕
3		Payment:								
4		Periods:	120					Row input cell:	$C$2	⬆
5								Column input cell:	$C$3	⬆
6					Rate					
7			$ -	3.50%	3.75%	4.00%	4.25%	OK	Cancel	
8			100	$14,343.25	$14,532.51	$14,724.98	$14,920.73			
9			150	$21,514.88	$21,798.76	$22,087.47	$22,381.09			
10			200	$28,686.50	$29,065.02	$29,449.96	$29,841.45			
11		Investment Amount (Payment)	250	$35,858.13	$36,331.27	$36,812.45	$37,301.82			
12			300	$43,029.75	$43,597.53	$44,174.94	$44,762.18			
13			350	$50,201.38	$50,863.78	$51,537.43	$52,222.54			
14			400	$57,373.00	$58,130.04	$58,899.92	$59,682.90			
15			450	$64,544.63	$65,396.29	$66,262.41	$67,143.27			
16			500	$71,716.26	$72,662.54	$73,624.90	$74,603.63			

This column contains the input values to enter in the formula instead of the existing payment value.

The results of the data table display here.

☁ **View the video "Creating One- and Two-Variable Data Tables."**

Data→Forecast→What-If Analysis→Data Table…

▌ DEVELOP YOUR SKILLS: E8-D4

In this exercise, you will create one- and two-variable data tables to analyze what happens to the payments when the loan amount changes and when both the loan amount and interest rate change. Airspace may want to negotiate a lower purchase price or look for a larger building, depending on the results of your analyses.

1. Save your file as: **E8-D4-ATCFinancials**
2. Go to the **Mortgage Variables** worksheet.

   The first step in creating a data table is to ensure the arguments are set up correctly. For your one-variable table, the constants are the rate and term in cells C3 and C4. You will enter the formula to use in cell D5.

3. In **cell D5**, enter the formula: **=PMT(C3/12,C4,-C5)**

   Cell C5 is a blank cell; it's the variable that will be replaced with the loan amount values in the table.

4. Apply the **White, Background 1** font color to **cell D5**.
5. Select the **range C5:D11** and choose **Data→Forecast→What-If Analysis→Data Table….**

6. In the Data Table dialog box, click in the **Column Input Cell** box and then click **cell C5** in the worksheet.

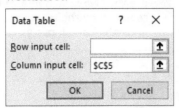

Cell C5 is the cell that will be replaced by the new values in the Loan Amount column.

7. Click **OK** to insert the data table.

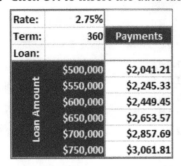

Rate:	2.75%	
Term:	360	**Payments**
Loan:		
	$500,000	$2,041.21
	$550,000	$2,245.33
	$600,000	$2,449.45
	$650,000	$2,653.57
	$700,000	$2,857.69
	$750,000	$3,061.81

The payment is the same as the original calculation on the Mortgage worksheet if the loan amount is $550,000. But if the loan amount goes up or down, you can see the change in the payment that would be required.

Now you will enter the PMT function again, using the same arguments, but in the upper-left corner of the two-variable table. The constant will be the term in cell C4, and this time the variables are both the Loan Amount (column) and the Rate (row).

8. In **cell G5**, enter the formula: `=PMT(C3/12,C4,-C5)`

Cells C3 and C5 will be replaced values in the table; C3 represents the variable interest rate and C5 represents the variable loan amount.

9. Apply the **White, Background 1** font color to **cell G5**.

10. Select the **range G5:K11** and choose **Data→Forecast→What-If Analysis→Data Table…**

11. In the Data Table dialog box, enter **C3** in the Row Input Cell box and **C5** in the Column Input Cell box and then click **OK**.

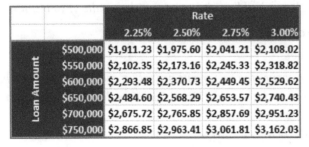

		Rate			
		2.25%	2.50%	2.75%	3.00%
	$500,000	$1,911.23	$1,975.60	$2,041.21	$2,108.02
	$550,000	$2,102.35	$2,173.16	$2,245.33	$2,318.82
	$600,000	$2,293.48	$2,370.73	$2,449.45	$2,529.62
	$650,000	$2,484.60	$2,568.29	$2,653.57	$2,740.43
	$700,000	$2,675.72	$2,765.85	$2,857.69	$2,951.23
	$750,000	$2,866.85	$2,963.41	$3,061.81	$3,162.03

12. Save the file.

Scenario Manager

Data tables give you a lot of information about the potential outcome of variables in your calculations. However, you might not always want all of that data; you may want to compare results for only two or three possibilities. The Scenario Manager uses variable inputs similar to data tables but with several additional benefits:

- The Scenario Manager can handle more than just one or two variables. In fact, you can have as many as 32 variables.
- You can show the effects of these variables on multiple formulas at the same time.

For each set of variables, called changing cells, you can either choose to show the results of each scenario directly in the worksheet or create a scenario summary report that shows the results of each scenario side by side. This can be useful when comparing potential outcomes for manufacturing decisions or financial investments.

The Scenario Manager allows you to add, edit, delete, and display your scenarios. Each scenario requires creating a name, identifying the changing cells, and entering the values for each of the changing cells. The changing cells are the input cells that contain the values being used in your formulas.

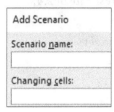

It's best to avoid using a formula cell as a changing cell, because the scenario will replace the formula with a constant value, which could cause errors or mistakes in your calculations.

> **TIP!** It's good practice to create names for your input cells so users can easily see which values are being replaced.

Data→Forecast→What-If Analysis→Scenario Manager...

DEVELOP YOUR SKILLS: E8-D5

In this exercise, you will create scenarios using the mortgage calculation to see what the result will be for a few specific situations that could arise.

1. Save your file as: **E8-D5-ATCFinancials**

   You will create three scenarios based on possible changes to the price, interest rate, down payment, and term. To begin, you will define names for the cells.

2. Switch to the **Mortgage** worksheet and select the **range B4:C11**.

3. Choose **Formulas→Defined Names→Create from Selection**.

4. Ensure **Left Column** is checked and click **OK**.

   This will name your input cells as well as the result cells in column C, using the labels in column B.

5. Select the **range C4:C7** (which will be the changing cells) and choose **Data→Forecast→ What-If Analysis→Scenario Manager...**.

6. In the Scenario Manager dialog box, which shows there are currently no scenarios created, click **Add**.

7. Enter **Best** for the scenario name, confirm the changing cells are C4:C7 based on your previous selection, and click **OK**.

8. For the Best scenario, enter these new values for the changing cells:

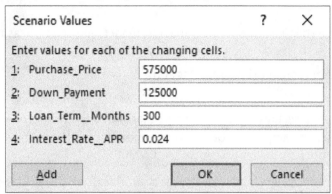

You believe the best possible situation allows you to negotiate a price of $575,000 for the property, pay $125,000 down, pay the mortgage off in 25 years (300 months), and obtain an interest rate of 2.4% (0.024).

9. Click **OK** to create the new scenario, which brings you back to the Scenario Manager.

10. Add another scenario named **Worst** that uses the same changing cells as step 5.

11. Enter the new values as indicated:

Purchase_Price	690000
Down_Payment	75000
Loan_Term__Months	420
Interest_Rate__APR	0.0299

The worst scenario is that the property costs $690,000, you can only pay a $75,000 down payment, the mortgage is for 35 years, and the interest rate goes up to 2.99%.

12. Add a third scenario named **Most Likely** using these values:

Purchase_Price	640000
Down_Payment	90000
Loan_Term__Months	360
Interest_Rate__APR	0.0269

The most likely situation is that the property costs $640,000, the down payment is $90,000, the mortgage term is 30 years, and the interest rate is 2.69%.

13. In the dialog box, choose the **Best** scenario and click **Show** to display the new values in the gray input cells, which automatically update the results in the blue formula cells.

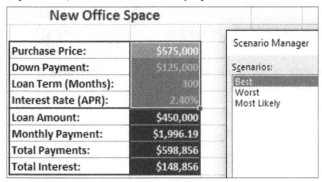

Note the changes to the loan amount, payments, and interest.

14. In the dialog box, click **Summary**.

15. Choose the **Scenario Summary** report type and the **range C8:C11** as the result cells and then click **OK**.

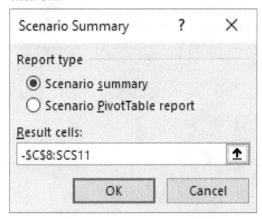

The Scenario Manager inserts a new sheet that shows the values of the changing cells and result cells listed for the three scenarios as well as the current values that match the best scenario.

Scenario Summary				
	Current Values:	Best	Worst	Most Likely
Changing Cells:				
Purchase_Price	$575,000	$575,000	$690,000	$640,000
Down_Payment	$125,000	$125,000	$75,000	$90,000
Loan_Term__Months	300	300	420	360
Interest_Rate__APR	2.40%	2.40%	2.99%	2.69%
Result Cells:				
Loan_Amount	$450,000	$450,000	$615,000	$550,000
Monthly_Payment	$1,996.19	$1,996.19	$2,363.40	$2,227.89
Total_Payments	$598,856	$598,856	$992,627	$802,039
Total_Interest	$148,856	$148,856	$377,627	$252,039
Notes: Current Values column represents values of changing cells at time Scenario Summary Report was created. Changing cells for each scenario are highlighted in gray.				

16. Save your work.

Goal Seek

Another What-If Analysis tool is Goal Seek, which is useful when you know the desired result and you want Excel to find the input required to achieve that result. For example, you might want your monthly car payment to be $400, and you know the interest rate and term. You could use Goal Seek to work backward to figure out how much you can afford to spend on the car (the loan amount).

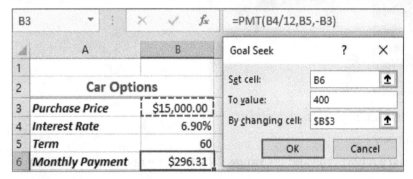

The set cell *must* contain a formula. In this example, cell B6 contains the formula *=PMT(B4/12,B5,-B3)*. The changing cell must be a cell reference that directly or indirectly impacts the result of the formula—in this case, cell B3. Goal Seek can take a few seconds, as Excel has to work through the hundreds or thousands of possible variables until a solution is found.

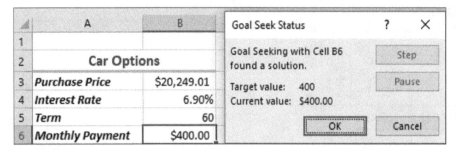

The new result displays in cell B3, showing you can afford to spend $20,249.01.

> Data→Forecast→What-If Analysis→Goal Seek...

DEVELOP YOUR SKILLS: E8-D6

Airspace is purchasing a new printer. In this exercise, you will use Goal Seek to determine the monthly payment required to pay for the new printer in four years (48 months).

1. Save your file as: **E8-D6-ATCFinancials**
2. Switch to the **Printer** sheet, select **cell C7** if necessary, and choose **Data→Forecast→What-If Analysis→Goal Seek...**.

   Because you selected cell C7 in the worksheet, C7 appears in the Set Cell box by default.

3. Enter **48** in the To Value box.

4. In the By Changing Cell box, select **cell C5** and click **OK**.

Goal Seek works through the possibilities and finds the solution. In the worksheet, the payment has been adjusted to $265 (rounded) and the loan term is now 48 months.

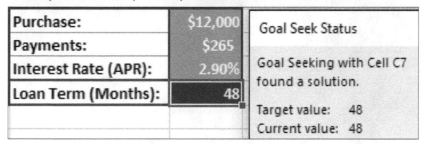

5. Click **OK** to close the Goal Seek window and keep the new values.

6. Select **cell C5** and increase the decimal to show two decimal places and the exact payment of $265.08.

7. Save and close the file.

Self-Assessment

Check your knowledge of this chapter's key concepts and skills using the online Self-Assessment Quiz.

Text Functions, Conditional Functions, and Formula Auditing

In this chapter, you will learn various functions that give you greater ability for analysis and decision making. You will create functions that sum or count values that meet your desired criteria. You will also explore functions used to clean up and rearrange text on your worksheet, as well as learn what you can do to find and prevent formula errors in your calculations.

LEARNING OBJECTIVES

- Use functions to format text
- Create conditional functions using IF and IFS criteria
- Create formulas using nested functions
- Find and correct errors in formulas
- Use 3-D cell references in formulas

CHAPTER TIMING

- Concepts & Practice: 01:20:00
- Self-Assessment: 00:15:00
- Total: 01:35:00

PROJECT: ANALYZING SALES INFORMATION

The Airspace Travel monthly sales results are in, and the data has been compiled for all company agents and managers in a worksheet for your review. Because the data was imported from different sources, you need to clean up the text entries. You'll also use various conditional functions to pull out important information about specific performance.

Learning Resources: **boostyourskills.lablearning.com**

Using Functions to Modify Text

Workbook data that comes from sources other than Excel may be formatted incorrectly. Data may also have been entered by multiple users, each using a different method of data entry. For example, one person might enter names into a worksheet using all capital letters, and another person might capitalize the first letter of the name only. Then when the two worksheets are combined, name entries will not be consistent. Another problem can occur when data is either entered in too few or too many columns, such as entering the first and last names together in one column when it is better to enter this data in separate columns.

> **TIP!** When storing data, it's best practice to use the smallest individual units for each field of information. In Excel, this means each column.

Although many people primarily think of Excel as a way to work with numbers, there are quite a few functions that allow you to work with text as well. You can use text functions to fix the issues mentioned or to manipulate text data to be used for a different purpose. There are functions that let you change case, combine or separate text, remove spaces, and extract or even replace text.

Changing Case

PROPER, UPPER, and LOWER are three functions that allow you to change the case of the input text. PROPER converts the first letter of each word to uppercase (capital) and all other letters to lowercase. As you can probably guess, UPPER converts all letters to uppercase and LOWER converts all letters to lowercase.

When using these functions, the function argument is simply the text to convert; you can use a cell reference or the text itself. For example, cell A2 shows text where some words are in all lowercase letters and another word is in all uppercase letters. The formula displayed in cell B2, =PROPER(A2), tells Excel to capitalize the first letter of each word from cell A2, and the result is *Use Your Imagination* (displayed in cell C2).

	A	B	C
1	**Text**	**Formula**	**Result**
2	use your IMAGINATION	=PROPER(A2)	Use Your Imagination
3		=LOWER("AND")	and
4	make some magic!	=UPPER(A4)	MAKE SOME MAGIC!

Extracting Text

In some cases, only a part of the cell's contents is needed, or there may be extra characters or spaces you don't want. The LEFT, MID, and RIGHT functions extract a certain number of characters from the text string. The TRIM function removes all spaces except for a single space between words.

The LEFT and RIGHT functions take two arguments: the text (which can be actual text or a cell reference) and the number of characters to extract.

	A	B	C
	Text	**Formula**	**Result**
1			
2	BASKabcdefg	=LEFT(A2,4)	BASK
3	abcdefgETB	=RIGHT(A3,3)	ETB
4	abcALLdefg	=MID(A4,4,3)	ALL
5	Who likes basketball?	=TRIM(A5)	Who likes basketball?

The TRIM function's only argument is the text from which to remove the spaces.

The MID function requires three arguments: the text, the position of the first character to extract, and then the number of characters to extract.

Merge and Modify Text with Functions and Flash Fill

There are several ways to merge, or concatenate, text in Excel. The CONCAT function, which replaces the CONCATENATE function from earlier versions of Excel (though it's still available for compatibility), allows you to combine two or more separate text entries or a range of text entries into one cell. TEXTJOIN is another function that combines text; it also inserts a character between each entry, called a *delimiter*.

Flash Fill can also be used to combine text, and it has other advantages too. Flash Fill can combine multiple entries into one cell or extract text from one text string into multiple entries, and it can perform many other tasks. After you have entered one or two examples, Flash Fill looks for patterns in your data entries and automatically fills in the remaining values.

> **TIP!** The CONCAT and TEXTJOIN functions are used as part of a formula, whereas Flash Fill is just a tool that enters text values into cells.

For example, if you have a column with First Name and another column with Last Name, CONCAT or TEXTJOIN can be used to combine the two names into one cell. Flash Fill can do this but can also do the opposite task; take one name and separate it into First and Last columns. You could use Flash Fill to extract one part of the cell only, such as the first three letters of the last name, or to extract the area code from a phone number. Flash Fill can even append or insert text, such as automatically creating email addresses from a list of employee names.

One big difference is that Flash Fill uses adjacent data only, whereas CONCAT and TEXTJOIN use a cell or range reference so the text could be anywhere on the worksheet or even on another worksheet. Another difference is that a function will update automatically if changes are made to the source of the text, but after Flash Fill is used the text becomes static.

Column C uses CONCAT to combine the text from columns A–B into one cell.

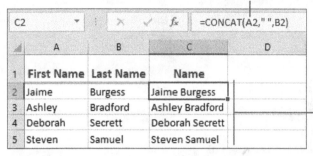

The function arguments are cell references or text. The second argument (" ") inserts the text within the quotation marks, in this case a space, between the first and last names from column A and B.

The original data is in column A.

The area code *232* was manually entered in cell B2 while Flash Fill was used to fill in the others.

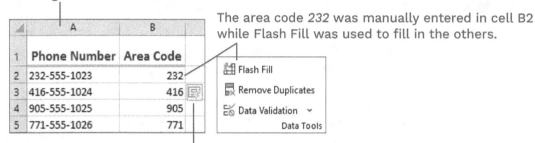

The Flash Fill Options button includes options to Accept and Undo the suggested entries.

Data→Data Tools→Flash Fill | Home→Editing→Fill→Flash Fill

Other Text Functions

Be sure to take some time to explore the other text functions available in Excel. There are text functions that allow you to replace or substitute text within a text string, functions for finding the text's position, and functions to calculate text length. You can even insert a function that will repeat a text character a specified number of times. These are just some examples; there is a long list of functions in the Text category of Excel's function library.

TEXT FUNCTIONS		
Function	**Description**	**Example**
REPLACE	Replaces part of a text string with another text string, such as replacing digits in a credit card number to display 8181-xxxx-xxxx-1188	Cell B1: 8181-3011-1103-1188 Formula: =REPLACE(B1,6,9,"xxxx-xxxx") *Result*: 8181-xxxx-xxxx-1188
SUBSTITUTE	Looks for an exact match (case-sensitive) and replaces old text with new text if found, such as replacing Mgr with Manager	Cell B4: Mgr Formula: =SUBSTITUTE(B4,"Mgr","Manager") *Result*: Manager
LEN	Determines the number of characters in a cell entry	Cell B7: 2223334444 Formula: =LEN(B7) *Result*: 10
REPT	Repeats text, such as the letter A five times	Formula: =REPT("A",5) *Result*: AAAAA

Formulas→Function Library→Text

DEVELOP YOUR SKILLS: E9-D1

In this exercise, you will use text functions to clean up the text entries in the Airspace Sales Results worksheet.

1. Start Excel, open **E9-D1-Sales** from your **Excel Chapter 9** folder, and save it as:
   E9-D1-SalesAnalysis

Change Case

The workbook opens to the Jul Sales sheet. Notice that the names in column A are not consistent in terms of the capitalization used. You want to correct that and, to begin, you will create a blank column in which the names can be converted to proper capitalization.

2. Insert a new column to the left of **column A**.

3. In **cell A5**, enter the formula **=PROPER(B5)** and then fill the formula down the column to **cell A33** and **AutoFit** the column width.

   The cells now display the text with the first letter of each name capitalized. To keep just the text and not the function, you will copy and paste the values only to the same range.

4. With the **range A5:A33** selected, choose **Home→Clipboard→Copy**.

5. Without changing the selection, choose **Home→Clipboard→Paste menu button ⌄→Values** to paste the values only (not the formulas) into the selected range.

   Instead of the PROPER function in the Formula Bar for cell A5, you should now see the text Amir Johnson, *with both names capitalized.*

6. Delete the names from the **range B5:B33**.

Extract Text

7. Insert a column to the left of **column E**.

   You will extract the first six characters of the employee ID numbers, removing the extra characters.

8. In **cell E5**, enter the function **=LEFT(D5,6)** and then fill the formula down the column.

9. With the **range E5:E33** still selected, copy the formulas and then paste the values only into **column D**.

10. Delete the formulas from the **range E5:E33**.

Combine Text

The location names that contain two words were mistakenly split into two columns, so you need to correct this by combining the two columns into one.

11. In **cell E5**, enter the function **=CONCAT(F5:G5)** and then fill the formula down the column.

    The cities with two names are missing a space between the two words. To fix this, the CONCAT function could be modified, but then a space would be added to each entry even if it isn't necessary. TEXTJOIN will work better because a space will only be added when needed.

12. Replace the formula in **cell E5** with the TEXTJOIN function:

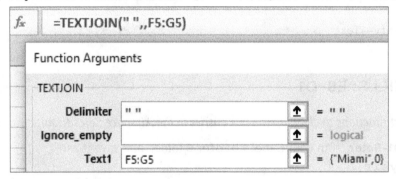

13. Fill the formula down **column E**; with the **range E5:E33** still selected, copy the formulas and paste the values only into **column F**.

14. Delete the formulas from **column E** (but keep the column) and delete **column G** (remove the entire column).

Use Flash Fill

Now you will fill in the blank columns and create a list of email addresses for the employees.

15. In **cell B5**, enter the name **Amir** and complete the entry.

16. Choose **Data→Data Tools→Flash Fill** to fill the first names down column B.

    Based on the first example you typed, Amir, Excel uses the text before the space in column A.

17. In **cell C5**, enter the name: **Johnson**

18. Use the **fill handle** in **cell C5** to copy the last name down **column C**, then click the **Auto Fill Options** button and choose **Flash Fill** to replace *Johnson* with each person's actual last name.

> **TIP!** Whether you use Flash Fill from the Ribbon or Auto Fill Options, the results will be the same.
>
> The advantage of Flash Fill is that if the result you want is text (not a formula) in each cell, Flash Fill skips the step of inserting a formula before copying and pasting values. The names are now in the appropriate column, so column A can be removed.

19. Delete **column A** entirely.

20. In **cell D4**, enter the heading: `Email`

21. In **cell D5**, enter this email address for Amir: `A.Johnson@airspace.com`

    Note that the email address automatically converts to a hyperlink. Although the email address is not fully visible, do not widen the column.

22. In **cell D6**, begin entering Robert's email address by typing **R** and stop when the suggested text appears in column D.

23. Tap `Enter` to accept the suggestions and insert the proper email addresses for all other employees in the column.

24. Save the file.

Creating Conditional Functions Using IF Criteria

Conditional functions allow you to sum, count, and find the average of a range of cells—if the cells meet your desired criteria.

IF CRITERIA FUNCTIONS	
Function	**Arguments (Optional)**
SUMIF	=SUMIF(range,criteria,(sum range))
AVERAGEIF	=AVERAGEIF(range,criteria,(average range))
COUNTIF	=COUNTIF(range,criteria)
SUMIFS	=SUMIFS(sum range,range1,criteria1,range2,criteria2...)
AVERAGEIFS	=AVERAGEIFS(average range,range1,criteria1,range2,criteria2...)
COUNTIFS	=COUNTIFS(range1,criteria1,range2,criteria2...)

In the preceding table, you may have noticed that a single criterion is entered for the IF functions, and multiple criteria are entered for the IFS functions. Think of IFS as the plural of IF!

IF CRITERIA FUNCTION ARGUMENTS	
Arguments	**Description**
Range	These are the cells to be compared with the criteria.
Criteria	They can be a comparison value or text, or an expression using a comparison operator such as =, >, <, >=, <=, <> (not equal to).
Sum range/Average range	This is the range to be summed or averaged, which can be different from the range being compared with the criteria. For IF functions, the sum/average range is optional; if omitted, the range from the first argument is used. For IFS functions, the sum/average range comes first and is required.

Using the conditional functions allows you to create formulas to find information such as:

- How many customers live in Florida?

- How many employees in the Human Resources division have salaries greater than $50,000?

- What are the total sales of product #2152?

For example, if you want to discover the total sales of product #2152 for employees in San Antonio, you would use the SUMIFS function because there are two criteria—the product and the city.

The Sum_range refers to the sales, to be added together from column C.

The formula in cell G3 is shown in the Formula Bar.

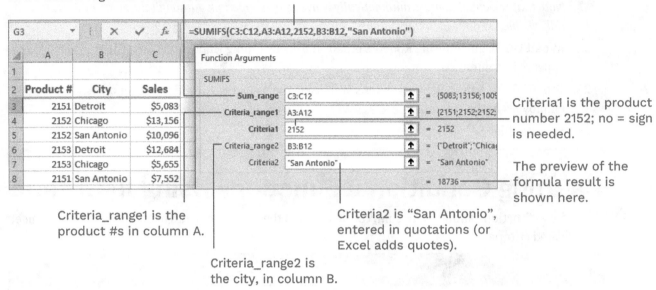

Criteria_range1 is the product #s in column A.

Criteria1 is the product number 2152; no = sign is needed.

Criteria_range2 is the city, in column B.

Criteria2 is "San Antonio", entered in quotations (or Excel adds quotes).

The preview of the formula result is shown here.

The Function Arguments dialog box makes it easier to enter the arguments because it can be difficult to keep track of the arguments when entering them directly in a cell. The dialog box also shows a preview of the formula result as you add more conditions. The result of the formula above is shown in the worksheet here:

=SUMIFS(C3:C12,A3:A12,2152,B3:B12,"San Antonio")

D	E	F	G	H
		Summary		
	Product	City	Total	
	2152	San Antonio	18736	

DEVELOP YOUR SKILLS: E9-D2

In this exercise, you will use conditional functions to obtain information about the Miami sales team's performance.

1. Save your file as: **E9-D2-SalesAnalysis**

   The description for each calculation is located in column K. You will enter the appropriate formula for each in column L.

Use Single Criterion Functions

2. In **cell L5**, enter this formula: **=COUNTIF(E5:E33,"Miami")**

   The formula looks for the criteria Miami and counts each cell that matches this text in the range E5:E33. The formula result shows nine sales employees listed in the Miami location. Next you will find the sum of the Miami sales employees' commissions.

3. In **cell L6**, insert the SUMIF function from the Math & Trig category in the Function Library.

4. In the Function Arguments dialog box, use these arguments:

Range	**E5:E33**
Criteria	**Miami**
Sum Range	**I5:I33**

Once complete, the formula in the Formula Bar shows: =SUMIF(E5:E33,"Miami",I5:I33)

The range and the criteria are the same as the COUNTIF function in step 2, but the SUMIF function also uses the sum range, which are the commissions in the range I5:I33. The result shows $6,876 in total commissions earned by employees in Miami.

5. Format **cell L6** as **Currency** with no decimals.

Now you will find Miami's average sales.

6. In **cell L7**, enter: **=AVERAGEIF(E5:E33,"Miami",H5:H33)**

NOTE! Remember, you can use the Function Arguments dialog box to enter formulas with several arguments.

This time the range to average is the sales data in column H. The result of the formula is 10643.22222, which you will reformat now.

7. Format **cell L7** as **Currency** with no decimals.

Work with Multiple Criteria Functions

The next thing you want to find is the number of Miami employees who achieved more than $10,000 in sales.

8. In **cell L8**, insert the COUNTIFS function and open the **Function Arguments** dialog box.

9. Enter **E5:E33** for the first criteria range and **Miami** for the criteria text.

As you insert the arguments, more boxes for additional criteria appear. You can select the ranges from the sheet with the mouse or type them, whatever you prefer.

10. Enter **H5:H33** for the second criteria range and **>10000** for the criteria.

You will leave the third criteria range blank.

11. Click **OK** to enter the function and compare your formula in the Formula Bar to this one: *=COUNTIFS(E5:E33,"Miami",H5:H33,">10000")*

The formula searches for Miami in the Location column and numbers higher than 10,000 in the Sales column, and then counts the employees that meet both criteria; the result is 4.

For comparison's sake, you also want to find out how many employees in Toronto had more than $10,000 in sales.

12. In **cell L8**, enter this formula: **=COUNTIFS(E5:E33,"Toronto",H5:H33,">10000")**

Use the Function Arguments dialog box, if desired.

The result is only three employees for Toronto. Now you want to find the total commissions paid out to Miami managers who had less than $10,000 in sales. There will be three conditions this time: Location (Miami), Position (Manager), and Sales (less than $10,000); the sum range will be Commissions.

13. In **cell L10**, insert the SUMIFS function and use these function arguments:

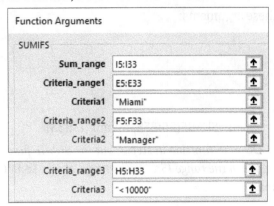

The complete formula in the Formula Bar should be:
=SUMIFS(I5:I33,E5:E33,"Miami",F5:F33,"Manager",H5:H33,"<10000")

This formula finds the sum for commissions if the criteria are met for Location, Position, and Sales. The result shows that $2,012 in commissions was paid out to managers in Miami who did not achieve $10,000 in sales.

14. Format **cell L10** as **Currency** with no decimals.

15. Save the file.

Nested Functions

There are times when you want to perform more than one function, without using two separate cells to do so. In those situations, it is possible to use functions inside of other functions. This is called *nesting* functions, or a *nested* function. Although this can be quite challenging with some functions, it can be fairly simple with others.

For example, when you use the AVERAGE function, you often get a long set of decimal places in the result. While you can adjust the number format, which will change the display of the number, the formula will store those decimal places for future calculations. In some cases, you might want to remove the decimal places altogether from the stored value, and this can be done by using a second function: the ROUND function. Thus, in the same cell, you could nest the AVERAGE function inside of the ROUND function to achieve the desired result.

This formula finds the average of the range F5:F52 and then rounds that result to zero decimal places.

Another example is, if you need more than one criterion to determine the result for an IF function, and there are more than two possible outcomes, you can nest an IF function in another IF function. For example, you could use the IF function to determine whether an employee achieved a sales goal and then inside that function place another IF function to determine if the employee also achieved a minimum number of sales.

The IFS Function

The IFS function also allows you to work with multiple conditions. With the IFS function, you are able to specify multiple criteria, and the function returns the value for the first one that is true. Depending on the situation, IFS can be used instead of nesting IF functions by rearranging the arguments slightly.

Rather than a value-if-false argument, like the IF function, one of the arguments in the IFS function *must* be true. This means you must carefully write your arguments to include at least one true possibility. Alternatively, the criteria for the last logical test can be entered as TRUE, which will return the corresponding value-if-true no matter what (as long as none of the previous logical tests are true).

For example, if a professor wants to assign letter grades rather than numbers to students, two different formulas can be used: a nested IF function or the IFS function. Previously, Excel allowed nested IF functions only, but with the addition of the newer IFS function, both options are now available. In the Letter Grade column below, the two possible functions are:

- =IF(C3>=80,"A",IF(C3>=70,"B",IF(C3>=60,"C",IF(C3>=50,"D","F"))))
- =IFS(C3>=80,"A",C3>=70,"B",C3>=60, "C",C3>=50,"D",C3<50,"F")

Again, both functions give the exact same result.

First	Last	Final Grade	Letter Grade
Sarah	Alamin	78	B
Ashley	Butler	83	A
Curtis	Coverdale	92	A
Yuel	Dolshi	75	B
Madison	Farrell	88	A
Trevor	Fischer	83	A
Nicolas	Gonzalez	67	C
Rohan	Kahar		F

The SWITCH Function

The SWITCH function is another logical function that can simplify nested functions in some situations. SWITCH performs an action similar to a lookup and similar to nested IF functions. Essentially the function compares "an expression" to a list and returns the desired result for the matching value. This means it can be used to replace (or "switch") one thing with another. Like other functions, SWITCH can be combined (nested) with different functions to become even more useful.

For example, the SWITCH function can be used to evaluate the WEEKDAY of a specific date and return the desired results, perhaps the number of employees needed on that day of the week or a short text entry.

◢	A	B	C	D	E	F	G	H	I
1		**Del's Restaurant**							
2		**Weekly Server Schedule**							
3									
4		Date	Feb 18	Feb 19	Feb 20	Feb 21	Feb 22	Feb 23	Feb 24
5		Weekday	M	T	W	Th	F	Sa	Su
6	Name	Staff Needed	3	4	4	6	9	10	CLOSED

In this example, the SWITCH function evaluates the date in row 4 to return a short text entry in row 5 and the number of staff needed in row 6. The functions in cell C5 and C6 are:

- =SWITCH(WEEKDAY(C4),1,"Su",2,"M",3,"T",4,"W",5,"Th",6,"F",7,"Sa")
- =SWITCH(WEEKDAY(C4),1,"CLOSED",2,3,3,4,4,4,5,6,6,9,7,10)

TIP! Remember, the WEEKDAY function examines the date and returns a *1* for Sunday, *2* for Monday, and so on.

Function arguments can be entered in any order, and up to 126 matching values can be entered. At least one value and one result are required, in addition to the expression to evaluate, and a default value can be entered if no matching values are found.

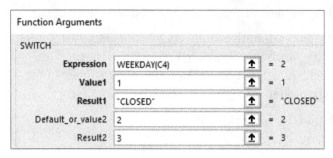

DEVELOP YOUR SKILLS: E9-D3

In this exercise, you will use a nested function to adjust the result of one formula and the IFS function to calculate an employee bonus in another formula.

1. Save your file as: **E9-D3-SalesAnalysis**
2. Select the Miami Average Sales amount in **cell L7**.
3. Increase the decimal to show three decimal places.

   The AVERAGEIF function results in a repeating decimal of .222.

4. Follow these steps to edit the formula:

   A. In the Formula Bar, click to place the insertion point between the = sign and AVERAGEIF and then type: **ROUND (**
   B. Click the right side of the Formula Bar and type **, 0)** at the end of the formula.
   C. Click **Enter** on the Formula Bar to complete the changes.

   The result displayed now shows $10,643.000, which is the average sales rounded to the nearest dollar.

5. In **cell L7**, decrease the decimal to remove the decimals from the display.

Using the IFS Function

6. Select **cell J4** and insert a new worksheet column.
7. In **cell J4**, apply a thick outside border and enter the heading: **Bonus**

   Because the commissions earned on sales can vary, you offer a 1% bonus to employees who met their sales target and a 2% bonus to employees whose commissions were also less than $1,000.

8. In **cell J5**, insert the **IFS** function from the Logical category of the Function Library.

   NOTE! The order of the logical tests is *very* important, since the function returns the value for the *first* test that is true!

9. Follow these steps to create the IFS function:

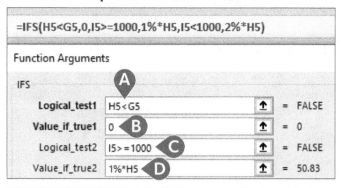

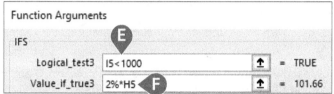

A. In the first logical test, enter **H5<G5** to determine which employees did not meet their target.

B. The Value_If_True for employees who did not meet their target is no bonus, so enter: **0**

C. If the first test is false, the employee did meet their target, so enter **I5>=1000** in the second logical test to determine if their commissions were greater than or equal to $1,000.

D. If the second test is true, the employee did meet their goal but had commissions greater than $1,000, so call for a 1% bonus by typing: **1%*H5**

E. In the third logical test type: **I5<1000**

F. Type **2%*H5** as the Value_If_True formula so employees who did meet their goal and had commissions less than $1,000 will receive a 2% bonus.

10. Click **OK** to enter the formula, modify the number format to show two decimals, and then fill the formula down the column for all other employees.

The result for the first employee is a bonus of $101.66.

11. Apply all borders to the **range J5:J33** to match the rest of the data and then reapply a thick outside border to **cell J4**.

Using the SWITCH Function

The company decided to modify the job titles, so you will use SWITCH to replace the existing names with new ones.

12. Select **cell G5** and insert a new column.

13. In **cell G5**, insert the **SWITCH** function with these arguments:

Function Arguments			
SWITCH			
Expression	F5	⬆	= "Agent"
Value1	"Agent"	⬆	= "Agent"
Result1	"Sales Rep"	⬆	= "Sales Rep"
Default_or_value2	"Manager"	⬆	= "Manager"
Result2	"Sales Director"	⬆	= "Sales Director"

If cell F5 contains Agent *it will be replaced with* Sales Rep, *and if it contains* Manager *it will be replaced with* Sales Director.

14. Fill the formula down for all employees, then copy the new positions from **column G** and paste the values only into **column F**; delete **column G**.

15. Save your work.

Troubleshooting Formulas

As you might have noticed, working with formulas can sometimes be complicated. Excel's auditing tools can help you make sense of your worksheet when it contains a complex set of formulas. The auditing tools can help you identify which cells were used to create a formula or where a particular cell is being used in other formulas, as well as locate and correct errors in formulas.

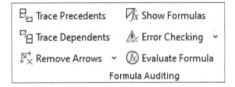

🖳 Trace Precedents	✔ₓ Show Formulas
🖳 Trace Dependents	⚠ Error Checking ⌄
🖳ₓ Remove Arrows ⌄	ⓕ Evaluate Formula
Formula Auditing	

Trace Precedents and Dependents

The Trace Precedents command displays arrows pointing to the current active cell from any cells that were used to produce the result. Trace Precedents works backward from the selected cell to show which cells affect the current result. Because the precedent cells could also use input from other cells to produce their results, there can be several layers of precedents. Repeating the Trace Precedents command will display the next level of precedents until a warning sound indicates there are no more levels.

Name	Goal	Sales	# Sales
Bert	$ 1,000	$ 900	18
Ernie	1,200	1,300	12
Jen	800	950	21
Sarah	1,000	1,200	17
Total	$ 4,000	$ 4,350	68
Sales Above Goal	$ 350		
Average Sale	$ 63.97		

Name	Goal	Sales	# Sales
Bert	$ 1,000	$ 900	18
Ernie	1,200	1,300	12
Jen	800	950	21
Sarah	1,000	1,200	17
Total	$ 4,000	$ 4,350	68
Sales Above Goal	$ 350		
Average Sale	$ 63.97		

With the current cell displaying the Sales Above Goal amount, Trace Precedents shows that the total Goal and Sales cells are used to calculate the above-goal amount of $350.

Adding another level to Trace Precedents shows that the totals use the information in the Goal and Sales columns.

Although you can see which cells are used in a formula by looking at the formula in the Formula Bar, tracing precedents is much quicker and gives you a better way to visualize the flow of data through the worksheet.

The Trace Dependents command shows the opposite of the precedents; it shows you any cells that use the current cell in a formula. Like precedents, there can be layers of dependent cells, which are displayed by repeating the Trace Dependents command. Changing the value in the current cell will therefore have an effect on all of the dependent cells.

Name	Goal	Sales	# Sales
Bert	$ 1,000	$ 900	18
Ernie	1,200	1,300	12
Jen	800	950	21
Sarah	1,000	1,200	17
Total	$ 4,000	$ 4,350	68
Sales Above Goal	$ 350		
Average Sale	$ 63.97		

Name	Goal	Sales	# Sales
Bert	$ 1,000	$ 900	18
Ernie	1,200	1,300	12
Jen	800	950	21
Sarah	1,000	1,200	17
Total	$ 4,000	$ 4,350	68
Sales Above Goal	$ 350		
Average Sale	$ 63.97		

The current cell shows Bert's number of sales, and by using Trace Dependents you see that Bert's sales amount is used to calculate total sales.

By adding another level, you see that total sales is then used to calculate the average sale.

Another way to think of it is to think of tracing precedents as looking backward, to see where the information comes from, and tracing dependents as looking forward, to see where the information is being used. When you no longer need the arrows, you can simply use the Remove Arrows command to remove them.

View the video "Tracing Your Formulas."

Checking for Errors

The Error Checking tool can help you spot and correct errors in formulas. This can be particularly useful if you are reviewing someone else's work and aren't sure where the errors are located. If it is your own work, you would usually fix errors as you go along.

Errors in cells are flagged with a green triangle, and sometimes with an error message in the cell instead of the formula result.

A green triangle indicates a cell that contains an error.

Selecting a cell with an error displays the warning sign.

Clicking the warning sign displays options for dealing with the error.

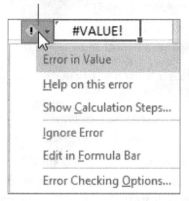

| #VALUE! |

| ◇ | #VALUE! |

| ! ▾ | #VALUE! |

Error in Value

<u>H</u>elp on this error

Show <u>C</u>alculation Steps...

<u>I</u>gnore Error

Edit in <u>F</u>ormula Bar

Error Checking <u>O</u>ptions...

> **NOTE!** Even if the formula displays a result, it might still contain an error, usually if the formula omits adjacent data. If this is done intentionally, you can click the warning sign and select Ignore Error to dismiss it.

COMMON EXCEL FORMULA ERRORS	
Error	**Description**
#DIV/0!	Dividing by zero is not possible, so this error displays if a formula attempts to divide by a cell that contains zero or by an empty cell.
#REF!	You will see this error if a formula contains an invalid cell reference; for example, if a formula refers to cell A1 and row 1 or column A is deleted.
#VALUE!	This error usually occurs because the formula is attempting to perform a mathematical operation using a cell that contains text.
#NAME?	This error occurs when a formula contains an incorrect function name or an undefined name for a cell or range.
Formula Omits Adjacent Cells	This error does not display in the result cell. It appears as a suggested error when a formula refers to a column or row of data but does not include all adjacent numerical values.

Evaluate a Formula

Not all mistakes result in Excel displaying an error; sometimes a valid formula is simply showing an incorrect result because it was not created with the correct cell references, functions, or operations. When reviewing a complex formula, it can be useful to break the formula down into steps and watch how Excel solves it. This can help you discover the source of an error or explain why the result does not look the way you expected. Evaluating a formula can also help you see how a formula with multiple operations is solved (by following the correct order of operations one step at a time).

The Watch Window

The Watch Window allows you to keep track of a particular formula, even when working on a different sheet or workbook. This is useful when you have multiple sheets with formulas that use data across many sheets, and you want to observe the effects of changes made on one sheet to the results of formulas on other sheets.

Formulas→Formula Auditing

DEVELOP YOUR SKILLS: E9-D4

In this exercise, you will use the Formula Auditing tools to analyze formulas and correct formula errors on the Aug Sales sheet.

1. Save your file as: **E9-D4-SalesAnalysis**
2. Go to the **Aug Sales** sheet and select **cell M10**.
3. Choose **Formulas→Formula Auditing→Trace Precedents**.

   You will now see lines drawn from the Location, Position, Sales, and Commissions columns, all pointing to cell M10. Because the formula refers to the range within the column, there is also a blue box around the entire range.

Location	Position	Target	Sales	Commissions	Bonus		Description	Amount
Miami	Sales Rep	$ 5,000	$ 5,286	$ 589	$105.72		Miami Employees	9
Miami	Sales Rep	10,000	13,419	1,351	$134.19		Miami Employee Commissions	$8,390
New York	Sales Rep	10,000	10,298	883	$205.96		Miami Average Sales	$10,890
New York	Sales Director	12,000	14,713	535	$294.26		Miami Employees - Sales >$10,000	4
Toronto	Sales Rep	5,000	5,485	437	$109.70		Toronto Employees - Sales >$10,000	4
Vancouver	Sales Director	10,000	5,815	614	$ -		Miami Mgr Comm's - Sales <$10,000	$0

   Tracing precedents also shows you that the position name has changed and needs to be updated in the formula.

4. In the Formula Bar, modify the formula for **cell M10** by replacing *Manager* with *Sales Director*: `=SUMIFS(I5:I33,E5:E33,"Miami",F5:F33,"Sales Director",H5:H33,"<10000")`

   The result in cell M10 displays $2,427. Modifying the formula also removes the arrows.

5. With **cell M10** still selected, choose **Formulas→Formula Auditing→Trace Precedents** two times.

   The first click shows the precedents again. On the second click, no arrows are added because the Location, Position, Sales, and Commissions columns all contain values—not formulas. If your volume is turned on, you may hear the warning sound indicating the command can't be completed.

6. With **cell M10** still selected, choose **Formulas→Formula Auditing→Trace Dependents**.

   You will see a warning box indicating there are no formulas that refer to the active cell.

7. Click **OK** to close the warning box.
8. Choose **Formulas→Formula Auditing→Remove Arrows**.

9. Select **cell M18** and choose **Formulas→Formula Auditing→Trace Precedents**.

   The Trace Precedents arrows indicate that cells M15, M16, and M17 are used in the formula to calculate the total paid out. Because the Sales amount is not paid to employees, this should not be included, and the formula will have to be corrected.

10. Edit the formula in **cell M18** to be: **=M16+M17**

11. With **cell M18** still selected, click the **Trace Precedents** button twice.

    The next level of precedents appears, showing that the formulas to calculate total commissions and bonuses use references to the data in the Sales and Commissions columns. This should be a warning that the formulas might be incorrect because Total Bonus does not refer to the Bonus column of data, and the ranges also do not include the entire column as they should.

12. Click the **Trace Dependents** button.

    The dependent arrow points to cell M19.

Check for Errors

Now you will find the errors on the sheet and correct them.

13. Remove the arrows from the worksheet.

14. Select **cell A1** and choose **Formulas→Formula Auditing→Error Checking**.

    The Error Checking dialog box opens and displays the first error in cell M15. The formula is =SUM(H5:H17), and the error is that the formula omits the adjacent cells.

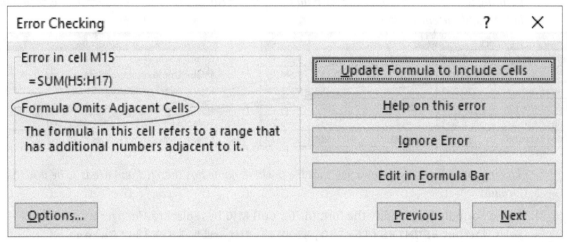

Because Excel anticipates that formulas will normally refer to an entire column or row and not just part, the error asks whether you want to update the formula to include cells. Of course, if the formula is meant to use only part of the column, you can ignore the error; in this case, you will correct it.

15. Click **Update Formula to Include Cells**.

    The error checker moves to the next error in cell M16. The error in cell M16 is the same error; the formula does not include all cells in the column.

16. Click **Update Formula to Include Cells** again.

    The error checker moves to the next error in cell M17. The error in cell M17 also omits adjacent cells; however, the formula also refers to the wrong column, so you can fix this by directly editing the formula.

17. Click **Edit in Formula Bar**.

18. In the Formula Bar, replace the existing range reference with **J5:J33** so the formula reads *=SUM(J5:J33)* and then click **Resume** in the Error Checking dialog box.

    This time the error in cell M19 is an error in value, meaning a value used in the formula is of the wrong data type, usually text instead of a number. The formula is =M18/M14, but cell M14 contains text. You can edit this formula in the Formula Bar so the formula is dividing Total Paid Out/Total Sales.

19. Click **Edit in Formula Bar**, then correct the formula to **=M18/M15** and click **Resume**.

    The rest of the worksheet is now error free.

20. Click **OK** in the dialog box and apply the **Percent Style** number format to **cell M19**.

Evaluate a Formula

21. With **cell M19** still selected, choose **Formulas→Formula Auditing→Evaluate Formula**.

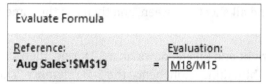

    The Evaluate Formula dialog box shows the reference to the cell being evaluated, cell M19 on the Aug Sales sheet, and the formula being evaluated, =M18/M15. The underline indicates the next part of the formula to evaluate.

22. Click **Evaluate**.

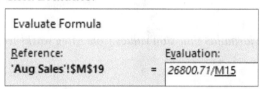

    Cell M18 is evaluated, and the value of cell M18 is displayed: 26800.71. Note that the cell's true value is shown, not the value displayed on the worksheet, which is affected by the number format (in this case no decimals). The second cell reference, M15, is underlined, indicating it is the next part of the formula that will be evaluated.

23. Click **Evaluate**.

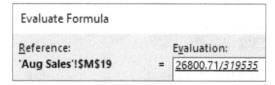

    Now the value of cell M15 is displayed: 319535.

24. Click **Evaluate** once more.

    The result of the formula 26800.71/319535 is now shown, which is 8%.

25. Click **Close** in the Evaluate Formula dialog box.

26. Save the file.

3-D Cell References

Excel formulas can refer to data on other worksheets or in other workbooks; however, sometimes a formula is required to refer to multiple sheets at the same time. For example, if cell A5 contains sales information for Product #1, and there is a different sales worksheet for each month, you might want to summarize the sales data by finding the total in cell A5 across multiple sheets. This can be done by adding each cell individually or by using a 3-D reference in your formula.

Compare these two formulas.

- =SUM(January!A5+February!A5+March!A5+April!A5+May!A5)
- =SUM(January:May!A5)

Similar to using a range instead of referring to each cell individually, a 3-D reference is quicker because you can refer to the range of sheets January to May and all sheets between, and then use the same cell (or range) from all sheets.

If you think of columns and rows as arranged left to right and up and down on a 2-D page, then stacking multiple worksheets on top of each other would be a third dimension, hence the 3-D reference. This is also useful because if a new sheet is inserted into the worksheet range, the data on the new sheet will automatically be included.

DEVELOP YOUR SKILLS: E9-D5

In this exercise, you will use 3-D cell references to create formulas that sum values from three worksheets.

1. Save your file as: **E9-D5-SalesSummary**
2. Go to the **Q3 Sales Summary** worksheet.

   For each employee you will summarize the total target, sales, and commission amounts for July, August, and September.

3. In **cell G5**, begin entering your formula by typing: **=SUM(**
4. Follow these steps to finish the formula using a 3-D reference:

   A. While editing the formula, click the **Jul Sales** worksheet tab.
   B. Click **cell G5** and see that the Formula Bar displays *=SUM('Jul Sales'!G5*.
   C. Hold down Shift+click the **Sept Sales** sheet tab to select the range of sheets Jul Sales:Sept Sales, which includes the Aug Sales sheet.

5. Complete the entry by clicking **Enter** ☑ on the Formula Bar, which automatically returns you to the Q3 Sales Summary worksheet.

> **WARNING!** Be careful when completing the entry. Do NOT click the Q3 Sales Summary tab or any other cells, as this will change the formula!

The completed formula is =SUM('Jul Sales:Sept Sales'!G5), which finds the sum of cell G5 on all three sheets. The result of the formula is $15,000.

6. Select **cell H5** and complete steps 3–5 again to create a formula that adds cell H5 on the Jul Sales, Aug Sales, and Sept Sales sheets.

   Your completed formula should be =SUM('Jul Sales:Sept Sales'!H5).

7. In **cell I5**, create a formula that adds cell I5 on the Jul Sales, Aug Sales, and Sept Sales sheets.

   Your completed formula should be =SUM('Jul Sales:Sept Sales'!I5). *The sum in cell H5 is $16,113, and the sum in cell I5 is $1,322.*

8. Select the **range G5:I5** and use the **fill handle** to copy the formulas down all three columns.

9. Save your work and close the file.

Self-Assessment

 Check your knowledge of this chapter's key concepts and skills using the online Self-Assessment Quiz.

10

Lookup Functions and Outlines

n this chapter, you will explore functions that can be used to find data from a large database or a small lookup table. You will also learn about the Outline feature, which can be used to group information or create subtotals and is also a handy tool for data analysis.

LEARNING OBJECTIVES

- Create formulas using lookup functions
- Use the Outline feature
- Create subtotals
- Use the Quick Analysis tool

CHAPTER TIMING

- Concepts & Practice: 01:20:00
- Self-Assessment: 00:15:00
- Total: 01:35:00

PROJECT: MANAGING EMPLOYEE RECORDS

LearnFast College provides fast-paced learning programs for college students. You're an instructor at the college, and you also assist the office with various Excel tasks. The college employee records are saved in an Excel spreadsheet and contain confidential information about employees, including their salaries. You have been asked to create a method for entering employees' names to quickly find their extension numbers and also to enter the tax rates for each employee based on salary. You will work with Excel to accomplish these tasks and use the outline tools to analyze the information further.

Learning Resources: **boostyourskills.lablearning.com**

Introducing Lookup Functions

Lookup functions are used to retrieve a piece of data from a table (usually a large table). By knowing one piece of information from a record, you can use it to find other information from that record. A phonebook is an example of a simple lookup. You know a person's name, so you look for it in the first column on the left, and when you find it you look across to the column that contains the phone number.

VLOOKUP and HLOOKUP

The VLOOKUP function is the most commonly used lookup function because it's used specifically to look up information arranged in columns, which is the format for many databases.

> **TIP!** The *V* in VLOOKUP stands for *vertical*; columns are vertical. Conversely, the *H* in HLOOKUP stands for *horizontal*; rows are horizontal.

The HLOOKUP function has the same arguments and is used when the data is arranged in rows. The LOOKUP function is another option, but it is primarily available because older versions of Excel did not have VLOOKUP and HLOOKUP.

The VLOOKUP function arguments are:

=VLOOKUP(Lookup Value, Table Array, Column Index Number, (Range Lookup(Optional)))

LOOKUP FUNCTION ARGUMENTS	
Argument	**Description**
Lookup_Value	This is the value to be found in the first column (VLOOKUP) or row (HLOOKUP) of the table.
Table_Array	This is the range of cells used to search for the lookup value and retrieve the result.
Col_Index_Num or Row_Index_Num (Column/Row Index Number)	This number indicates the column (VLOOKUP) or row (HLOOKUP) in the table from which the matching value will be retrieved; the first column/row in the Table Array is always 1.
Range_Lookup (Optional)	If TRUE or omitted, this function searches for the value closest to but less than the lookup value; if FALSE, it searches for exact matches only. If TRUE or omitted, the data must be sorted in ascending order.

Looking up a tax rate or discount rate is a good example of when you might use the VLOOKUP function. To encourage customer spending, a business may offer a discount based on annual spending. The various discount levels would be contained in a table.

> **NOTE!** Because the information is arranged in two columns, you would use the VLOOKUP function.

	E	F
1	Discount Table	
2	**Annual Spending**	**Discount Rate**
3	$0	0.00%
4	$20,000	2.00%
5	$30,000	3.00%
6	$40,000	4.50%
7	$50,000	6.50%

For each customer, you would look up the amount of money spent to date to determine the discount.

This is the full formula in cell C3.

The Lookup_Value is in cell B3, Robert's total spending to date (*$28,000*).

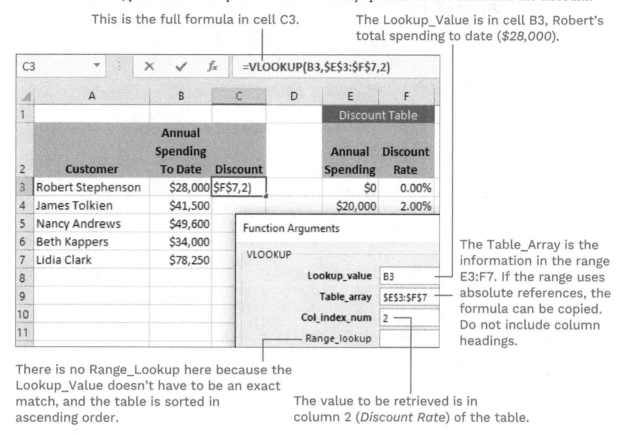

=VLOOKUP(B3,$E$3:$F$7,2)

The Table_Array is the information in the range E3:F7. If the range uses absolute references, the formula can be copied. Do not include column headings.

There is no Range_Lookup here because the Lookup_Value doesn't have to be an exact match, and the table is sorted in ascending order.

The value to be retrieved is in column 2 (*Discount Rate*) of the table.

The result for the first customer, Robert, is 2% because he spent more than $20,000 but less than the $30,000 required to qualify for a 3% discount; $20,000 is the closest value that *does not exceed* the $28,000 lookup value. The remaining customer discounts can then be calculated by copying the formula down the column.

	A	B	C	D	E	F
1					Discount Table	
2	Customer	Annual Spending To Date	Discount		Annual Spending	Discount Rate
3	Robert Stephenson	$28,000	2.0%		$0	0.00%
4	James Tolkien	$41,500	4.5%		$20,000	2.00%
5	Nancy Andrews	$49,600	4.5%		$30,000	3.00%
6	Beth Kappers	$34,000	3.0%		$40,000	4.50%
7	Lidia Clark	$78,250	6.5%		$50,000	6.50%

DEVELOP YOUR SKILLS: E10-D1

In this exercise, you will use the VLOOKUP function to both find an employee's phone extension by typing in the name and look up the tax rates for all employees in a tax table.

1. Start Excel, open **E10-D1-Database** from your **Excel Chapter 10** folder, and save it as:
   E10-D1-DataLookup

   To make it possible to search through the employee list and find the extension number, you will create a formula with the VLOOKUP function.

2. In **cell B5**, enter the name: **Ed Neal**

3. Select **cell E5** and choose **Formulas→Function Library→Lookup & Reference→VLOOKUP**.

4. Follow these steps to create a formula using VLOOKUP:

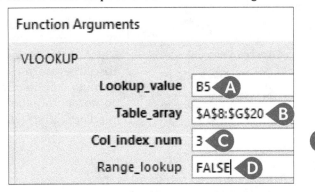

A. For the lookup value argument, select **cell B5**.

B. For the table array value, select the **range A8:G20** and tap F4 to make the range reference absolute (cells A8 and G20 both need to be absolute).

C. Type **3** in the Col_Index_Num box.

D. Type **FALSE** in the Range_Lookup box. (You're looking for an exact match here, so this argument should not be omitted.)

E. Click **OK**.

The formula in the Formula Bar displays =VLOOKUP(B5,$A$8:$G$20,3,FALSE) *and the result in cell E5 is* x222.

5. Select **cell B5** and enter: **Patty Mills**

   The result in cell E5 updates to show the extension for Patty Mills, x227.

   Next you will look up the tax rate for each employee on the Tax Rate sheet.

6. Select **cell G8** and insert the VLOOKUP function.

7. Select **cell F8** for the Lookup_Value argument.

8. To specify the table array argument, choose the **Tax Rate** sheet, select the table without the headings, and press F4.

9. Enter **2** as the Col_Index_Num argument.

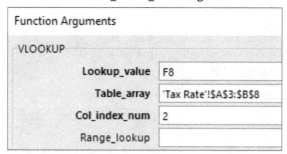

Function Arguments	
VLOOKUP	
Lookup_value	F8
Table_array	'Tax Rate'!$A$3:$B$8
Col_index_num	2
Range_lookup	

A range lookup is not necessary because you're not looking for an exact match.

10. Click **OK**.

The result for the first employee, Ed Neal, is 0.34.

11. Apply the **Percent Style** number format and increase the decimal places to one.

12. Copy the formula down the column for the other employees.

13. Save the file.

The Outline Feature

You can use the Outline feature to group related information, which can also be useful for quickly calculating subtotals and totals. Groups can be created by either rows or columns. Having an outline means you can control which data to display and hide, and you can choose between a detailed view of data or to hide the details and view only a summary. Outlines are best used with normal data ranges, rather than tables.

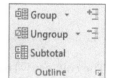

You can create an outline manually or by using Auto Outline. To use Auto Outline, you must have inserted formulas that sum or subtotal information from groups of rows or columns. For example, in the following illustration there is a sum below each Position category (rows 6, 12, and 18). The Auto Outline command will recognize these as distinct areas of data and group each accordingly. Likewise, column H is a sum of the sales figures contained in columns F and G.

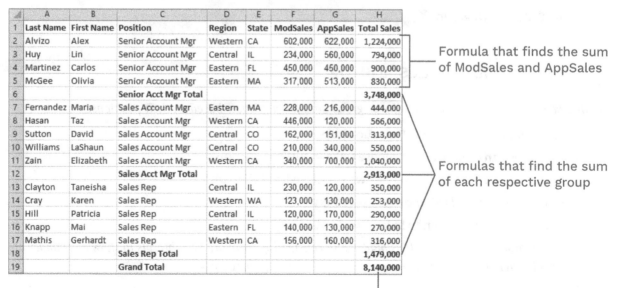

	A	B	C	D	E	F	G	H
1	Last Name	First Name	Position	Region	State	ModSales	AppSales	Total Sales
2	Alvizo	Alex	Senior Account Mgr	Western	CA	602,000	622,000	1,224,000
3	Huy	Lin	Senior Account Mgr	Central	IL	234,000	560,000	794,000
4	Martinez	Carlos	Senior Account Mgr	Eastern	FL	450,000	450,000	900,000
5	McGee	Olivia	Senior Account Mgr	Eastern	MA	317,000	513,000	830,000
6			Senior Acct Mgr Total					3,748,000
7	Fernandez	Maria	Sales Account Mgr	Eastern	MA	228,000	216,000	444,000
8	Hasan	Taz	Sales Account Mgr	Western	CA	446,000	120,000	566,000
9	Sutton	David	Sales Account Mgr	Central	CO	162,000	151,000	313,000
10	Williams	LaShaun	Sales Account Mgr	Central	CO	210,000	340,000	550,000
11	Zain	Elizabeth	Sales Account Mgr	Western	CA	340,000	700,000	1,040,000
12			Sales Acct Mgr Total					2,913,000
13	Clayton	Taneisha	Sales Rep	Central	IL	230,000	120,000	350,000
14	Cray	Karen	Sales Rep	Western	WA	123,000	130,000	253,000
15	Hill	Patricia	Sales Rep	Central	IL	120,000	170,000	290,000
16	Knapp	Mai	Sales Rep	Eastern	FL	140,000	130,000	270,000
17	Mathis	Gerhardt	Sales Rep	Western	CA	156,000	160,000	316,000
18			Sales Rep Total					1,479,000
19			Grand Total					8,140,000

Formula that finds the sum of ModSales and AppSales

Formulas that find the sum of each respective group

Formula that finds the sum of the three subtotals

Auto Outline then adds the outline structure along the top and left sides of the worksheet that contains the outline symbols for adjusting the view.

Row levels show three layers of detail, where 1 shows the least and 3 shows the most detail; all groups in a level are collapsed/expanded together.

Column levels show/hide the column details.

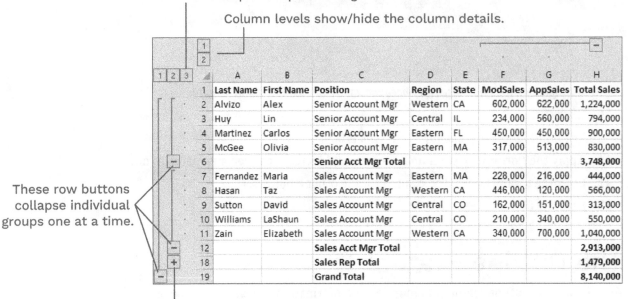

These row buttons collapse individual groups one at a time.

Rows 13–17 are hidden; clicking the expand ⊞ button would redisplay them.

The collapse ⊟ buttons show less information by hiding the detail in a group of rows or columns, while the expand ⊞ buttons show the hidden group. And removing an outline is easy; just use the Clear Outline command.

👀 **View the video "Creating Outlines and Subtotals."**

Data→Outline→Group ⊞

Data→Outline→Ungroup ⊞

DEVELOP YOUR SKILLS: E10-D2

In this exercise, you will create an outline to group data for employees based on their positions.

1. Save your file as: **E10-D2-DataLookup**

2. Select the **range E8:E15** and choose **Data→Outline→Group**.

3. In the Group dialog box, ensure **Rows** is selected and click **OK**.

   One group level is added, encompassing rows 8–15.

4. Click the collapse button to hide **rows 8–15**.

   The information in rows 8–15 is hidden but, considering there are no subtotals to show a summary of the hidden information, there is no real benefit to hiding these rows.

5. Choose **Data→Outline→Ungroup menu button ∨→Clear Outline**.

    The outline is cleared. Now you will insert subtotal formulas and a grand total and then use Auto Outline to group the data.

6. Insert a new row above **row 16** then enter **Instructor Total** in the empty **cell D16**.

7. In **cell F16**, choose **Home→Editing→AutoSum** and insert the formula to calculate the combined total for instructor salaries.

    The remaining employee positions are grouped together as administrative positions.

8. In **cell D22**, enter **Administrative Total** and then use **AutoSum** in **cell F22** to calculate the sum of the remaining employee salaries.

    Notice that AutoSum recognizes the subtotal in cell F16 and automatically selects the range F17:F21.

9. In **cell D23**, enter **Grand Total** and then use **AutoSum** in **cell F23**.

    This time AutoSum uses the two subtotals in cells F22 and F16.

10. Apply bold formatting to the **ranges D16:F16** and **D22:F23**.

11. Now select a single cell only, anywhere on the worksheet.

    Auto Outline will not work while a range of cells is selected.

12. Choose **Data→Outline→Group menu button ∨→Auto Outline**.

    Auto Outline adds groups to the rows for each subtotal and one group for the grand total.

13. Click the **2** outline symbol to show the second level of detail.

    The Instructor and Administrative groups are collapsed, but both subtotals as well as the grand total are visible.

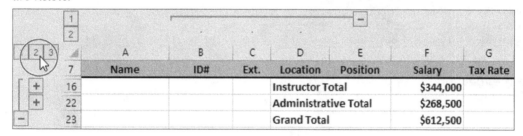

14. Save your work and close the file.

Subtotals

In some ways, using the Subtotal command is simpler and quicker than grouping rows or using Auto Outline, although there are a few more steps in the process. Which option to use depends on the existing state of your data. For example, if your data already has subtotals inserted, then using Auto Outline will be quick and easy for you. If your data is in one large block with *no dividers or subtotals*, then the Subtotal command will add the outline and create the subtotals by group all at once.

To use the Subtotal command, start by sorting the list on the column you will use to group the subtotals. For example, to create a subtotal for each city, your data must be sorted by city.

Last Name	First Name	Position	Region	State	ModSales	AppSales	Total Sales
Huy	Lin	Senior Account Mgr	Central	IL	234,000	560,000	794,000
Sutton	David	Sales Account Mgr	Central	CO	162,000	151,000	313,000
Williams	LaShaun	Sales Account Mgr	Central	CO	210,000	340,000	550,000
Clayton	Taneisha	Sales Rep	Central	IL	230,000	120,000	350,000
Hill	Patricia	Sales Rep	Central	IL	120,000	170,000	290,000
Martinez	Carlos	Senior Account Mgr	Eastern	FL	450,000	450,000	900,000
McGee	Olivia	Senior Account Mgr	Eastern	MA	317,000	513,000	830,000
Fernandez	Maria	Sales Account Mgr	Eastern	MA	228,000	216,000	444,000
Knapp	Mai	Sales Rep	Eastern	FL	140,000	130,000	270,000
Alvizo	Alex	Senior Account Mgr	Western	CA	602,000	622,000	1,224,000
Hasan	Taz	Sales Account Mgr	Western	CA	446,000	120,000	566,000
Zain	Elizabeth	Sales Account Mgr	Western	CA	340,000	700,000	1,040,000
Cray	Karen	Sales Rep	Western	WA	123,000	130,000	253,000
Mathis	Gerhardt	Sales Rep	Western	CA	156,000	160,000	316,000

This worksheet, sorted by Region, is ready for the user to create a Subtotal to sum the sales for each region.

The Subtotal Dialog Box

The Subtotal dialog box gives you a step-by-step process to simplify creating the subtotals.

Indicate the column to use for grouping. Data should be sorted by this column; in this case, you want a subtotal for each region. ———

Indicate the function to use in ——— the subtotal calculation (SUM, COUNT, AVERAGE, MIN, MAX).

Indicate the column(s) to ——— calculate a subtotal. In this case, the ModSales, AppSales, and Total Sales columns will be summed by region.

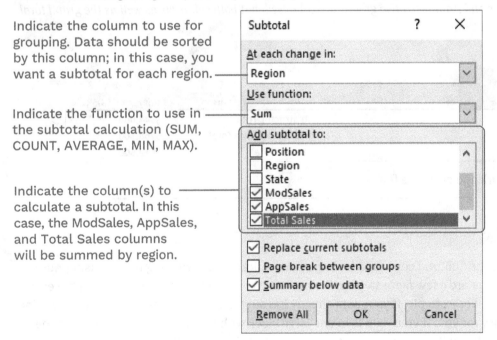

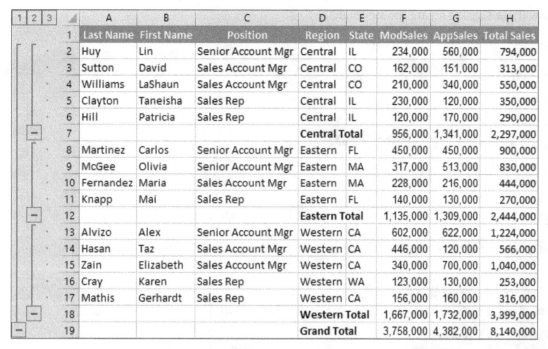

1 2 3	▲	A	B	C	D	E	F	G	H
	1	Last Name	First Name	Position	Region	State	ModSales	AppSales	Total Sales
	2	Huy	Lin	Senior Account Mgr	Central	IL	234,000	560,000	794,000
	3	Sutton	David	Sales Account Mgr	Central	CO	162,000	151,000	313,000
	4	Williams	LaShaun	Sales Account Mgr	Central	CO	210,000	340,000	550,000
	5	Clayton	Taneisha	Sales Rep	Central	IL	230,000	120,000	350,000
	6	Hill	Patricia	Sales Rep	Central	IL	120,000	170,000	290,000
	7				**Central Total**		956,000	1,341,000	2,297,000
	8	Martinez	Carlos	Senior Account Mgr	Eastern	FL	450,000	450,000	900,000
	9	McGee	Olivia	Senior Account Mgr	Eastern	MA	317,000	513,000	830,000
	10	Fernandez	Maria	Sales Account Mgr	Eastern	MA	228,000	216,000	444,000
	11	Knapp	Mai	Sales Rep	Eastern	FL	140,000	130,000	270,000
	12				**Eastern Total**		1,135,000	1,309,000	2,444,000
	13	Alvizo	Alex	Senior Account Mgr	Western	CA	602,000	622,000	1,224,000
	14	Hasan	Taz	Sales Account Mgr	Western	CA	446,000	120,000	566,000
	15	Zain	Elizabeth	Sales Account Mgr	Western	CA	340,000	700,000	1,040,000
	16	Cray	Karen	Sales Rep	Western	WA	123,000	130,000	253,000
	17	Mathis	Gerhardt	Sales Rep	Western	CA	156,000	160,000	316,000
	18				**Western Total**		1,667,000	1,732,000	3,399,000
	19				**Grand Total**		3,758,000	4,382,000	8,140,000

This figure shows the results after the Subtotal on the previous page is applied to sales data.

DEVELOP YOUR SKILLS: E10-D3

In this exercise, you will rearrange the employee data to find average salaries for each location by creating an outline using the Subtotal command.

1. Open **E10-D3-Database** from your **Excel Chapter 10** folder and save it as:
   E10-D3-DataOutline

   You have to sort the data by location first to create subtotals for each location.

2. Select a cell in **column D** below the *Location* heading and choose **Home→Editing→ Sort & Filter→Sort A to Z**.

3. Choose **Data→Outline→Subtotal**.

4. Follow these steps to create the subtotal:

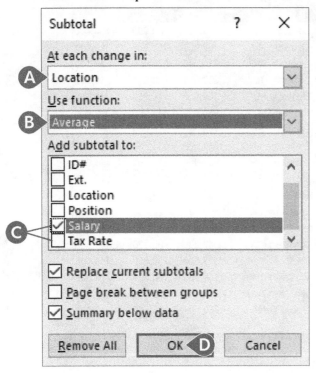

A. Choose **Location** as the column for grouping.

B. Choose **Average** as the function.

C. Select **Salary** and deselect the **Tax Rate** checkbox.

D. Keep the other default settings and click **OK**.

Notice the options to remove all subtotals or to insert page breaks between groups.

5. Save your work.

The Quick Analysis Tool

The Quick Analysis tool offers quick and easy access to several popular analysis options also available from the Ribbon. For example, you might have a list of expense data, and you want to quickly highlight the expenses that went over budget with conditional formatting or insert a chart of all expenses.

To access the Quick Analysis tool, simply select any range of two or more cells that contain data.

NOTE! The Quick Analysis tool button appears only when the mouse is near the selected range of data!

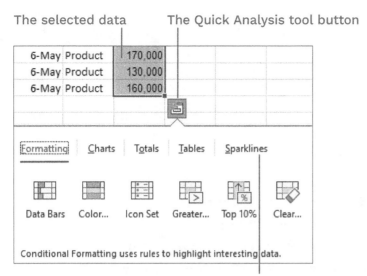

The selected data   The Quick Analysis tool button

The Quick Analysis options, which contain five categories and are based on the type of data selected

Each category name will display the menu of options, which include:

- Adding conditional formatting to your selection
- Creating a chart
- Inserting totals such as sum, average, or count, either in the row below or the column to the right of the selection
- Inserting tables, including PivotTables (depending on the data), or sparklines

You can see a preview of each option by holding the mouse pointer over the option.

DEVELOP YOUR SKILLS: E10-D4

In this exercise, you will use the Quick Analysis tool to add conditional formatting and then create a chart using the employee salary and tax rate data.

1. Save your file as: **E10-D4-DataAnalysis**
2. Begin by selecting a cell in the Salary column, **column F.**

   You will sort the data by Salary first before creating your chart.
3. Choose **Home→Editing→Sort & Filter→Sort Smallest to Largest.**

   You will see a warning window that tells you that sorting will remove the subtotals.
4. Click **OK** to accept and remove the subtotals.
5. Select the Salary and Tax Rate headings and data in the **range F7:G20.**
6. Click the **Quick Analysis** tool button.

   Hint: If you don't see the button, move the mouse pointer near the bottom-right corner of the selection.

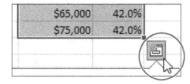

7. Click **Charts** and then click the second chart option (**Clustered Column**).

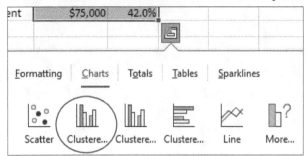

8. Edit the chart title to: `Salary and Tax Rate Comparison`
9. Move the chart to a new sheet called: `Comparison Chart`
10. Return to the **Database** sheet and select the salary data in the **range F8:F20**.
11. Click **Quick Analysis** and then choose **Icon Set** from the Formatting category.
12. Select the tax rate data in the **range G8:G20**.
13. Click **Quick Analysis** and then choose **Color Scales** from the Formatting category.

    The arrow icons are added to the salaries, and the red and green fill is added to the tax rate data to show groups of low, middle, and high data for each column side by side.

14. Save your work and close the file.

Self-Assessment

Check your knowledge of this chapter's key concepts and skills using the online Self-Assessment Quiz.

MICROSOFT EXCEL 2021/365

Working with Tables

11

I n this chapter, you will explore the table tools available in Excel as you discover the advantages of creating and using tables. You will also create formulas that use structured references and insert sparklines for quick and simple data trend analysis.

LEARNING OBJECTIVES

- Manage data using a table
- Create a custom filter
- Name a table
- Use structured references in a formula
- Create sparklines

CHAPTER TIMING

- Concepts & Practice: 01:30:00
- Self-Assessment: 00:15:00
- Total: 01:45:00

PROJECT: ANALYZING EXAM PERFORMANCE

You are an instructor at LearnFast College. Your business students completed their final exams recently, and you are reviewing the grades. To help you assess individual exam grades and find the class average, you are going to create a table and use the table tools. For further analysis, you will create a series of formulas that use structured references to the table data and insert sparklines to show trends in the exam grades.

Learning Resources: **boostyourskills.lablearning.com**

Working with Tables

Tables can be a valuable feature in Excel if they are used properly. An Excel table is comprised of a group of related data within a defined range. Formatting the data as a table enables the use of the table features.

Tables are useful, not only for managing and organizing data, but also when it comes to creating advanced formulas and analyzing data. In addition, table features allow you to manage the data in the table rows and columns independently from the data in other rows and columns on the worksheet. You can create a table by converting existing data into a table, or you can start by creating a blank table and then fill in the information later. You can even create multiple tables on the same worksheet.

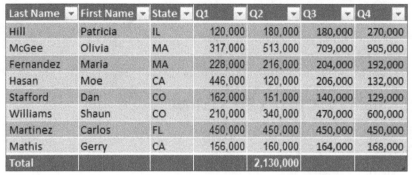

Last Name	First Name	State	Q1	Q2	Q3	Q4
Hill	Patricia	IL	120,000	180,000	180,000	270,000
McGee	Olivia	MA	317,000	513,000	709,000	905,000
Fernandez	Maria	MA	228,000	216,000	204,000	192,000
Hasan	Moe	CA	446,000	120,000	206,000	132,000
Stafford	Dan	CO	162,000	151,000	140,000	129,000
Williams	Shaun	CO	210,000	340,000	470,000	600,000
Martinez	Carlos	FL	450,000	450,000	450,000	450,000
Mathis	Gerry	CA	156,000	160,000	164,000	168,000
Total				2,130,000		

This table of sales data displays the header row, banded rows (alternating colors), and a total row.

Insert and Delete Table Rows and Columns

Generally, working with a table is not very different from working with a regular data range. You can add rows or columns into the middle of a table just as you would with a normal range—by selecting a cell below the desired location of the new row, or to the right of the location of the new column, and using the Insert command. To delete a row or column, you use the Delete command.

The simplest way to add rows, however, is to add them at the bottom of the table, as entering new data in the row directly below a table will automatically expand the table to include the new row. Likewise, if you add new data in the column to the right, it will be included in the table as well. Table formatting will also be automatically applied to any new rows or columns to stay consistent with the rest of the table.

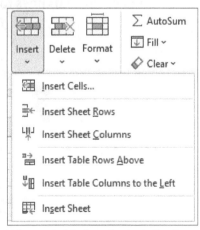
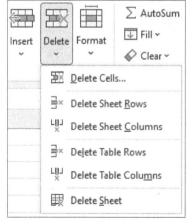

When a table is selected, the Insert and Delete menus have the additional table options to Insert/Delete Table Rows or Columns.

The difference between inserting a table row/column or a sheet row/column is that the Table commands do not affect the rest of the worksheet. For example, inserting a table row will insert the row into the table only, but inserting a sheet row will insert the row for the table and the entire worksheet.

> **TIP!** If the table includes a total row, you can insert a new row at the bottom but above the total row by selecting the bottom-right table cell and pressing Tab.

Calculated Columns

Table columns can contain text values, numerical values, or formulas. When you enter a formula into a table cell, it will automatically become a calculated column, which instantly copies the formula to all cells in the column. In the same fashion, editing a formula in one cell will update the formula for the entire column. This eliminates the need to use the fill handle to copy your formula, making the task quick and easy.

Apply a Sort or Filter

Another advantage of tables is the ability to quickly sort and filter the information contained in them. A sort will arrange all the information in the table according to your preference, and a filter allows you to decide which data to display and which to hide. Sorts and filters can be performed on both a normal range or a table, but a table automatically displays a filter button at the top of each column. Depending on the actions taken in that column, the filter button may show the down-arrow, the filter symbol, a sort arrow, or some combination of these.

Last Name	First Name	State	Q1	Q2	Q3	Q4
McGee	Olivia	MA	317,000	513,000	709,000	905,000
Fernandez	Maria	MA	228,000	216,000	204,000	192,000

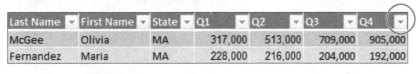

Insert→Tables→Table

Home→Cells→Insert or Delete

DEVELOP YOUR SKILLS: E11-D1

In this exercise, you will create a table from existing data (the exam grades) and then edit and sort the students' exam data.

1. Start Excel, open **E11-D1-Exam** from your **Excel Chapter 11** folder, and save it as: **E11-D1-ExamRevised**

2. Select **cell A5** and choose **Insert→Tables→Table**.

   The Create Table dialog box suggested range is A5:J17 (as an absolute reference), which is correct. The My Table Has Headers box has a checkmark to indicate there are headers.

3. Click **OK** to create the table.

   The table is created. Notice the filter buttons beside each heading and the formatting changes. The Table Tools Design tab is activated on the Ribbon.

4. Select **cell D5** and choose **Home→Cells→Insert menu button ⌄→Insert Table Columns to the Left**.

   Notice the inserted column does not affect the data in the range A20:D22.

5. Type **Date** to replace *Column1* in **cell D5**.

6. In **cell D6**, enter **=$A$3** to copy the date from **cell A3** using an absolute reference.

   After you complete the formula entry in cell D6, the formula is automatically added to all other cells in the table column. The results display only the #### symbols because the column needs to be resized.

7. Select the **range D6:D17**, change the number format to **Short Date**, and then autofit the width of **column D**.

8. Set the width of **column I** to: **6**

9. Select **cell K17** and tap ⌜Tab⌟.

   A new row is added to the bottom of the table in row 18.

10. Enter the information for another student in the new table row:

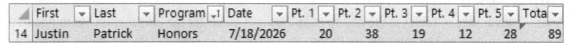

First	Last	Program	Date	Pt. 1	Pt. 2	Pt. 3	Pt. 4	Pt. 5	Total
14 Justin	Patrick	Honors	7/18/2026	20	38	19	12	28	89

   Notice that the Date and Total column formulas for Justin are automatically added for you.

11. Use the **Total filter** button ▼ to sort the students by their total mark, **Smallest to Largest**.

12. Sort the students by program, from **A to Z**.

    Because you already sorted by the totals first, the students are still arranged lowest to highest within the Applied group and Honors group.

13. Save the file.

| **NOTE!** Always leave your file open at the end of an exercise unless instructed to close it.

Special Table Features

The special features of a table include the ability to rename the table for quick reference to its data, the header row (used to label columns of information), and the total row (summarizes table data). You can also quickly adjust the formatting of a table by applying a table style, and you can modify table styles by adding or removing options such as banded rows, banded columns, or special first/last column formatting. For other formatting changes, you can select a table row or column with one click without selecting the rest of the worksheet.

| **NOTE!** The Table Tools tab is a contextual Ribbon tab; you must have a cell within the table selected to prompt it.

Table Name

The default name for the first table in a workbook is *Table1*, the second is *Table2*, and so on. Although you can keep the default names, more descriptive names can be useful, especially if the table data will be used in formulas. You can change a table name by editing the name directly in the Table Tools Properties menu. As with defining names for a cell or range, table names cannot contain spaces but may include underscores.

Header Row

Most tables will contain categories of information in columns, so including a header row at the top of the table provides a label for each column. It's good practice to limit each column to one piece of information, such as having two separate columns for first name and last name, to enable full sorting and filtering. Each column heading in a table should be unique.

> **WARNING!** Avoid the characters @, #, ( ), and ' in column headings because they have special meanings in formulas.

When scrolling through a large table, a table's header row will remain visible across the top of the worksheet, eliminating the need to freeze the top row. The headings replace the normal worksheet column headings A, B, C, etc.

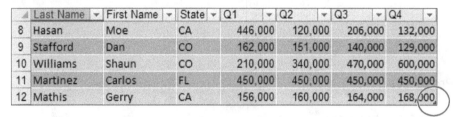

	Last Name	First Name	State	Q1	Q2	Q3	Q4
8	Hasan	Moe	CA	446,000	120,000	206,000	132,000
9	Stafford	Dan	CO	162,000	151,000	140,000	129,000
10	Williams	Shaun	CO	210,000	340,000	470,000	600,000
11	Martinez	Carlos	FL	450,000	450,000	450,000	450,000
12	Mathis	Gerry	CA	156,000	160,000	164,000	168,000

You can drag the table resize handle to add and remove columns and rows.

Table Style Options

You can add and remove table formatting using the Table Style Options checkboxes. These options can help make the information easier to read by differentiating certain rows and columns. Clear the Filter Button checkbox to hide the filter buttons in the header row.

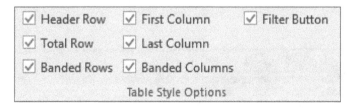

Total Row

Checking the Total Row option in the Table Style Options group will automatically add a row to the bottom of your table with the text *Total* in the left column and a sum in the far-right column. Although a total row is often used to sum the values in a column, there are other summary functions that can be used as well. The total row is formatted to match the style of the rest of the table but may be a different shade to stand out from the other data.

Williams	Shaun	Central	CO	210,000	340,000
Martinez	Carlos	Eastern	FL	450,000	450,000
Mathis	Gerhardt	Western	CA	156,000	160,000
Total					4,252,000

This total row adds a sum in the last column on the right, but if the last column contained text or dates, it would simply count the populated cells.

Selecting a cell in the total row will display a menu button ▼ that shows a list of the available summary formulas. For example, rather than a sum, you may wish to display the average of the column data.

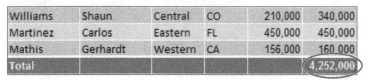

Table Tools→Design→Properties

Table Tools→Design→Table Style Options

DEVELOP YOUR SKILLS: E11-D2

In this exercise, you will rename the table and add a total row to calculate the average exam grades for the students.

1. Save your file as: **E11-D2-ExamRevised**

2. Go to **Table Tools→Design→Properties** and click in the **Table Name** box to select the existing name, type **Exams** to replace that, and tap Enter.

   The new table name is now saved as part of the table properties.

3. Scroll down on the worksheet so **row 6** is the first visible row. (You may need to use the up/down arrows on the scroll bar to move up/down one row at a time to get the worksheet to display precisely this way.)

   The table headers now replace the worksheet column headers.

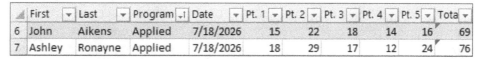

4. Point to the **First** table header, which changes your pointer to the table column selector arrow.

5. Drag one column to the right, to the **Last** table header, to select both table columns.

   Notice that the selection does not include the cells below the table.

6. Apply **Bold** formatting to the selection.

7. Add a total row by going to **Table Tools→Design→Table Style Options** and clicking the **Total Row** checkbox.

   The total row is added to the bottom of the table. The number 0 appears in the bottom-right cell because there is no data in the % column yet (the sum for that column is zero).

8. Select **cell A19** and replace the text *Total* with: **Average**

9. Select the cell that contains the zero in the total row, **cell K19**, under the % heading.

10. Use the **menu** button ▼ to select **None** from the drop-down list, which removes the *0*.

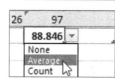

11. Move one cell to the left, to **cell J19** below the exam totals.

12. To find the average exam grade, click the **menu** button ▼ and select **Average** from the drop-down list.

13. Decrease the decimal places to show only one decimal.

14. Go to **Table Tools→Design** and in the Table Style Options group, click the **Last Column** checkbox and change the table style to **Blue, Table Style Medium 13**.

    Only certain table styles have different last column shading, Medium 13 being one of them.

15. Save your work.

Structured References

A structured reference is created when you use a formula with cell/range references to data contained in a table. The advantage of structured references is that they adjust formula results automatically when new rows or columns are added to a table. They also make it easier to identify the data source because the reference name includes information such as the table name and header name. The reference name, once used in a formula, will also update automatically if you rename the table or column header.

The syntax for a structured reference varies depending on whether it is a reference to a cell, an entire column, or even an entire table.

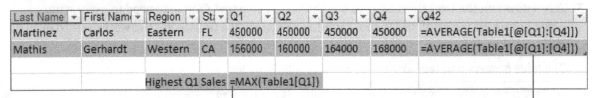

Last Name ▾	First Nam ▾	Region ▾	St ▾	Q1 ▾	Q2 ▾	Q3 ▾	Q4 ▾	Q42 ▾
Martinez	Carlos	Eastern	FL	450000	450000	450000	450000	=AVERAGE(Table1[@[Q1]:[Q4]])
Mathis	Gerhardt	Western	CA	156000	160000	164000	168000	=AVERAGE(Table1[@[Q1]:[Q4]])
		Highest Q1 Sales	=MAX(Table1[Q1])					

A formula with a structured reference to the column Q1 in Table1

A formula with a structured reference to one row of data in the range from Q1:Q4 in Table1

 View the video "Creating Formulas with Structured References."

Formulas with Structured References

The best way to create structured references is to use the point-and-click method to select the table cell or column, which adds all the appropriate formatting/syntax based on the cell or range selected. Trying to type a structured reference manually is much more difficult and can lead to mistakes in your formula.

Compare the formulas in the following illustrations. The formula in the left figure was typed in, and the formula in the right figure was created by clicking on the cells in the Q1 and Q2 columns. In the formula on the right, it's easy to see that the information from Q1 and Q2 is being added together, whereas the formula on the left would require finding the cells H5 and I5 first to understand the meaning.

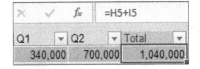

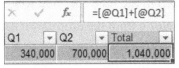

DEVELOP YOUR SKILLS: E11-D3

In this exercise, you will create formulas that use structured references to calculate the percentage grades, fix the total calculation, and insert summary calculations below the table.

1. Save your file as: **E11-D3-ExamRevised**

   You will create a formula to find the percent each student scored by dividing the total mark by 150.

2. Select **cell K6** in the first row below the % table header.

3. Type **=** and use the mouse to select **cell J6**, one cell to the left, below the Total table header.

   The cell reference is automatically inserted as a structured reference. Due to the dark fill color in the column (the image shows a lighter blue for visibility), you may not be able to see the text in the cell. If that's the case, check the Formula Bar.

4. Type **/150** and complete the formula entry.

   The formula is calculated in cell K6, the result is 0.46, and the formula is automatically copied down to the rest of the column.

5. Point to the % column header, click to select the table column, and apply **Bold** and the **Percent Style** number format.

   You may notice the marks seem unusually low, and you may have already noticed an error in the Total column, which you will fix now.

6. Select **cell J6**, the first cell below the Total header.

   The sum formula finds the total for the range E6:H6, and the error indicates that there are adjacent cells omitted from the formula. Rather than edit the formula, you will reenter the SUM formula using AutoSum.

7. Choose **Home→Editing→AutoSum**.

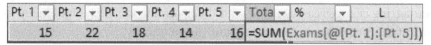

   The new formula calculates the SUM using a structured reference that includes the table name Exams *and the table column headers in the range reference @[Pt. 1]:[Pt. 5].*

8. Complete the formula entry, which again automatically updates all formulas in the column as well as the % grades in the next column.

9. Select **cell K19** in the total row below % and add the **Average** calculation for the % column.

   Now you will enter some additional formulas outside of the table that use structured references to the table data.

10. Select **cell D21** in the box beside *Highest Exam Grade*.

    To find the highest exam grade, you will use the MAX function referring to the % table column.

11. Type **=MAX (** and then use the mouse to select the **range K6:K18**. Complete the formula while keeping **cell D21** active.

    The formula converts the range reference to Exams[%], *and the Formula Bar displays* =MAX(Exams[%]).

12. Apply the **Percent Style** number format.

13. In **cell D22**, enter the formula **=COUNTIF (Exams [Program] , "Honors")** and then use the mouse to select the program information (starting in **cell C6**, below the heading).

    The result shows there are eight Honors students.

14. In **cell D23**, enter this formula using the mouse to select the table ranges, program information, and the marks for each criteria range:
    =COUNTIFS (Exams [Program] , "Honors" , Exams [%] , ">80%")

    The result shows two Honors students scored higher than 80% on the exam. Notice the criteria ranges and corresponding criteria are easier to understand than a regular cell reference: The program must be Honors and the percentage score must be greater than 80%.

15. Save the file.

Creating Sparklines

In addition to creating charts and adding conditional formatting, Excel has another tool for visualizing data trends. A sparkline is a miniature chart inserted as an object into an individual cell. Sparklines are smaller, simpler versions of charts, and any changes made to the data are immediately updated in the sparklines, just as with a normal chart. Each sparkline can contain data for only one column or row at a time.

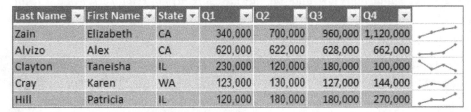

Last Name	First Name	State	Q1	Q2	Q3	Q4	
Zain	Elizabeth	CA	340,000	700,000	960,000	1,120,000	
Alvizo	Alex	CA	620,000	622,000	628,000	662,000	
Clayton	Taneisha	IL	230,000	120,000	180,000	100,000	
Cray	Karen	WA	123,000	130,000	127,000	144,000	
Hill	Patricia	IL	120,000	180,000	180,000	270,000	

Sparkline types include Line, Column, or Win/Loss, and you can change the type even after the sparkline has been created. Formatting changes can be made with the Sparkline tools. Changes made to one sparkline are applied to all of the sparklines in the same group automatically.

Insert→Sparklines

DEVELOP YOUR SKILLS: E11-D4

In this exercise, you will insert sparklines to spot trends in the students' exam marks.

1. Save your file as: **E11-D4-ExamRevised**
2. Select the **range L6:L18** immediately to the right of the table.
3. Choose **Insert→Sparklines→Line** to open the Create Sparklines dialog box.
4. Click in the **Data Range** box and then use the mouse to select the **range E6:I18**.

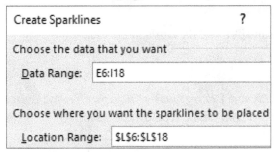

> *Because you already selected the desired range, the Location Range is already entered.*

5. Click **OK** to insert the sparklines.

   The sparklines are displayed in column L and show a comparison for each student, displaying the trends for the marks across the five different parts of the exam.

6. Go to **Sparkline Tools→Design→Show** and check the **Markers** option to display the markers on the sparklines.

7. Select **cell K20** and choose **Insert→Sparklines→Column**.

8. Select the **range K6:K18** as the data range, ensure K20 shows as the location, and click **OK**.

9. Go to **Sparkline Tools→Design→Show** and check the options for **High Point** and **Low Point**.

    The columns with the highest and lowest marks are indicated in red.

10. Save the file and close Excel.

Self-Assessment

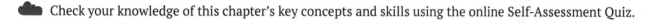 Check your knowledge of this chapter's key concepts and skills using the online Self-Assessment Quiz.

MICROSOFT EXCEL 2021/365

PivotTables and PivotCharts

PivotTables and PivotCharts are powerful, interactive Excel features that help you deal with large worksheets because they allow you to analyze your data in different ways. In this chapter, you will create and format PivotTables and PivotCharts. You will also filter data, add slicers, and create calculated fields.

LEARNING OBJECTIVES

- Create PivotTables
- Modify and format PivotTables
- Apply a filter to a PivotTable
- Insert a slicer to filter a PivotTable
- Create a calculated field
- Create PivotCharts

CHAPTER TIMING

- Concepts & Practice: 01:30:00
- Self-Assessment: 00:15:00
- Total: 01:45:00

PROJECT: ANALYZING SALES DATA

You work with Airspace Travel, which provides luxurious vacation packages to tropical destinations. You have been given an Excel file containing all the sales information for Airspace Travel's employees for Q3 (July through September). To analyze the employees' performance, you will create a variety of PivotTables and PivotCharts to highlight important details within the data.

Learning Resources: **boostyourskills.lablearning.com**

Creating PivotTables

A PivotTable is a powerful and cooperative Excel tool used to summarize complex information. PivotTables make it easy to understand large amounts of information by creating a summary report of your data. They are created by taking existing data in a worksheet and organizing the various fields into columns and rows, which can then be used to display different results. The purpose of a PivotTable is to take large amounts of data and to help you determine, for example, which products are selling the best, which employees are performing the best, which day of the week or time of day you need to have more staff on hand to reduce wait times for customers, etc.

To create a PivotTable, you can start with a blank table and add fields, or you can use one of the recommended PivotTables that Excel suggests based on your data.

 View the video "Making a PivotTable."

What Is a PivotTable?

A PivotTable combines some of the features of both tables and outlines, along with additional unique features that make it extremely flexible. You can arrange your data in different ways, which is where the term *pivot* (to turn or rotate) comes from, and you can quickly switch between the different views rather than creating a separate table each time. PivotTables are made up of rows and columns that contain field labels, and the value fields are then summarized within. PivotTable fields can be used to subtotal, compare, count, or perform other calculations on your data, as well.

The following PivotTable uses this data (only a small part of the worksheet data is shown) to compare the sum of product and service sales side by side for the employees, who are grouped by position:

Last Name	First Name	Position	Region	State	Date	Type	Amount
Louis	Lin	Senior Account Mgr	Central	IL	2-May	Service	234,000
Darko	David	Sales Account Mgr	Central	CO	3-May	Product	162,000
Lemmon	LaShaun	Sales Account Mgr	Central	CO	3-May	Product	210,000
Tavares	Taneisha	Sales Rep	Central	IL	4-May	Service	230,000
Plumlee	Patricia	Sales Rep	Central	IL	4-May	Product	120,000
Louis	Lin	Senior Account Mgr	Central	IL	5-May	Service	560,000
Darko	David	Sales Account Mgr	Central	CO	6-May	Service	151,000
Lemmon	LaShaun	Sales Account Mgr	Central	CO	6-May	Product	340,000
Tavares	Taneisha	Sales Rep	Central	IL	6-May	Service	120,000
Plumlee	Patricia	Sales Rep	Central	IL	6-May	Product	170,000

The Row Labels field also includes a filter button to apply a Sort or Filter to the rows in the PivotTable.

The values for product and service sales are shown in two columns.

The Row Labels include position and last name.

Rows are grouped by position, and each group can be collapsed or expanded as needed.

Row Labels	Sum of Product	Sum of Service
⊟ Sales Account Mgr	1,386,000	1,527,000
Darko	162,000	151,000
Eggles	340,000	700,000
Lemmon	210,000	340,000
Mandel	228,000	216,000
Tucker	446,000	120,000
⊞ Sales Rep	769,000	710,000
⊞ Senior Account Mgr	1,603,000	2,145,000
Grand Total	3,758,000	4,382,000

Arranging the Source Data

To create a PivotTable, you must know where to get the source data and what state the data has to be in. Because a PivotTable summarizes data, the source data should not be summarized in any way. You can also think of this as being the *raw* data.

Typically, you want the source data to have fields (column headings) listed across the top, and then each row in the worksheet should contain a unique list entry. For example, the source should not have a list of employees and then list a summary of sales for each month in the same row. Rather, the source should be the raw sales data with a separate row for each individual sale.

The source can be a list of data formatted as either a normal range or a table. The source should not contain any blank rows or columns, or duplicate values.

Remove Duplicates

When entering data or combining data from different sources, there is a chance of having the same information listed twice. This duplicate information can cause your information to be incorrect, which in turn causes incorrect evaluations, analysis, and perhaps important decisions based on flawed data. To check for and remove duplicates, you can use the Remove Duplicates command. For the tool to determine whether a record is considered a duplicate, you indicate which columns must match. In some cases, it requires only one or two columns to determine that a record is a duplicate; for other data, you may want to match all columns.

Data→Data Tools→Remove Duplicates

Adding PivotTable Fields

Whether you start with a blank PivotTable or use a recommended one, you can add and remove fields to manipulate the table data after it's created. The PivotTable Fields pane allows you to quickly add and remove fields by either clicking or dragging.

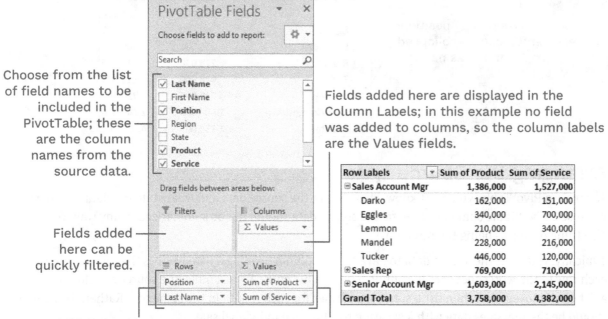

Choose from the list of field names to be included in the PivotTable; these are the column names from the source data.

Fields added here are displayed in the Column Labels; in this example no field was added to columns, so the column labels are the Values fields.

Fields added here can be quickly filtered.

Fields added here are displayed in the Row Labels; note in the PivotTable on the right that position comes first, followed by last names.

This area displays the Value fields added to the PivotTable and the function being performed.

Insert→Tables

DEVELOP YOUR SKILLS: E12-D1

In this exercise, you will check the source data for duplicates, insert a blank PivotTable, and add fields to the PivotTable to show a summary of sales for each location.

1. Start Excel, open **E12-D1-Sales** from your **Excel Chapter 12** folder, and save it as: **E12-D1-SalesTargets**

2. Begin by quickly scrolling down through the worksheet to verify the data.

   You want to ensure there are no blank rows separating the data. Note that the data ends at row 93. Considering there are that many rows, you likely didn't find any duplicates visually, so you will check for them now.

3. Choose **Data→Data Tools→Remove Duplicates**.

   In some cases, you may want to match only one or two fields to remove duplicates, but in this case, each record could have a repeated value such as name, position, or month. If all the fields match—including target, sales, and commissions—you know there is a true duplicate.

4. Leave all columns checked and click **OK**.

   You will see a dialog box telling you that four duplicates were found and 86 values remain.

5. Click **OK** to close the dialog box.

6. Quickly navigate to the last row of data by pressing [Ctrl]+[↓] and notice the data stops at row 89.

   Now you are ready to insert a PivotTable. You will start with a blank PivotTable.

7. Choose **Insert→Tables→PivotTable**.

   The Create PivotTable dialog box selects all adjacent data, and the PivotTable will be created on a new worksheet by default.

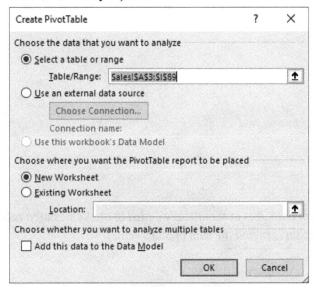

8. Confirm the range is *Sales!$A$3:$I$89* and click **OK** to create the PivotTable.

   The next step is to add the fields to the PivotTable. You will first add the rows, then the columns, and finally the values.

9. Click the **Location** and **Position** checkboxes (in that order) in the PivotTable Fields pane to add those fields as row labels and then drag the **Month** field into the Columns box.

NOTE! Adding row labels can be done with a simple click, but column labels are usually added by dragging or right-clicking.

10. Click the **Sales** checkbox (scroll down the field list as necessary) in the PivotTable Fields pane to add that field to the Values area.

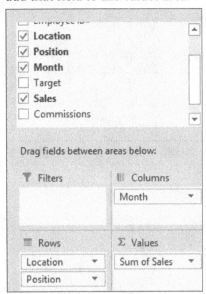

Because the Sales field contains numerical data, it is automatically added to the Values area rather than the Rows area, and the default function is to find the sum of Sales values.

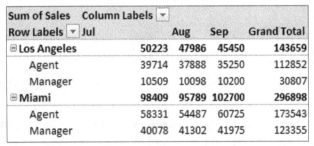

Sum of Sales	Column Labels			
Row Labels	Jul	Aug	Sep	Grand Total
⊟ Los Angeles	50223	47986	45450	143659
Agent	39714	37888	35250	112852
Manager	10509	10098	10200	30807
⊟ Miami	98409	95789	102700	296898
Agent	58331	54487	60725	173543
Manager	40078	41302	41975	123355

Your PivotTable shows a sum of the sales for each location for each month, with each location also showing a breakdown of sales by agents and sales by managers. A grand total is automatically added on the right side to sum all three months and at the bottom to sum all locations.

11. Rename the worksheet: `Sum of Sales by Location`

12. Save the file.

Using PivotTables for Analysis

After you have created a PivotTable, you can modify it at any time by adding or removing fields, or by changing the positioning and order of fields. This is done by checking/unchecking the boxes next to the field names or by dragging the field names in and out of the various areas. Each time you make a change, the PivotTable automatically reconfigures to display the new data.

> **NOTE!** Checking a box next to a field name places it in the default location, usually rows for text and values for numeric data. If you drag a text field into the Values area, Excel will use the COUNT function instead of SUM since text cannot be added!

Changing the order of fields in either the row or column area creates different data groupings, and this can be done by dragging and dropping the field names into the new positioning. Or you might want to switch a field label from row to column or column to row—pivoting the data.

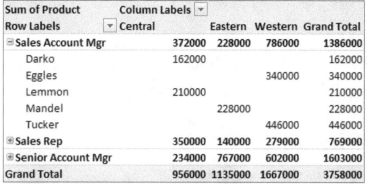

Sum of Product	Column Labels			
Row Labels	Central	Eastern	Western	Grand Total
⊟ Sales Account Mgr	372000	228000	786000	1386000
Darko	162000			162000
Eggles			340000	340000
Lemmon	210000			210000
Mandel		228000		228000
Tucker			446000	446000
⊞ Sales Rep	350000	140000	279000	769000
⊞ Senior Account Mgr	234000	767000	602000	1603000
Grand Total	956000	1135000	1667000	3758000

Here, product sales are grouped by position and then last name in the rows, while the columns are organized by region.

Row Labels	Sum of Product
⊟ Central	956000
⊟ Sales Account Mgr	372000
Darko	162000
Lemmon	210000
⊞ Sales Rep	350000
⊞ Senior Account Mgr	234000
⊟ Eastern	1135000
⊟ Sales Account Mgr	228000
Mandel	228000
⊞ Sales Rep	140000
⊞ Senior Account Mgr	767000
⊟ Western	1667000
⊟ Sales Account Mgr	786000
Eggles	340000
Tucker	446000
⊞ Sales Rep	279000
⊞ Senior Account Mgr	602000
Grand Total	3758000

Now the PivotTable shows the product sales with rows grouped by region, then position, then last name. It's the same data, it's just organized differently.

Arranging fields appropriately is perhaps the most important skill for working with PivotTables because each change in the data's organization tells a new story. It is important to practice organizing your fields in a variety of ways to see how the information can be shaped to answer different questions.

View the video "Changing a PivotTable."

Formatting PivotTables

Changing the PivotTable's format can help make the information easier to read and understand. Similar to tables, there are a number of styles to choose from in the gallery on the Design tab. There are also a number of layout and style options to choose from.

Report Layout options include Compact, Outline, and Tabular. Subtotals can either be displayed at the top or bottom of each category or group or turned off altogether, and grand totals can also be turned on or off for rows and columns.

Number formatting does not automatically transfer from the source data, but you can quickly change the number format for an entire value field by selecting a value and using the Field Settings command or by right-clicking a value and choosing Number Format.

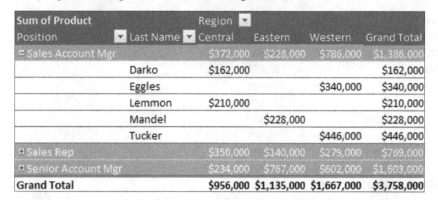

Sum of Product		Region			
Position	Last Name	Central	Eastern	Western	Grand Total
⊟Sales Account Mgr		$372,000	$228,000	$786,000	$1,386,000
	Darko	$162,000			$162,000
	Eggles			$340,000	$340,000
	Lemmon	$210,000			$210,000
	Mandel		$228,000		$228,000
	Tucker			$446,000	$446,000
⊞Sales Rep		$350,000	$140,000	$279,000	$769,000
⊞Senior Account Mgr		$234,000	$767,000	$602,000	$1,603,000
Grand Total		$956,000	$1,135,000	$1,667,000	$3,758,000

This PivotTable has a style and number formatting applied. The report layout is displayed in outline form, which takes up more space but makes it easier to see the row labels.

Changing Value Field Settings

For each value field, the settings can be changed to better suit the information you want to show. The field name can be customized, the number format can be modified, and a function other than Sum can be used to summarize values. For example, instead of showing the sum of sales for each region, you might want to show the average sales by region. Then, instead of *Average of Product*, you could adjust the custom name to *Avg Product Sales* and the number format to Currency.

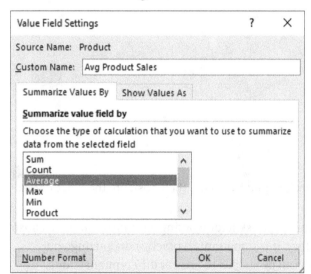

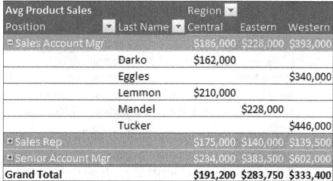

Avg Product Sales		Region		
Position	Last Name	Central	Eastern	Western
⊟Sales Account Mgr		$186,000	$228,000	$393,000
	Darko	$162,000		
	Eggles			$340,000
	Lemmon	$210,000		
	Mandel		$228,000	
	Tucker			$446,000
⊞Sales Rep		$175,000	$140,000	$139,500
⊞Senior Account Mgr		$234,000	$383,500	$602,000
Grand Total		$191,200	$283,750	$333,400

DEVELOP YOUR SKILLS: E12-D2

In this exercise, you will create another PivotTable and adjust the fields and value field settings to show the average by position for commissions, sales, and targets.

1. Save your file as: **E12-D2-SalesTargets**

2. Go to the **Sales** worksheet and choose **Insert→Tables→Recommended PivotTables**.

   The dialog box gives a list of suggested PivotTables on the left and a preview of the selected PivotTable on the right.

3. Select the third option on the left, **Sum of Commissions, Sum of Sales and Sum of Target by Location**, and click **OK** to insert the PivotTable.

4. Uncheck the **Location** box in the PivotTable Fields pane to remove the Location field from the PivotTable.

5. Now check the **Position** box in the Fields pane to add that field.

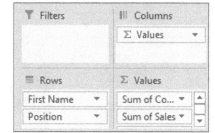

Row Labels	Sum of Commissions	Sum of Sales	Sum of Target
⊟ Adam	805.479	14647	15000
Manager	805.479	14647	15000
⊟ Alexander	1083.608	17471	15000
Agent	1083.608	17471	15000
⊟ Cam	4189.56	68904	75000
Agent	4189.56	68904	75000

The PivotTable shows employees by first name and then lists their data again in a separate row with their positions, which does not make the information displayed very useful at the moment!

6. Drag the **Position** field above the First Name field in the Rows area to change the order of the fields.

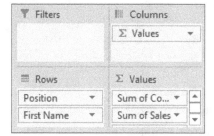

Row Labels	Sum of Commissions	Sum of Sales	Sum of Target
⊟ Agent	31288.38	504496	471000
Alexander	1083.608	17471	15000
Cam	4189.56	68904	75000
Cassie	1804.5	26250	24000
Cynthia	2384.273	41188	30000
Debra	2893.21	54870	45000

Now the PivotTable shows the results for each employee grouped by position, which is much more useful. Next you will make another change to see a different result.

7. Check the **Month** box to add that field and then remove the **First Name** field by dragging it out of the Rows area and onto the worksheet (this is an alternative to removing the checkmark).

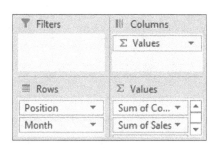

Row Labels	Sum of Commissions	Sum of Sales	Sum of Target
⊟ Agent	31288.38	504496	471000
Jul	9466.241	158462	156000
Aug	11183	176881	156000
Sep	10639.139	169153	159000
⊟ Manager	29018.726	464380	459000
Jul	9587.954	150754	153000
Aug	8974	150612	153000
Sep	10456.772	163014	153000
Grand Total	**60307.106**	**968876**	**930000**

This PivotTable shows a different story by displaying the monthly results for agents and managers separately. Next you will apply a new PivotTable style to change the colors of the table.

8. Choose **Design→PivotTable Styles→Dark Blue, Pivot Style Dark 20**.

Now you will adjust the field name and number format for the three value fields.

9. In the Values area, click **Sum of Commissions** and choose **Value Field Settings...**.

The full field name may be cut off from view; hover the mouse pointer over the field to see the full name.

10. Follow these steps to change the field settings:

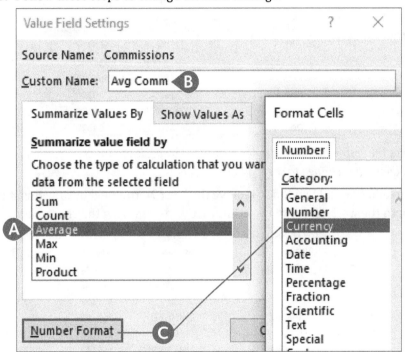

A. Choose **Average** in Summarize Value Field By.

B. In the Custom Name box, type: **Avg Comm**

C. Click **Number Format** and then choose **Currency** and click **OK**.

11. Click **OK** to close the Value Field Settings dialog box.

12. Repeat this process for the Sum of Sales and Sum of Target fields, including using the **Average** summary function and the **Currency** number format. Use the custom names: **Avg Sales** and **Avg Target**

13. Choose **Design→Layout→Report Layout→Show in Outline Form**.

Position	Month	Avg Comm	Avg Sales	Avg Target
⊟ Agent		$711.10	$11,465.82	$10,704.55
	Jul	$676.16	$11,318.71	$11,142.86
	Aug	$745.53	$11,792.07	$10,400.00
	Sep	$709.28	$11,276.87	$10,600.00
⊟ Manager		$690.92	$11,056.67	$10,928.57
	Jul	$684.85	$10,768.14	$10,928.57
	Aug	$641.00	$10,758.00	$10,928.57
	Sep	$746.91	$11,643.86	$10,928.57
Grand Total		$701.25	$11,266.00	$10,813.95

14. Rename the worksheet: `Averages by Position`

15. Save your work.

Filtering a PivotTable

You can filter a PivotTable to remove unnecessary data and focus on the data that is important. To add a filter you can use AutoFilter, add a filter field, or add a slicer. Each time you filter a PivotTable, the totals and subtotals instantly recalculate throughout the table.

Filtering with AutoFilter

The row labels and column labels have an AutoFilter menu button ▼ that provides the same sorting and filtering options available in worksheet lists and tables.

This PivotTable has been filtered to show the Sales Account Mgr and Senior Account Mgr positions only, and to sort those positions alphabetically.

Filtering with a Filter Field

Adding a field to the Filters area simplifies the process of filtering the data to display one or more categories of data at a time. To turn on the option for showing more than one category, click the Select

Multiple Items checkbox in the filter menu. The filtered field and the current filter setting will always display directly above the PivotTable.

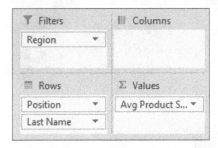

Adding the Region field to the Filters area displays that filter above the PivotTable (next figure).

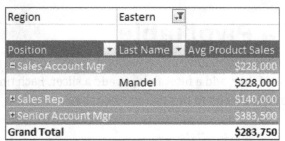

This PivotTable has been filtered to show only the Eastern region.

Filtering with Slicers

Slicers are menu frames placed on a worksheet that contain all filtering choices for one field. Selected items are highlighted in the slicer, making it easy to identify the applied criteria. To select multiple fields in a slicer, you can use the Multi-Select feature or use the Ctrl key.

Slicers are appealing because they can be moved around, resized, and styled to match the PivotTable, but the real benefit is that slicers can be shared with other sheets in the same workbook for other PivotTables that use the same source data. Changing the filtered selections in a shared slicer automatically updates all connected PivotTables.

The PivotTable with a slicer used to display only the Central and Eastern region data

DEVELOP YOUR SKILLS: E12-D3

In this exercise, you will add filters to the existing PivotTables using two different methods.

1. Save your file as: **E12-D3-SalesTargets**

   Ensure the PivotTable on the Averages by Position worksheet is selected and the Fields list is visible.

2. Drag the **Location** field into the Filters area.

   You will now see the field name Location *in cell A1. The filter in cell B1 displays* (All), *indicating all data is showing with no filter applied.*

3. Click the **Location filter** button ▼ above the PivotTable, select **New York** to display the information for New York only, and then click **OK**.

   The filter now shows New York, *and the data in the PivotTable show the averages for the New York location only.*

   Next you will adjust the Sum of Sales by Location PivotTable by adding a slicer for Position.

4. Go to the **Sum of Sales by Location** sheet and, if necessary, select any cell in the PivotTable.

5. Click the **Position** field in the Rows area and choose **Remove Field**.

6. Choose **PivotTable Analyze→Filter→Insert Slicer**.

7. In the Insert Slicers dialog box, click the **Position** checkbox and then click **OK**.

The slicer window is displayed on the sheet, and the Slicer Tools are displayed on the Ribbon.

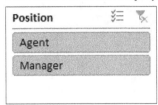

8. Drag the slicer window directly beside the PivotTable, with the tops of both roughly aligned.

9. Go to **Slicer Tools→Options→Size** and resize the slicer to exactly **1"** high and **1.5"** wide.

10. Apply the **Light Blue, Slicer Style Dark 5** style (**Slicer Tools→ Options→Slicer Styles**) to the slicer.

11. Click **Agent** in the slicer window to display the sales data for agents only.

   Now you will adjust the number format for sales values.

12. Right-click **cell E5** and choose **Number Format...**, then choose **Currency**, set to zero decimals, and click **OK**.

   Notice the entire range of values is now formatted with the Currency style.

13. Select **Manager** in the slicer window to display the sales data for managers only.

14. Save the file.

Creating Calculated Fields

You may want to create your own calculations and add them to your PivotTables. A *calculated field* uses a formula containing values from one or more of the existing fields. For example, you could take Sales values and multiply by 5% or take the Cost field from a PivotTable and subtract the Sales field.

In this example, a calculated field is created by taking Product field values and multiplying them by 105% to get the expected product sales growth, which is 5% above the current product value.

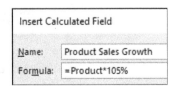

PivotTable Analyze→Calculations→Fields, Items, & Sets

Show Values As

Another option for displaying PivotTable values is to use comparison operations, which are also available from the Value Field Settings dialog box. There are options already created to determine calculations such as a percentage of a grand total, the difference between values in two fields, or a ranking order.

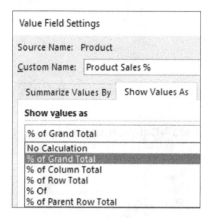

This PivotTable shows each employee's sales in dollars and as a percentage of the grand total.

Refreshing PivotTable Data

Whenever you change the source data, you must also refresh your PivotTable to reflect the updated data. You can refresh only the current PivotTable or all of them at once. You can also set up an option to refresh the data each time the file is opened.

> PivotTable Analyze→Data→Refresh

Referencing PivotTable Data

Extracting data from a PivotTable requires using the GETPIVOTDATA function. This function is much easier to use than most functions because it can be created with just a click. Using the point-and-click method to create a reference to data in a PivotTable inserts the function *and* all the required arguments simultaneously.

▌ DEVELOP YOUR SKILLS: E12-D4

In this exercise, you will create a new PivotTable that shows which employees achieved their sales targets.

1. Save your file as: **E12-D4-SalesTargets**
2. Go to the **Sales** sheet and create a new PivotTable using the default values.
3. Rename the new sheet: **% of Target**
4. Add the **Location**, **Position**, and **Last Name** fields to the Rows area, in that order.

5. Add **Sales** and **Target** to the Values area, in that order.

   Values are automatically added to the Columns area as well.

   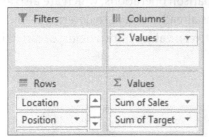

6. In the Values area, adjust the value field settings of each to **Currency** with no decimals and use the custom names: **Total Sales** and **Total Target**

7. Choose **PivotTable Analyze→Calculations→Fields, Items, & Sets→Calculated Field....**

8. Follow these steps to create a calculated field:

   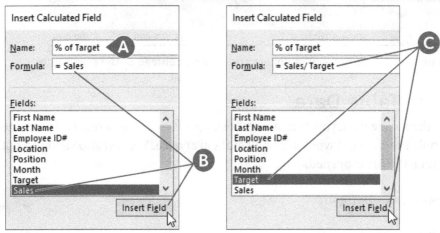

   A. In the Name box, enter: **% of Target**

   B. Delete the number **0** in the Formula box, select **Sales,** and click **Insert Field.**

   C. Type **/** and then select **Target** and click **Insert Field.**

9. Click **OK** to create the calculated field, which will divide sales by the target and be displayed in the Values quadrant.

   The calculated field will only display mostly 1s until the number format is changed.

10. Right-click **cell D4** and open the Value Field Settings for the calculated field, change the name to **Total % of Target** and the Number Format to **Percentage** with two decimal places.

    Now the calculated field displays percentages above and below 100%, where 100% represents reaching their target.

11. Click the collapse buttons for the Agent and Manager labels to display locations and positions only.

Row Labels	Total Sales	Total Target	Total % of Target
⊟Los Angeles	$143,659	$141,000	101.89%
⊟Agent	$112,852	$111,000	101.67%
Bryant	$43,948	$36,000	122.08%
Owens	$68,904	$75,000	91.87%
⊟Manager	$30,807	$30,000	102.69%
Curry	$30,807	$30,000	102.69%

Row Labels	Total Sales	Total Target	Total % of Target
⊟Los Angeles	$143,659	$141,000	101.89%
⊞Agent	$112,852	$111,000	101.67%
⊞Manager	$30,807	$30,000	102.69%

12. Change the PivotTable style to **Dark Blue, Pivot Style Dark 20**.

13. Now go to the **Sales** sheet and select **cell H7**.

   New sales information has come in for Sarah Mckinnon for July, so you will enter the new information.

14. Enter the correct information by typing **12900** in **cell H7**.

15. Return to the **% of Target** sheet and choose **PivotTable Analyze→Data→Refresh menu button ∨→Refresh All**.

   The data in all PivotTables is now updated to reflect the correction.

16. Save the file.

Creating PivotCharts

PivotCharts are charts based on PivotTable data. PivotCharts can be created simultaneously with the PivotTable or after the PivotTable has been created, but a PivotChart must have an associated PivotTable. The fields on the Values area of the PivotTable are displayed as data series on the chart. The row labels are used as the axis labels, and the column labels are used in the chart legend. The PivotChart Tools tab contains all of normal options for chart formatting, in addition to the Analyze options for PivotTables.

Filtering PivotCharts

A PivotChart also includes AutoFilter buttons directly in the chart for quick and easy access to filter options. Filtering the PivotChart also filters the associated PivotTable, and vice versa. If a slicer has been added to the PivotTable, filtering can also be performed with the slicer for the PivotChart.

The PivotTable Legend values indicate the columns being displayed.

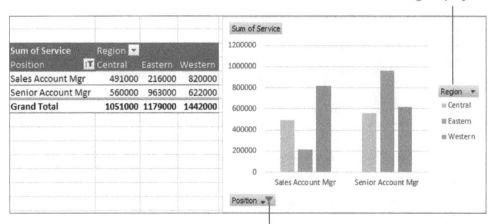

Filter buttons can be used to filter the data; in this example, the filter for position displays the Sales and Senior Account Mgr positions but hides the Sales Reps.

DEVELOP YOUR SKILLS: E12-D5

In this exercise, you will insert a PivotChart for an existing PivotTable and then build a new PivotChart while creating the adjoined PivotTable at the same time.

1. Save your file as: **E12-D5-SalesTargets**
2. Go to the **Sum of Sales by Location** sheet.
3. Select the pivot table, if necessary, and then choose **PivotTable Analyze→Tools→PivotChart**.
4. Click **OK** to insert the clustered column chart.
5. Drag the chart so it is directly below the PivotTable.
6. In the slicer, click the **Multi-Select**  button and then click **Agent** to display data for both positions in the chart.
7. Go to the **Sales** worksheet and choose **Insert→Charts→PivotChart**.
8. In the Create PivotChart dialog box, click **OK**.
9. In the PivotChart Fields pane, add **Location** to the Axis area, **Month** to the Legend area, and **Commissions** to the Values area.

   Use whatever method you prefer to add fields, as long as they are added to the correct area.

10. In the PivotChart legend, click the **Month** button, click to remove the checkmark from **Sep**, and click **OK**.

    In the PivotChart, the September data is removed and only July and August are displayed.

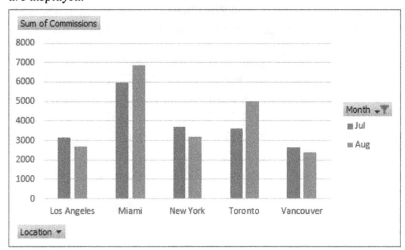

11. Rename the worksheet: **Commissions by Month**
12. Drag the chart so it is directly below the PivotTable.
13. Save your work and close the file.

Self-Assessment

Check your knowledge of this chapter's key concepts and skills using the online Self-Assessment Quiz.

MICROSOFT EXCEL 2021/365

Working with Macros

13

Many Excel workbooks you create will be used over and over and the same tasks will be performed repeatedly, like transferring data from one worksheet to another. Being able to automate certain tasks is more efficient and can reduce the risk of errors. In this chapter, you will change the security settings to allow macros in Excel that will enable you to automate common, repetitive tasks.

LEARNING OBJECTIVES

- Change the macro security settings
- Create macros to automate tasks
- Run macros
- Create macro buttons to run macros quickly

CHAPTER TIMING

- Concepts & Practice: 01:30:00
- Self-Assessment: 00:15:00
- Total: 01:45:00

PROJECT: CREATING MACROS TO SIMPLIFY TASKS

The sales data for Airspace Travel is used frequently and is often sorted in different ways to compare results. In order to make it quick and easy for any team member to use the data, you will create macros to do the sorting for you. You'll also create custom buttons so a complex sort can be done with just one click.

Learning Resources: **boostyourskills.lablearning.com**

Introducing Macros

A macro is a recorded set of mouse and keyboard actions that can be played back at any time. Essentially, a macro records the actions so a repetitive series of tasks can be completed with a single click of the mouse. For example, if the first thing you do when you create a new workbook is enter the company name in the header and the date in the footer, you can create a macro that performs these actions with one click, saving you valuable time.

Changing Macro Security

Macros are a way of programming Excel to take shortcuts, but they can contain viruses, so you should be aware of the added security features associated with using macros. You can change macro security settings in the Trust Center, and these settings take effect for all Excel workbooks opened on that computer. There are four options for macro security:

- Disable all macros without notification
- Disable all macros with notification
- Disable all macros except digitally signed macros
- Enable all macros

> **WARNING!** Choosing to enable all macros is not recommended due to potentially unsafe macros.

Disabling all macros with a notification is the default and recommended option because this gives you the option of allowing or disabling macros as you see fit, each time you open a macro-enabled workbook.

File→Options→Trust Center→Trust Center Settings→Macro Settings

DEVELOP YOUR SKILLS: E13-D1

In this exercise, you will verify the macro security settings and then open a workbook and enable the macros.

1. Start Excel and open a new, blank workbook.
2. Choose **File→Options→Trust Center**.
3. Click the **Trust Center Settings** button, choose the **Macro Settings** category, and if necessary choose **Disable VBA macros with notification**.
4. Choose the **Message Bar** category from the left side of the window and verify that the **Show the Message Bar...** option is selected.
5. Click **OK** twice to close both dialog boxes.
6. Open **E13-D1-MacroTest** from your **Excel Chapter 13** folder.
7. On the message bar, click the **Enable Content** button to enable the macros for this workbook.

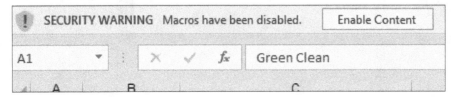

8. Save the file as: **E13-D1-Macro**

Note the default file type is a macro-enabled workbook because it was saved that way previously.

The workbook has macros in it, which enable the user to click a custom-made button to sort the data.

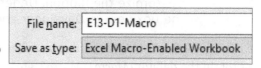

| File name: | E13-D1-Macro |
| Save as type: | Excel Macro-Enabled Workbook |

9. Click the **Sort by Leader** button at the top of the worksheet.

The list is now sorted alphabetically (A–Z) by the Team Leader column.

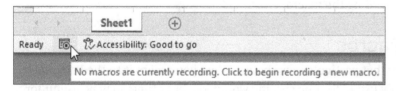

	A	B	C	D	E	F	G
1	**Green Clean**		Capital Campaign	Sort by Category	Sort by Sponsor		Sort by Leader
3	Pledge	Team Leader	Sponsor Category	Sponsor Name	Year 1	Year 2	To Date
4	Level 3	Abbott	Organization Contribution	Child Advocate Society	50,000	50,000	100,00
5	Level 4	Abbott	Organization Contribution	Hands Across Foundation	20,000	15,500	35,50
6	Level 4	Abbott	Organization Contribution	Chamber of Commerce	10,000	12,500	22,50
7	Level 5	Abbott	Organization Contribution	Accountancy Association	0	15,000	15,00
8	Level 5	Abbott	Organization Contribution	Business Roundtable	0	15,000	15,00

| WARNING! Running a macro cannot be reversed by clicking the Undo button.

10. Save and close the file.

Recording Macros

To create a macro, you can record a series of actions that you perform in a way that's similar to using a video camera. You click a button to start recording and then click again to stop recording when finished. You can then run the macro again and again to repeat the same series of actions, including keystrokes and mouse clicks.

There are several options for recording macros. One quick method is the button on the status bar.

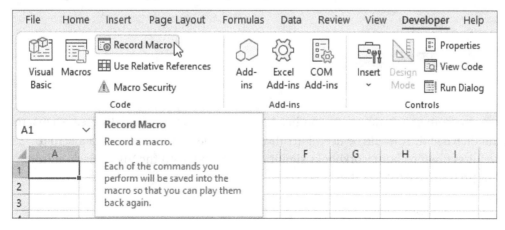

There's also a button on the Developer tab. (After the Record Macro button is clicked, the Stop Recording button will appear in both places.)

Clicking the Record Macro button launches the Record Macro window, where you can rename the macro or retain the default (*Macro1*, *Macro2*, etc.) and assign a keyboard shortcut if desired. Macro names may not contain spaces.

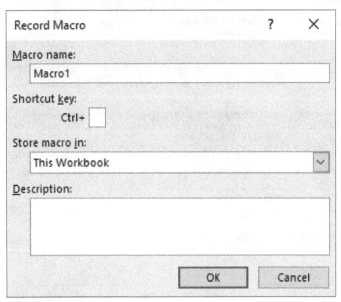

Recording the Macro Steps

Most actions you perform are recorded in the macro, including mouse actions, choosing Ribbon commands, selecting options in dialog boxes, using arrow keys to navigate the worksheet, and typing text. Any mistakes or corrections made during the recording are saved as part of the macro. As long as the final result is correct, you can keep the recording with the mistakes and corrections, rather than recording a new macro; the macro will still give the proper results when you run it. That said, it's a good idea to practice the steps before actually recording the macro.

Storing and Sharing Macros

The macro you record is saved only for that particular workbook, unless you assign it to the Personal Macro Workbook. Some macros are only useful for one specific workbook, but others may be useful for any Excel file. The Personal Macro Workbook is a hidden folder, and any macros saved there are available to all open workbooks.

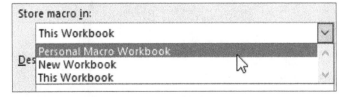

You can also copy a macro from one workbook to another. For example, you may initially create a macro for one workbook and then decide it would be useful in other workbooks as well. Copying a macro to another workbook requires opening both workbooks simultaneously and, with the Visual Basic editor open, dragging the macro from one to the other.

Saving a Workbook Containing Macros

To save a normal Excel file after recording and saving macros, you must use the Save As command and choose the Excel Macro-Enabled Workbook file type. If you use the Save command, Excel will display a warning message.

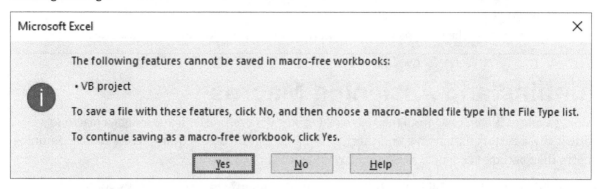

This is a safety feature that prevents you from accidentally losing the macros you create. Clicking No in the message window opens the Save As dialog box so you can change the file type. Files saved with the Excel Macro-Enabled Workbook file type have the extension *.xlsm* (the "m" is for "macro").

DEVELOP YOUR SKILLS: E13-D2

In this exercise, you will record a macro to sort the employee list by location, position, and first name, in that order. You will save the workbook in the macro-enabled file format.

1. Open **E13-D2-Sales** from your **Excel Chapter 13** folder and save it as:
   E13-D2-SalesReport

2. Click **Record Macro** [img] on the status bar in the bottom-left corner of the Excel window.

   If the Record Macro button is not showing, right-click the status bar and select Macro Recording to add it to the status bar.

3. In the Record Macro dialog box, type **SortbyLocation** as the macro name and click **OK**.

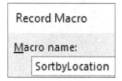

4. Ensure **cell A5** is selected and choose **Home→Editing→Sort & Filter→Custom Sort**.

5. Create this sort, using the **Add Level** button for each new sort type and clicking **OK** when finished:

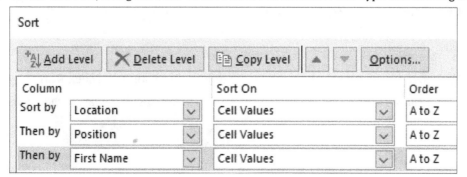

6. Click **Stop Recording** ☐ on the status bar.

   The data is sorted. You want to save the macro so you can perform the same sort in the future by simply running the macro.

7. Click **Save**, which opens the warning to alert you that the macro will be lost unless you change the file type.

8. Click **No**, change the file type to **Excel Macro-Enabled Workbook**, and click **Save**.

Running and Assigning Macros

Running a macro is easy to do from the Macro dialog box. It's even easier if you assign a macro to a shortcut key, a custom button on a worksheet, or a custom button on the Quick Access toolbar. Running a macro then becomes as simple as clicking any other Ribbon button.

You can assign a macro to a shortcut key either when you initially create it or later by editing its options. Or you can insert a shape onto the worksheet and then assign a macro to that shape, creating a custom button.

City	Region	Participants	Volunteers	Funds Raised	
Oakland	West	260	14	$48,658	**Sort By Region**
Atlanta	South	177	16	$46,494	
Denver	West	209	21	$46,218	**Sort By Funds**
Dallas	South	205	17	$45,884	
Baltimore	East	220	16	$44,225	

To create a keyboard shortcut, the keys Ctrl or Ctrl+Shift must be part of the combination. A shortcut you assign will override any existing shortcut; keep this in mind when assigning shortcut keys. For example, if you assign Ctrl+B to a macro, you won't be able to use that shortcut to apply bold formatting. As a way around this, you can use Ctrl+Shift+B for the macro shortcut instead.

> View→Macros→Macros | Developer→Code→Macros

DEVELOP YOUR SKILLS: E13-D3

In this exercise, you will run an unassigned macro, record a new macro and assign a shortcut to it, and then create custom buttons for the two macros.

1. Save your file as: **E13-D3-SalesReport**

2. Select **cell C5** and then choose **Home→Editing→Sort & Filter→Sort A to Z**.

   To re-sort the data by location, you will run the macro you recorded earlier.

3. Choose **View→Macros→Macros**.

4. Ensure **SortbyLocation** is selected (it should be the only macro listed) and click **Run**.

   The data is once again sorted by location, then position, then first name. Running the macro also closes the Macro window.

Assign a Macro to a Shortcut Key

To make it easier to run the macro, you will assign a shortcut key.

5. Choose **View→Macros→Macros**.

6. Ensure **SortbyLocation** is selected and choose **Options**.

7. With the insertion point in the Shortcut Key box, press [Shift]+[D].

8. Click **OK** to close the dialog box and then close the Macro window.

9. Select **cell G5** and then choose **Home→Editing→Sort & Filter→Sort Smallest to Largest** to sort employees by number of sales.

10. Now press [Ctrl]+[Shift]+[D] to once again sort by location, position, and first name.

Create Custom Buttons

To make it easier to remember and run the macros, you will create custom buttons using shapes.

11. Click **Record Macro** ⊡ on the status bar.

12. In the Record Macro dialog box, type **SalesbyPosition** under Macro Name and click **OK**.

13. Choose **Home→Editing→Sort & Filter→Custom Sort**.

14. Create this sort, removing a level and editing the levels as needed.

    Hint: Use the Delete Level button and note the order to sort by.

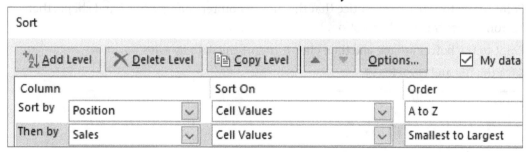

15. Click **OK** in the Sort dialog box then click **Stop Recording** ▢ on the status bar.

    The data is sorted and the macro is saved. The Sales column should be arranged from largest to smallest for agents and then for managers.

16. Choose **Insert→Illustrations→Shapes** and select **Rectangle: Rounded Corners**.

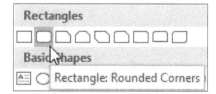

17. Draw the rectangle shape from **cell J3** to **cell K4**, approximately two rows high and two columns wide.

18. With the shape still selected type: `Sort by Location`

19. Insert another rounded rectangle shape, this time drawing the shape from **cell J6** to **cell K7**.

20. With the shape still selected, type: `Sort by Sales`

   Your buttons need not exactly match the size and position shown here:

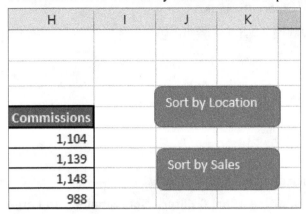

21. Right-click the **Sort by Location** shape and choose **Assign Macro…**.

22. In the Assign Macro dialog box, select the **SortbyLocation** macro and click **OK**.

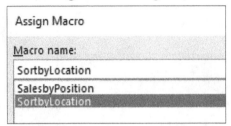

23. Right-click the **Sort by Sales** shape and assign the **SalesbyPosition** macro to it.

24. Deselect the shape by clicking any cell on the worksheet.

25. Point to the top shape and notice that the mouse pointer changes to a hand shape, then click the button to sort the data by location.

26. Point to the bottom shape and then click it to sort the data by sales.

27. Save the file and close Excel.

Self-Assessment

 Check your knowledge of this chapter's key concepts and skills using the online Self-Assessment Quiz.

MICROSOFT EXCEL 2021/365

Data Management for Business

14

In this chapter, you will explore some of the tools businesses use to manage vast amounts of data collected on customers, transactions, employees, and more. While not going into great depth, you will be introduced to the terminology, concepts, and tools available for analyzing and managing data.

LEARNING OBJECTIVES

- Import data from various sources
- Consolidate data from multiple sheets into one sheet
- Create a series of data using different methods
- Chart trends and save chart templates
- Use additional functions for lookups and logic

CHAPTER TIMING

- Concepts & Practice: 01:30:00
- Self-Assessment: 00:15:00
- Total: 01:45:00

PROJECT: WORKING WITH MULTIPLE DATA SOURCES

You have been maintaining the quarter one (Q1) sales data for the five Airspace Travel office locations in individual files. Now you want to put it all in one file for better analysis and as a model for how data for the rest of the year should be organized. You will also be summarizing and analyzing the Q1 sales data to create projections for Q2.

Learning Resources: **boostyourskills.lablearning.com**

Importing and Exporting Data

Excel is certainly useful, but companies also use many other apps for a variety of business-related tasks. This means that data needs to be transferable between apps that are used for different purposes; for example, a business might use accounting software to perform the bookkeeping tasks and then import the financial data from the accounting software into Excel to create financial forecasts.

To effectively work with data from different sources, you must understand common database terminology and functionality. Databases are typically made up of numerous tables, which are made up of fields and records. For example, a coffee shop might have a database with tables for inventory, customers, and employees. The employees table would have fields for employees' names, IDs, and contact information, and the information for each employee would be their record.

To work across different applications, you should save the data in one of several common formats that most programs understand. This allows you to import and export data in and out of various programs that are otherwise incompatible. Characters such as commas, spaces, and tabs can be used as delimiters, which are any characters used to specify a boundary between fields when working with data.

One of the more common file formats for importing and exporting data is CSV (*.csv*), which stands for *comma separated values*. Data in a CSV file typically comes from a database, where data from each field is separated by a comma. Text files (*.txt*) are also common and usually use either a tab or a space to separate values rather than a comma. Excel will normally recognize the character being used, but you can also choose which delimiter to use during the import process. You can use CSV files to import and export data between Word, Excel, Access, and many more programs, including most accounting and database software.

Importing

Importing data creates a query. A query is essentially a request for information from an external data source, which could be a CSV or XML file, a website, an Access table, or other various sources and databases. The query then creates a connection between the Excel workbook and the data source, and you can choose how the data is imported and managed. Sometimes you may want to import the data once only, and other times you may want to ensure the data is updated continuously.

After importing data with a query, you can edit the query with the Power Query Editor, enabling you to manipulate the data inside the query instead of on the worksheet. Since some sources contain huge amounts of raw data, the query can summarize the data and eliminate the need to store the information on a worksheet to create summary tables or PivotTables, or to conduct further data analysis.

Exporting

To export data, you can save any file as a CSV version from the Save as Type option in the Save As window. Saving a file as a CSV will only save the active worksheet, because the CSV format does not support multiple worksheets. Other formats in which to save an Excel file include PDF, for a read-only file, and HTML, to create a web page.

Mail Merge with Microsoft Word

You might want to send a custom letter or discount offer via snail mail to a large list of customers. To do this, you would perform a Mail Merge in Microsoft Word. A Mail Merge has a main document with the same message for everyone, and then personalized information for customers using fields for each recipient, such as name and address. The list of recipients and fields can be created in a program like Excel or Access then exported by saving as a CSV, imported into Word, and used to perform the merge. The merge then replaces the fields for each recipient to create a unique document for each customer.

File→Save As→Save as Type

Data→Get & Transform Data→Get Data

DEVELOP YOUR SKILLS: E14-D1

In this exercise, you will import the February sales data from a separate file into your Q1 workbook. Once you have all data for the quarter in one file, you will be able to conduct analysis on it.

1. Start Excel, open **E14-D1-Q1** from your **Excel Chapter 14** folder, and save it as:
   E14-D1-Q1Summary

   There is some data in the January sheet already, but notice that all information is missing for February and March. The February data is contained in a CSV file.

2. Go to the **Feb** sheet and choose **Data→Get & Transform Data→From Text/CSV**.

3. In the Import Data window, navigate to your **Excel Chapter 14** folder, select the **E14-D1-Q1 feb data** file, and click **Import**.

   A new window opens, displaying the contents of the CSV file. Note the Delimiter type is Comma.

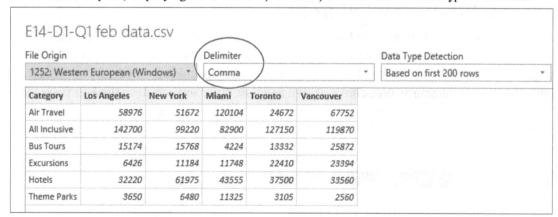

Rather than using the default settings, which would insert a new sheet in the workbook, you will change the load settings now.

4. Near the bottom of the window, click the **Load menu** button ▾ and choose **Load To....**

   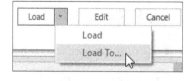

   In the Import Data window, you can see options for how and where the data will be inserted. Options for how to import include as a table, PivotTable, and PivotChart, any of which can be placed either on an existing or a new sheet. The other option is creating a data connection only and not actually pasting any information into the sheet.

5. Leave **Table** selected, choose the option to put the data onto an existing worksheet, which will position it in cell A5 (the selected cell), and click **OK** to insert the data.

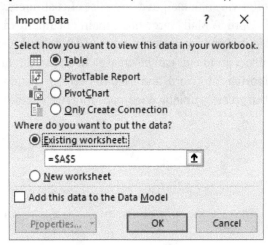

The data is inserted as a table, and the Queries & Connections pane opens on the right side of the Excel window, showing there is a query created to the E14-D1-Q1 feb data file.

In addition to the Table Tools contextual tab on the Ribbon, you will also see the Query Tools contextual tab, which allows you to edit, refresh, and perform other actions with the query.

6. Save your work.

Importing Tables from Microsoft Access

Information can be shared between Excel and Access without converting to a CSV, as the programs are directly compatible.

External Workbook References

If the data you need exists in another Excel workbook, the data can be referenced between workbooks without importing the data. Creating an external reference creates a link to the data, so if the source data changes, the information in the destination workbook will be updated automatically by default. You can modify links, open the source, break links, as well as adjust other settings from the Edit Links dialog box.

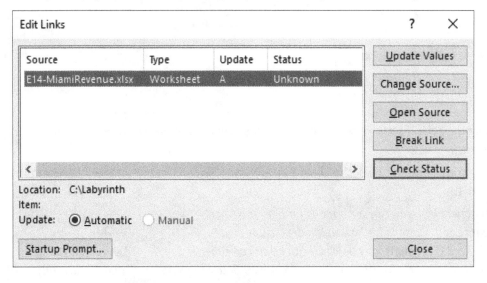

Data→Queries & Connections→Edit Links

DEVELOP YOUR SKILLS: E14-D2

In this exercise, you will import the March data from an Access table. Then you will create a link to the data for Vancouver's January results, which is currently missing.

1. Save your file as: **E14-D2-Q1Summary**

2. Go to the **Mar** sheet and choose **Data→Get & Transform Data→Get Data→From Database→From Microsoft Access Database**.

3. In the Import Data window, navigate to your **Excel Chapter 14** folder, select **E14-D2-March data.accdb**, and click **Import**.

   A new window opens, displaying the name of the database file, with March Results below.

4. Click **March Results** to preview its contents.

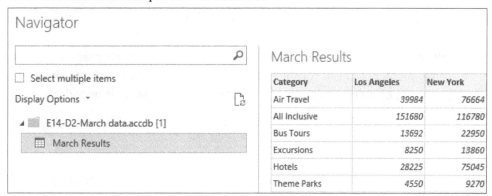

5. Click the **Load menu** button ▼ and choose **Load To....**

6. In the dialog box, choose to insert the data on an existing worksheet and click **OK**.

   The data for February and March is now complete, and you can see two items in the Queries & Connections pane.

   The last piece of missing information is the January Vancouver data. This data is in an Excel file and can be referenced directly.

7. Switch to the **Jan** sheet and then open **E14-D2-Vancouver** from your **Excel Chapter 14** folder.

8. Switch back to **E14-D2-Q1Summary** and select **cell F6**.

TIP! You can switch between open windows in several ways: ⎀Alt⎀+⎀Tab⎀, the taskbar, or View→Window→Switch Windows. Or, to have multiple workbooks visible at the same time, you can use View→Window→Arrange All.

9. Type **=** to begin the formula, then switch to **E14-D2-Vancouver** and, on the **Jan** sheet, click **cell B6** and tap ⎀Enter⎀.

   The formula in cell F6 on the Jan sheet in E14-D2-Q1Summary is:
   ='(E14-D2-Vancouver.xlsx)Jan'!$B$6

   This formula includes a reference to the workbook, sheet, and cell. The result is $44,528.

NOTE! References to other workbooks are absolute references by default.

10. In **cell F7**, repeat the process from step 9 to create a reference to the January results for Vancouver All Inclusive sales.

11. Edit the reference in **cell F7** to make it relative.

    Hint: Click the Formula Bar to place the insertion point at the end of the reference and tap F4 *three times.*

12. Copy the formula from **cell F7** down to **cell F11**.

13. Close the **E14-D2-Vancouver** file.

    The formulas and references in column F of the Q1Summary file now include the path to the Vancouver file's storage location on your computer.

    The data from the Vancouver file is linked and can be accessed, updated, or changed at any point via the Edit Links dialog box.

14. Save your work.

Summarizing Data

You can use PivotTables and 3-D references to summarize data, but when working with different data sources across platforms, you may want to consider other options. In some cases, it may be necessary to import the data first; in other cases, you can use some of Excel's built-in tools or add-ons to get the job done:

- Queries
- Power Pivot
- Data models
- Cube functions

These require external data sources and extensive knowledge of the data you are working with. While a database is made up of fields and records, a data cube (like a PivotTable) summarizes the information across multiple groupings, such as dates, locations, and product categories. With a data model, such as a data cube, you can analyze data using cube functions instead of creating PivotTables. For example, CUBEMEMBER, CUBESET, and CUBEVALUE are some of the functions used to pull information out of the data cube.

Data Consolidation

You can also summarize data using the Consolidate command on the Data tab. If your data has similar labels across multiple worksheets, such as income or expenses from several different company offices, you can combine the data into one range in a few simple steps.

Data→Data Tools→Consolidate

DEVELOP YOUR SKILLS: E14-D3

In this exercise, you will consolidate the first quarter data from the Jan, Feb, and Mar sheets into the Q1 Summary sheet.

1. Save your file as: **E14-D3-Q1Summary**

2. Go to the **Q1 Summary** sheet and choose **Data→Data Tools→Consolidate**.

3. Follow these steps to consolidate the Q1 data:

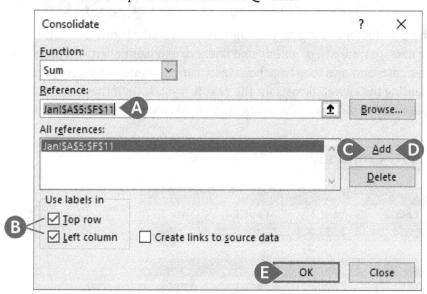

The desired function, Sum, is already selected.

A. Click in the **Reference** box and then go to the **Jan** sheet and select the **range A5:F11**.

B. Check the boxes beside **Top Row** and **Left Column**.

C. Click **Add** to add the selected range to the All References box.

   Selecting additional sheets will automatically use the same cell locations on those sheets.

D. Click the **Feb** sheet, click **Add**, click the **Mar** sheet, and click **Add**.

E. Once all three references are added, click **OK**.

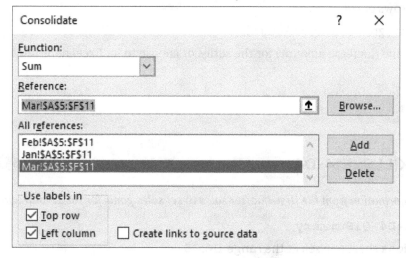

The consolidated data remains saved as part of the current worksheet and can be reused if desired.

4. In **cell A15**, enter the heading: **Q1 Averages**

5. Select the **range A3:G5** and then use **Format Painter** to copy the formatting and apply it to the **range A15:G17**.

6. Select **cell A17** and open the **Consolidate** tool, change the function to **Average**, and click **OK**.

7. Select the **range B18:F23** and change the number format to the **Comma Style** and remove the decimals.

8. Save your work.

Advanced Options for Filling a Data Series

Creating a series of values can be useful for making predictions and business decisions. You can create a data series based on existing data, past trends, or anticipated linear or exponential growth rates. For example, if a business examines costs and sees they have been increasing at a rate of 2% per year, they can create a set of data representing the expected costs for the next five years. Or, if they anticipate sales to increase from $10 million to $12 million in five years, they could create a set of data for that increase.

ABC Company					
Sales					
Current	Year 1	Year 2	Year 3	Year 4	Year 5
$10,000,000	$10,400,000	$10,800,000	$11,200,000	$11,600,000	$12,000,000
Expenses					
Current	Year 1	Year 2	Year 3	Year 4	Year 5
$ 8,000,000	$ 8,160,000	$ 8,323,200	$ 8,489,664	$ 8,659,457	$ 8,832,646

The values highlighted in yellow are created using the Fill Series command.

A linear series increases by the same number, while a growth series increases by the same percentage.

You can also select existing data and let Excel determine the trend for an increasing series of data. Or, start with a beginning value and an ending value, and let Excel fill in the missing values. There are many options; it all depends on how you want to use the information you do have to fill in the missing pieces of data.

- A series can be created in rows or columns.
- The series type can be linear, growth, date, or AutoFill.
- You can choose the step value (increase amount) for the series or choose to let Excel determine the trend.

Home→Editing→Fill ⬇

DEVELOP YOUR SKILLS: E14-D4

In this exercise, you will use information from the first-quarter sales to set sales goals for the second quarter.

1. Save your file as: **E14-D4-Q1Summary**
2. Go to the **Q2 Projections** sheet and select the **range D6:G6**.

   After examining the Air Travel sales, you have determined a sales goal of 3% growth for the next three months.

3. Choose **Home→Editing→Fill→Series...**.

4. In the Series dialog box, choose **Growth** in the Type section, type **1.03** in the Step Value box, and click **OK**.

   1.03 is equal to 103%, or an increase of 3%.

   The goal for All Inclusive travel sales is to increase sales to $615,000 in June, with steady growth in April and May to reach that goal.

5. In **cell G7**, enter: **615000**

6. Select the **range D7:G7** and choose **Home→Editing→Fill→Series...**.

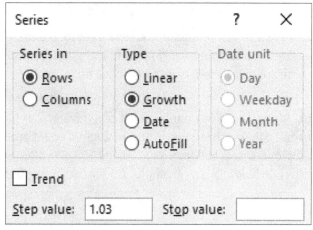

7. Leaving all settings as they are, note that the step value *11500* is identified and already entered and click **OK**.

   The values 592,000 and 603,500 are entered to fill in the missing months that represent an increase of 11,500 per month.

   Bus Tours and Excursions are seeing slower growth and unpredictable sales, so you want to be more conservative with these estimates.

8. Select the **range D8:G9** and fill in the two series using a **Linear** increase and a step value of: **3000**

   Based on your market research and increasing advertising efforts, you believe Hotels is going to be an excellent source of revenue and will continue its rapid growth for the next three months.

9. Select the **range C10:G10** (February and March data) and fill in the series using the **Growth** increase type and selecting the **Trend** option.

   The resulting series shows values between 210,000 and 243,000, increasing by roughly 7% per month.

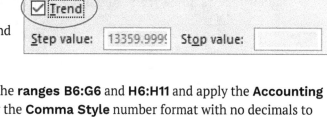

10. Select the **range C11:G11** (February and March data) and fill in the series using the **Linear** trend.

11. Insert the heading **Total** in **cell H5** and then use AutoSum to insert totals for each category in the **range H6:H11**.

12. To make the data easier to read, select the **ranges B6:G6** and **H6:H11** and apply the **Accounting** number format with no decimals; apply the **Comma Style** number format with no decimals to the **range B7:G11**.

13. Save your work.

Additional Charts and Chart Tools

After creating sets of data, you may want to explore ways to visualize the information and make it easier to understand. In addition to the simpler column charts, bar charts, line charts and pie charts, there are many more charts to choose from.

A histogram chart can be useful for grouping large amounts of data and showing the distribution of the data in groups. For example, a list of a thousand or more employee salaries would not produce a very useful column chart; however, a histogram could group those salaries into a chart showing how many employees earn between $20,000 and $30,000, $30,000 and $40,000, and so on. The histogram groups are called *bins*. In this example, the bin width is $10,000 (and can be adjusted).

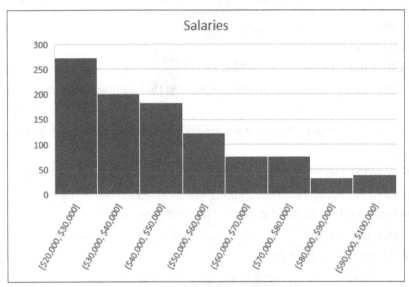

Another useful chart is the Pareto chart, which shows the significance of contributions of parts relative to the whole. For example, you could identify which sales categories contribute the most to the company's total revenue. The Pareto chart organizes the categories from highest to lowest, with a secondary axis and line indicating the increasing overall total.

> **TIP!** The Pareto principle (also commonly known as the *80/20 rule*) states that 80% of your results come from 20% of your efforts!

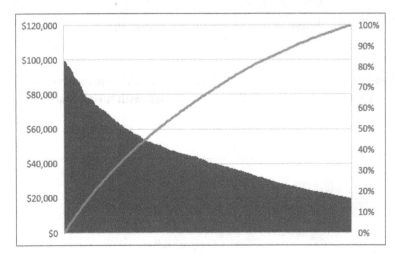

MORE CHART TYPES	
Chart Name	**Description**
Waterfall	Displays cumulative effects of positive and negative values, such as cash flow
Funnel	Displays progressively declining values as part of a process, such as sales conversions through the sales process
Sunburst	Shows data proportionally across levels, displayed as rings for each level
Box and Whisker	Displays variations in a data set when there are many sets of related data, such as tracking stock prices
Stock	Similar to Box and Whisker but requires data to be organized in a specific way

Adding Trendlines

A trendline is an indicator of overall increases or decreases in data and can be useful to help create future projections; for example, this is particularly useful for predicting income or expenses for budget purposes. You can add trendlines using a number of methods, similar to creating a data series. The trendline can be linear or exponential, or it can be created as a linear forecast or moving average. When tracking stock prices, for example, a useful chart might include the 50-day or 200-day moving average.

Saving a Chart as a Template

Once you have created and modified a chart to suit your specific purpose, you may want to save the chart as a template. Saving a chart as a template allows you to insert a new chart using the same chart settings but with different data. This can be a significant time saver.

DEVELOP YOUR SKILLS: E14-D5

In this exercise, you will create a Pareto chart for all sales categories and then create a column chart and add a trendline.

1. Save your file as: **E14-D5-Q1Summary**
2. Select the **ranges A5:A11** and **H5:H11**.

   Hint: Use Ctrl *to select them.*
3. Choose **Insert→Charts→Insert Statistic Chart→Pareto**.

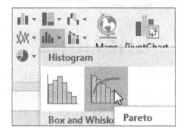

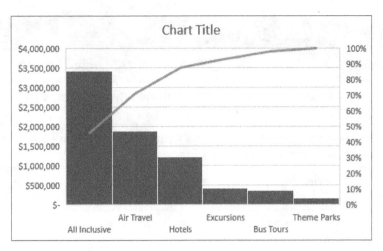

This chart shows the order of the sales categories from largest to smallest, with the line indicating the increasing percentage of the whole. The last category, Theme Parks, is the smallest, and adding it to all the other categories places the line at 100%.

4. Drag the chart to place it below the data and delete the chart title.

5. To create the next chart, select the **range A5:G7** and insert a 2-D clustered column chart.

6. Drag the chart and position it to the right of the data (if the Queries & Connections pane is still open, you can close it).

7. Choose **Chart Design→Chart Layouts→Add Chart Element→Trendline→Linear**.

8. In the dialog box, choose **All Inclusive** and click **OK**.

9. Format the chart with **Style 14** and monochromatic colors of your choice, and then add the title: **Projected Revenue**

10. Right-click inside the chart area and choose **Save As Template**.

> **TIP!** You must point to the chart area, not a chart element like a column, line, or axis, to see the Save As Template option. The blank space to the left or right of the chart title is the easiest place to click.

11. Save the chart template in the default location as: **Linear Trend**

12. For the next chart, select the **ranges A5:G5** and **A8:G9** and choose **Insert→Charts→ Recommended Charts**.

13. In the Insert Chart dialog box, click the **All Charts** tab, choose **Templates** on the left to display your saved Linear Trend template, and click **OK** to insert the chart.

14. Drag the chart to position it below the Projected Revenue chart and then edit the chart title to: **Projected Revenue**

15. Save your work.

Additional Lookup and Logical Functions

When you search for data in a large database, the VLOOKUP and HLOOKUP functions are useful, but they do have limitations: The data usually has to be sorted, and the functions can only look up values from left to right, or top to bottom. There may be situations in which alternative methods are required.

Nesting the MATCH function inside the INDEX function allows for more flexibility in performing a data lookup. The INDEX function returns a value from a specific cell location, and the MATCH function determines what that location should be.

XLOOKUP

Microsoft has introduced a new Excel function, XLOOKUP, which can replace the other lookups and simplifies the process. There are some great advantages to using XLOOKUP over VLOOKUP, and it is easier to use than INDEX and MATCH because there is no need to nest multiple functions. XLOOKUP looks for an exact match by default and allows you to search in any direction: up, down, left, or right.

For example, imagine you are looking for the first name of an employee whose ID number is 1323 (in cell F2) in a table where the first name is in column A and the ID number is in column C. The VLOOKUP function would not work because the ID column is to the right of the name column. Instead, you could choose between using INDEX and MATCH together, or the XLOOKUP function.

The formula used in the figure on the left, visible in the Formula Bar, is =INDEX(A2:A11,MATCH(F2,C2:C11,0)). In the figure on the right, the formula is =XLOOKUP(F2,C2:C11,A2:A11).

Review the image at the left above. The MATCH function looks in the range C2:C11 for the cell that exactly matches the value in cell F2 and returns the matching row number; the INDEX function then returns the value from the range A2:A11 from that row, in this case James.

Now review the image at the right above. The XLOOKUP function uses the same information, just organized differently. In this formula, cell F2 contains the ID number (lookup value), the range C2:C11 (lookup array) is the range in which to search for the value in cell F2, and the range A2:A11 (return array) contains the names. The function enters the corresponding name, James, as the formula result.

Other Logical Functions

In many cases you can use the IF function to determine one of two possible outcomes, true or false, based on a logical test. For other situations you may need to use additional functions such as AND, OR, as well as NOT, either independently or combined with other functions to create even more possibilities. The AND function simply checks whether *all* arguments are true and returns TRUE if they are and FALSE if they are not. The OR function, on the other hand, checks whether *any* of the arguments are true and returns TRUE if at least one is. The NOT function is used to reverse the results of a logical function so TRUE becomes FALSE and FALSE becomes TRUE.

DEVELOP YOUR SKILLS: E14-D6

In this exercise, you will look up the employee names from the list and determine which employees should have a salary review.

1. Save your file as: **E14-D6-Q1Summary**

2. Go to the **Employees** sheet.

   The Employee Lookup section has been completed for all fields except the name fields. Within this section, the ID# is used to find the corresponding position, location, and salary. You will add functions to insert the employees' names as well.

3. Enter this formula into **cell K6**: `=INDEX(A5:A33,MATCH(K5,C5:C33,0))`

   The formula returns the name Kristen. The INDEX function returns the contents of the cell in the range A5:A33, in the position returned by the MATCH function; the MATCH function returns the correct position by finding the position of the contents of cell K5 in the range C5:C33 (the 0 argument means it must match exactly).

4. In **cell K7**, use the **XLOOKUP** function to find the employee's last name by looking up the ID# in **cell K5** within the **range C5:C33** and returning the last name from the **range B5:B33**.

   The name Chambers is entered into cell K7 as a result. One of the benefits of XLOOKUP is that you can choose what is entered in the cell if the lookup value is not found, rather than seeing an error.

5. Edit the formula in **cell K7** (either by opening the function arguments or typing directly into the Formula Bar) to: `=XLOOKUP(K5,C5:C33,B5:B33,"Not Found")`

6. Delete the contents of **cell K5**.

   As you can see, the other lookups return errors while the XLOOKUP shows the text Not Found.

7. Enter a new ID# to search for in **cell K5**: **#13041**

   The lookup formulas will now show the information for Sarah Goldman.

   Now you want to determine if all the managers' salaries are at least $50,000.

8. Enter this formula into **cell H5**: `=AND(F5="Manager",G5<50000)`

   This formula checks if the position is Manager and salary is less than $50,000. If both conditions are met, it will return TRUE. The result in cell H5 is FALSE.

9. Copy the formula in **cell H5** down the column for all employees.

   Since TRUE and FALSE are not very useful, the AND function can be nested inside the IF function to return one result if the outcome is TRUE and another if FALSE.

10. Modify the formula in **cell H5** by nesting the AND function as follows:
    `=IF(AND(F5="Manager",G5<50000),"Review"," ")`

    Since the result of the first function was FALSE, the IF function returns the result for the value if false, which is a blank space; therefore, you will see nothing in cell H5 if the formula is entered correctly.

11. Copy the new formula down for all employees.

12. Use the **fill handle** to copy **cell G4** into **cell H4** and then edit the **column H** heading to:
    Salary Review

13. Save the file and close Excel.

Self-Assessment

Check your knowledge of this chapter's key concepts and skills using the online Self-Assessment Quiz.

Workbook Completion

15

In this chapter, you will learn how to put the finishing touches on a workbook before sharing or submitting your work.

LEARNING OBJECTIVES

- Create hyperlinks for navigation
- Insert comments
- Add alt text to objects
- Inspect your workbook for issues
- Create forms
- Protect your workbook

CHAPTER TIMING

- Concepts & Practice: 01:30:00
- Self-Assessment: 00:15:00
- Total: 01:45:00

PROJECT: GRADE BOOK SUBMISSION

Now that you have finished all the grading for the Business class at LearnFast College, you are ready to finalize your workbook before ultimately submitting the end-of-semester grades. You will create hyperlinks for easy navigation, add alt text to objects to ensure all users have access to the content in them, and then inspect and protect the workbook to finish your work.

Learning Resources: **boostyourskills.lablearning.com**

Inserting Hyperlinks for Navigation

Hyperlinks (or *links*) are often used to create links to websites or email addresses. Hyperlinks can also be used for navigation in Excel. You can create hyperlinks to give the user a quick link to navigate to a cell in another workbook, worksheet, or just a cell in another area of the same worksheet. Rather than using Find or Go To, which require opening a dialog box and typing or selecting the desired destination, the hyperlink is created right on the worksheet, and clicking the link takes you to a predetermined location. You can add a hyperlink to any text, shape, or picture.

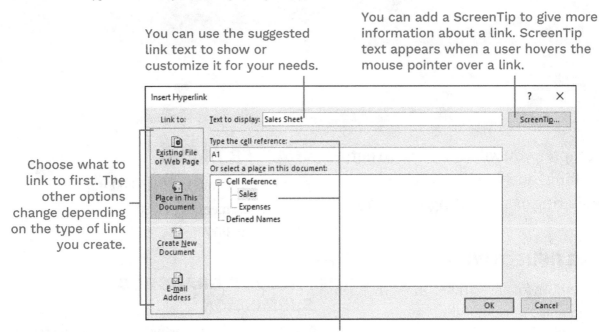

You can use the suggested link text to show or customize it for your needs.

You can add a ScreenTip to give more information about a link. ScreenTip text appears when a user hovers the mouse pointer over a link.

Choose what to link to first. The other options change depending on the type of link you create.

You can link to a specific cell or to a more general area, such as another sheet or a defined name.

You always have the option to edit or remove a hyperlink you have created, and it's as simple as right-clicking the cell, shape, or picture that contains the hyperlink and choosing Remove Hyperlink.

Insert→Links→Link

DEVELOP YOUR SKILLS: E15-D1

In this exercise, you will insert hyperlinks to create shortcuts to each of the worksheets containing the different parts of each student's grades.

1. Start Excel, open **E15-D1-Grades** from your **Excel Chapter 15** folder, and save it as: **E15-D1-GradesFinal**

2. Click in the **Name** box and then type **D5** and ⏎Enter.

   Cell D5 contains the heading for the overall quiz grades. You will create a hyperlink to the sheet that contains the individual quiz grades.

3. Choose **Insert→Links→Link**.

4. Select **Place in This Document** in the Link To section, select the **Quizzes** sheet on the right to create a link to that sheet, and click **OK**.

   The text to display and cell reference can be left as they are.

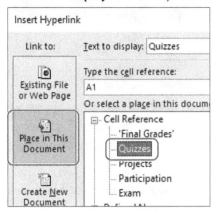

   Notice that the word Quizzes in cell D5 changes to a blue color with an underline to indicate the text is now linked.

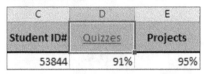

5. Point to **cell D5** and click with the mouse.

   This takes you to the Quizzes worksheet.

6. Return to the **Final Grades** worksheet and select **cell E5**.

   You may notice the word Quizzes in cell D5 has changed to a purple color. The default workbook theme has different settings for the font color of hyperlinks (blue) and followed hyperlinks (purple).

7. Choose **Insert→Links→Link**.

8. Ensure **Place in This Document** is selected in the Link To section, select the **Projects** sheet on the right to create a link to that sheet, and click **OK**.

9. Repeat this process to create hyperlinks for **cells F5** and **G5** to the **Participation** sheet and **Exam** sheet, respectively.

10. Save the file.

Working with Notes and Comments

Before sending a workbook to someone else to view or use, you may wish to include commentary about the file's contents. Comments and notes make it easy to collaborate with others working on the same file, without cluttering up the normal view of the workbook. You can use comments to have a conversation with other file viewers; for example, you can ask questions about worksheet data, provide additional information, explain complex data and formulas, and so on. Comments can be shown individually or all at once, and if the workbook is large or if you aren't sure where the comments are located, you can use the Ribbon commands to navigate to the next (or previous) comment.

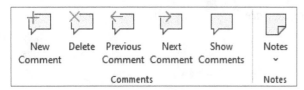

The Ribbon options for adding, deleting, and navigating through comments

Comments are indicated by a purple marker in the upper-right corner of the cell; notes appear with a red triangle in the same location. When you hover the mouse pointer over the cell with a marker, the author's name and comment will appear. Clicking Show Comments opens the Comments pane, which displays all comments for the worksheet.

Excel changed the way comments work, so for continuity with older versions and older Excel files, comments created previously now appear as notes. You can still create and use notes as in previous versions; you can reposition and resize an open note, and when you do, the note remains attached to the same cell. Notes from old files can also be converted into comments to take advantage of the new features.

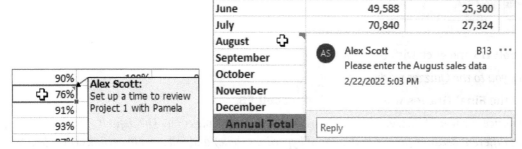

At left is a note and at right is a comment. Comments allow for easier conversations; each comment is time-stamped and threaded to make it easy to reply to.

Review→Comments→New Comment

DEVELOP YOUR SKILLS: E15-D2

In this exercise, you will insert comments for some of the students whose grades require additional work.

1. Save your file as: **E15-D2-GradesFinal**

   You need to review Project 1 with Pamela, so you want to insert a comment to remind to yourself.

2. Select **cell E15** and choose **Review→Comments→New Comment**.

   Another way to insert a comment is to use the shortcut menu that appears when you right-click a cell.

3. Type **Set up a time to review Project 1 with Pamela** and click **Post** (tapping **Enter** will not save the comment); then click any other cell on the worksheet.

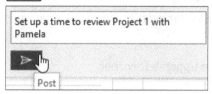

You may notice that the comment is no longer visible, but the purple marker remains in the upper-right corner of the cell. Moving the pointer back over that cell will display the comment again.

| 90% | 100% |
| 76% | 90% |

4. Right-click **cell G13** and choose **New Note**.

5. Type **Schedule exam retake** and then click any cell.

6. Hover the mouse pointer over **cell G13** to view the note and then right-click and choose **Edit Note**.

7. Type for **Oct. 1** to add the date to the end of the note and then click anywhere on the worksheet to finish editing.

8. Choose **Review→Notes→Notes→Convert to Comments** and, when the warning box appears, click **Convert All Notes** to continue.

9. Save your work.

Adding Alternative Text to Objects for Accessibility

To make your workbook accessible to individuals with visual impairments, you can add alternative text (or *alt text*) to the object properties. Alt text provides a descriptive representation of the information contained in charts, pictures, and shapes, which is useful for people who may not be able to see or understand the object otherwise.

For pictures, charts, and other illustrations, you can access the Alt Text pane through the contextual tabs on the Ribbon (for example, the Shape Format tab). Another option is to access it via the shortcut (or context) menu that appears when you right-click the object. In the Alt Text pane, enter a brief description of what the object is or what information it contains. Good alt text is clear and concise and conveys the purpose of the visual element for someone who can't see it.

> **TIP!** If a picture or shape doesn't contain any useful or important information, it can be marked as decorative.

Shape Format→Accessibility→Alt Text

Picture Format→Accessibility→Alt Text

In this exercise, you will add alt text to illustrations in your workbook for people with visual impairments.

1. Save your file as: **E15-D3-GradesFinal**

2. Go to the **Exam** sheet and select the small picture in the upper-left corner.

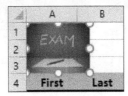

3. Choose **Picture Format→Accessibility→Alt Text**.

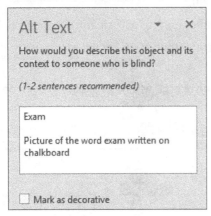

In the Alt Text pane on the right, notice that alt text is already added; a title and a description of the picture have been included.

4. Return to the **Final Grades** sheet and click in the chart area of the chart to select it.

Remember that the chart area is the empty space surrounding the title, plot area, and axes. The Alt Text pane is blank for this object.

5. Click in the **Alt Text** pane box and type: **Final Grade Line Chart**

6. Tap [Enter] twice and type: **The line chart shows the final grades for all students, ranging from 74% to 91%**

7. Close the Alt Text pane and then click **cell A7** to deselect the chart.

8. Save the file.

Inspecting Your Workbook

When you are finished editing a workbook, you might want others to see or use it. It's a good idea to check certain aspects of a workbook before sharing it. For example, you might want to check for personal information, accessibility issues, or compatibility. And if you will share your workbook with those in other parts of the world, you may want to set language options as well.

Inspect a Workbook for Hidden Properties or Personal Information

The Document Inspector searches your workbook for certain information you may not wish others to see. This table gives examples of data that you may include in a search, as well as items that will not be searched:

DOCUMENT INSPECTOR	
Items Included	**Items Not Included**
• Hidden worksheets, rows, columns, and names • Comments, ink annotations, and invisible content • Document properties and personal information • Scenarios in the Scenario Manager • Headers and footers	• Data entered in remote areas of a worksheet • White text on a white background • Data on a worksheet covered by a picture or shape

Before running the Document Inspector, it's a good idea to save a copy of your workbook. The Document Inspector will prompt you to save the file, but it's wise to have a backup. You also have the option of choosing which items to inspect and which to omit from the inspection.

After performing the inspection, the Document Inspector displays the search results. Nothing is removed until you choose to do so. Once you choose Remove All, however, the removal may be permanent. You cannot choose whether to keep or remove specific items within a category.

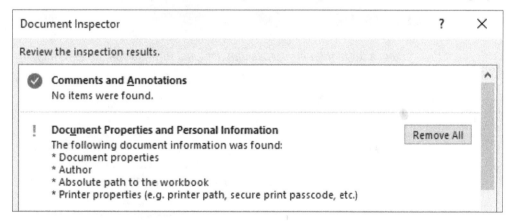

Inspect a Workbook for Accessibility

Similar to how the spelling checker tells you about possible spelling errors, the Accessibility Checker can alert you to possible accessibility issues in your workbook. You can then fix the identified issues so someone with an impairment can access and understand your content. Issues are classified into two groups:

- Errors: Content that will be very difficult for people with disabilities to understand
- Warnings: Content that might be difficult for people with disabilities to understand

Examples of issues you might find in your workbook include pictures without alt text, text that is similar in color to the background, blank sheets, or merged cells.

Inspect a Workbook for Compatibility

If you're sending a workbook to someone using an earlier version of Excel, you may want to first check to see whether there is content that won't be available to that person. You can select which version to check or just check all versions of Excel since 1997. The summary will indicate what might cause issues and how many occurrences there are of each issue.

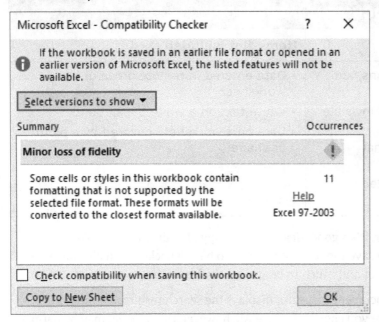

DEVELOP YOUR SKILLS: E15-D4

In this exercise, you will check the workbook for hidden properties and personal information, accessibility, and compatibility.

1. Save your file as: **E15-D4-GradesFinal**

2. Click the **File** tab and click the **Info** tab, if necessary.

   The Info tab shows the backstage options for protecting, inspecting, and managing your workbook. There is already a list of items below Inspect Workbook that you should be aware of, but you will inspect the workbook anyway to find exactly where these items or issues occur. Your screen may differ slightly.

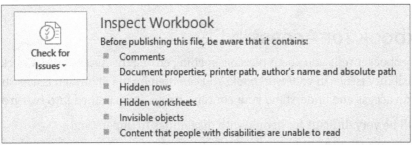

3. Choose **Check for Issues→Inspect Document**.

4. In the Document Inspector window, leave all options checked and click **Inspect**.

   The report shows you any areas that might be of concern, including comments and document properties.

5. Scroll through the report and notice the results show the file contains comments, document properties, one hidden row, and one hidden sheet.

   You will ignore the comments and hidden content.

6. Scroll back to the top and click **Remove All** next to *Document Properties and Personal Information.*

7. Click **Close** to finish using the Document Inspector.

Check for Accessibility Issues

8. Choose **File→Info→Check for Issues→Check Accessibility**.

   The Accessibility Checker pane opens on the right side of the Excel window and shows a summary of errors and warnings for the workbook.

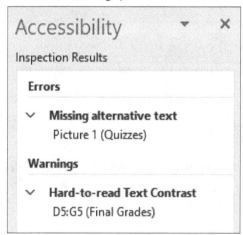

   If necessary, click the arrows next to Errors and Warnings to expand them. There is one error for missing alt text and one warning for text that is hard to read. You will ignore the warning but fix the error now.

9. Click the **Picture 1 (Quizzes)** item below *Errors*.

   This brings you to the Quizzes worksheet and selects the picture.

10. Right-click the picture and choose **Edit Alt Text**.

11. Type **Cartoon picture of a quiz and pencil** in the Alt Text pane and then close it.

    The error is removed from the Accessibility Checker pane.

12. Close the Accessibility Checker pane.

Check for Compatibility Issues

13. Choose **File→Info→Check for Issues→Check Compatibility**.

The summary shows two significant compatibility issues, since the two comments will be removed if the file is opened in Excel 2019 or older. There are also 13 cells that may have minor formatting changes if the file is opened in Excel 97–2003.

It's important to be aware of the possible loss of information in the comments, but you don't need to make changes in this case.

14. Click **OK** to close the Compatibility Checker.

15. Save the file.

Configure Editing and Display Languages

When collaborating with people from different areas of the world, you may need to modify the language settings in Excel. Excel also has a tool that can translate selected text into another language.

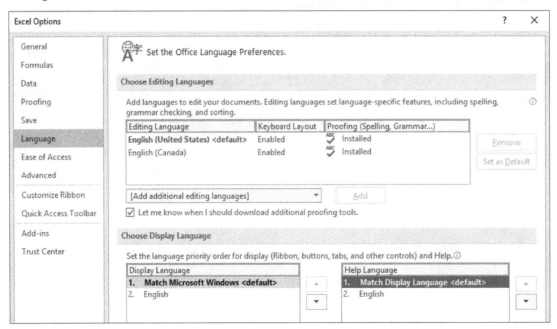

The Language section in Excel Options allows you to manage language settings.

Creating Forms

Another useful way of entering large amounts of data into Excel is through forms. You can create a form in Excel and then print it, complete with blank spaces for filling in data, or the user can fill it out directly in Excel. For example, when new clients come into the Raritan Clinic East office, they typically need to provide personal information. They could be given a form to fill out themselves on paper or it could be entered directly into the program by an assistant.

Data forms make it easier to enter information across a wide table without scrolling horizontally. Form tools like list boxes, checkboxes, spin buttons, and toggle buttons make data entry quick and easy—and less prone to error.

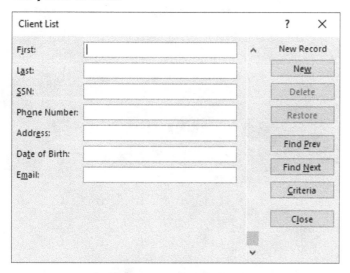

A data form for entering new client data.

Form controls and ActiveX controls are inserted from the Developer tab, which must be added to the Ribbon, and to use a data form you must add the Form command to either the Ribbon or Quick Access toolbar.

> **TIP!** You can customize the Ribbon and the Quick Access toolbar by right-clicking anywhere on the Ribbon.

You can also protect your forms so users can only enter information in the appropriate places, and the rest of the workbook is inaccessible.

DEVELOP YOUR SKILLS: E15-D5

In this exercise, you will insert a form for adding new students into the class and create a list box to identify students who passed the course.

1. Save your file as: **E15-D5-GradesFinal**

   Depending on your current setup, you may need to first show the Quick Access toolbar and/or move it above the Ribbon to match the following images.

2. As necessary, right-click the Ribbon and choose **Show Quick Access Toolbar** and then click the **Customize Quick Access Toolbar** button and choose **Show Above the Ribbon**.

3. Click the **Customize Quick Access Toolbar** button again and, this time, choose **More Commands...** to open the Excel Options window.

4. Follow these steps to add the Form button to the Quick Access toolbar:

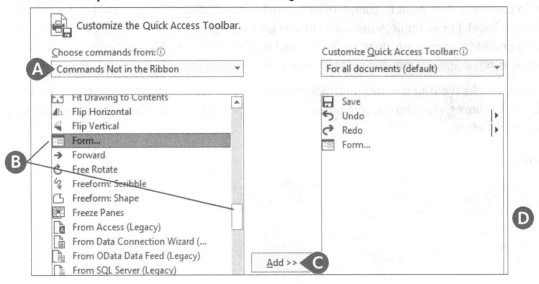

A. Choose **Commands Not in the Ribbon**.

B. Scroll down the list and choose **Form...**.

C. Click **Add**.

D. Click **OK** to close the Excel Options window.

The Form command is now visible on the Quick Access toolbar.

5. Go to the **Final Grades** sheet and ensure **cell A7** is selected.

6. Click the **Form** button on the Quick Access toolbar and then click **New** and enter this information for a new student:

NOTE! The fields for quizzes and other grades are not available because these columns contain formulas for calculating the grades.

7. Click **Close** and see the new student's info in row 19, with zeros filling in the formulas. (Grades can be entered later, and this will update the formulas.)

8. The form controls are located on the Developer tab, so if necessary, right-click the **Ribbon** and add the Developer tab.

9. Enter **Pass** in **cell K7** and **Fail** in **cell K8**.

10. Choose **Developer→Controls→Insert→Combo Box (Form Control)**, which is the second option in the top row.

11. Starting in the top-left corner of **cell I7**, drag to insert a combo box roughly the same size as the cell (ensure the box fits entirely inside the cell).

12. With the combo box still selected, choose **Developer→Controls→Properties** to modify the combo box options.

13. Click in the **Input Range** box, select the **range K7:K8** in the worksheet, and click **OK**.

    Hint: You may need to drag or collapse the dialog box to see the range K7:K8.

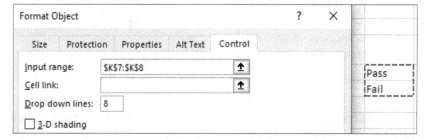

14. Hide **column K** and then click the form control in **cell I7** and select **Pass**.

15. Right-click the form control, copy the object, and paste it into **cell I8** (you may need to reposition it after pasting).

16. Repeat pasting the combo box beside each student.

17. Once each student has a form control in **column I**, select **cell H19** and set the form control for Alex Santiago to **Fail**. Until his grades are entered, he does not pass the course.

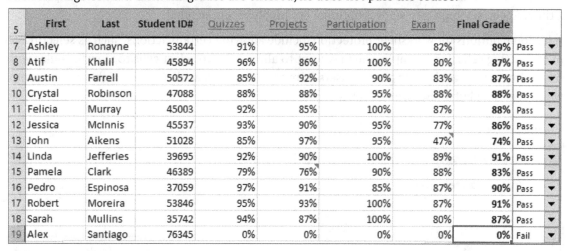

5	First	Last	Student ID#	Quizzes	Projects	Participation	Exam	Final Grade		
7	Ashley	Ronayne	53844	91%	95%	100%	82%	89%	Pass	▼
8	Atif	Khalil	45894	96%	86%	100%	80%	87%	Pass	▼
9	Austin	Farrell	50572	85%	92%	90%	83%	87%	Pass	▼
10	Crystal	Robinson	47088	88%	88%	95%	88%	88%	Pass	▼
11	Felicia	Murray	45003	92%	85%	100%	87%	88%	Pass	▼
12	Jessica	McInnis	45537	93%	90%	95%	77%	86%	Pass	▼
13	John	Aikens	51028	85%	97%	95%	47%	74%	Pass	▼
14	Linda	Jefferies	39695	92%	90%	100%	89%	91%	Pass	▼
15	Pamela	Clark	46389	79%	76%	90%	88%	83%	Pass	▼
16	Pedro	Espinosa	37059	97%	91%	85%	87%	90%	Pass	▼
17	Robert	Moreira	53846	95%	93%	100%	87%	91%	Pass	▼
18	Sarah	Mullins	35742	94%	87%	100%	80%	87%	Pass	▼
19	Alex	Santiago	76345	0%	0%	0%	0%	0%	Fail	▼

18. Save your work.

Protecting Workbooks

Another option to consider is how to protect your workbook. When sending a workbook to another user, you may want to protect some aspects of the file from being changed, either accidentally or intentionally. There are many options to choose from that allow you to limit who has access to the file and what they can see and do with the file.

Protect Workbook Structure

To prevent structural changes from being made to the workbook, you can turn on Protect Workbook Structure. This prevents users from making such changes as adding, deleting, renaming, moving, or copying worksheets.

There is an optional password to turn off protection. If a password is not set, any user can turn off the protection, so it's highly recommended to use a password.

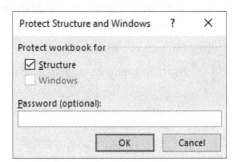

> **WARNING!** Use a password you will remember (or write it down). If you forget the password, there is *no way* to recover it and regain access to the protected elements of the workbook.

Be aware that protecting the workbook structure *does not* include worksheet protection, so the contents of each worksheet can still be edited, copied, or deleted. Protecting your data involves a separate process that you must perform.

Protect a Worksheet

To protect the data on your worksheets from changes, you can restrict edits using the options in the Restrict Access or Protect Worksheet commands. Restrict Access allows you to grant specific users access while removing their ability to edit, copy, or print. The simplest way to restrict edits is to use the Protect Sheet command. Worksheet protection must be done for each sheet you want to protect, one at a time. Again, setting a password is optional but highly recommended.

Additional options for worksheet protection include allowing certain actions, such as selecting cells or formatting cells. For example, you may want to allow users to select cells to view formulas without the ability to change them or prevent users from selecting cells at all. Or you might want to protect the worksheet data but allow format changes to be made.

By default, the options to allow users to select locked and unlocked cells are checked. To change this option, simply remove the check.

Lock Cells and Hide Formulas

Another option is to allow users to edit *some* but not *all* cells. For example, you may want to send a workbook to someone to enter input data in one range but not allow changes to the formulas you have already entered in another range. You can do this by first unlocking the cells you want unlocked and then turning on worksheet protection. By default, all cells are locked until you unlock them, which is done in the Format Cells dialog box.

To hide the formulas on a worksheet, you can mark cells as hidden. This does not hide the results—only the formula remains hidden. (If the cell does not contain a formula, hiding it has no effect.)

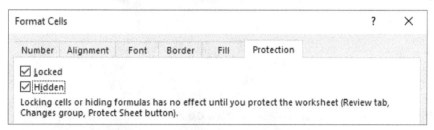

Configure Formula Calculation Options

Normally you want Excel to recalculate all formulas automatically each time a value changes. This is the default Excel setting, but you can change this in Excel Options if necessary.

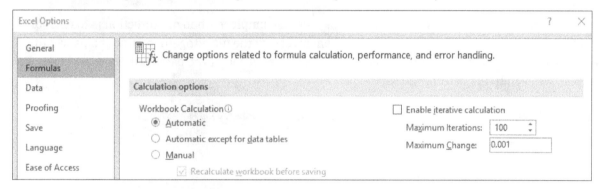

Manage Workbook Versions

It's always a good idea to save your work periodically. However, all Office apps, including Excel, have AutoRecover features that make it very rare that you would actually lose any unsaved work. Even if you close a workbook and accidentally forget to save it, you can still recover the file; the key is knowing where to look and how to recover the unsaved workbook versions.

In Excel Options you can view and/or modify where and how often AutoRecover files are saved.

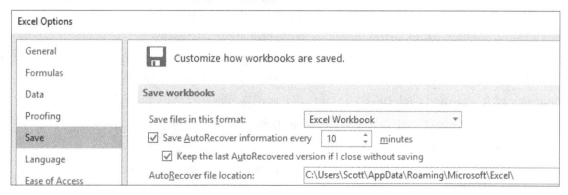

To recover an unsaved workbook after closing it, reopen Excel and go to Backstage view. On the Info tab, choose Manage Workbook. Note that you can also view a previous version of the current file. This might be useful if you make changes that cannot be reversed using the Undo command, such as deleting a worksheet!

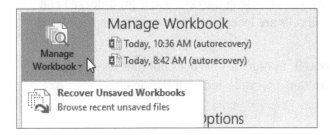

Mark as Final

If no more changes need to be made to a workbook, you can mark the document as final. This is perhaps the simplest method of protection because it allows no changes at all to the workbook, worksheets, or cells. However, any user can turn off this setting. You can tell a file is marked as final when the Mark as Final icon is displayed on the status bar.

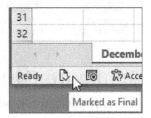

Encrypt with a Password

To prevent unauthorized access to your workbook, another simple method of protection is to encrypt the file with a password. This prevents anyone from accessing the file altogether without a password. Remember that passwords are not recoverable, so if you lose or forget the password, the file will be inaccessible even to the person who set the password!

File→Info→Protect Workbook | Review→Protect

DEVELOP YOUR SKILLS: E15-D6

In this exercise, you will add protection to the workbook and worksheet, unlock and hide cells, and mark the document as final.

1. Save your file as: **E15-D6-GradesFinal**
2. On the **Final Grades** worksheet, choose **Review→Protect→Protect Workbook**.
3. In the Protect Structure and Windows dialog box, type **abc123** for the password and click **OK**.

TIP! For the purposes of this book, all exercise passwords are the same, simple, and easy to remember. Of course, for true security, you should use different passwords and make them complex.

Because the password you entered is not visible, the next step asks you to confirm what you just entered, before the protection is applied, to ensure you did not make a mistake when typing the password.

4. Type **abc123** again and click **OK**.

The workbook is now protected from any structural changes.

5. Right-click the **Final Grades** worksheet tab.

Notice the options to insert, delete, rename, move, or copy are no longer available.

6. From the context menu, choose **Protect Sheet**.

7. In the Protect Sheet dialog box, type **abc123** for the password.

8. Uncheck the boxes beside **Select Locked Cells** and **Select Unlocked Cells** and click **OK**.

9. Type **abc123** to confirm the password and click **OK**.

   If you click around on the worksheet, you will not be able to select any cells, meaning you cannot make changes to any cells. The exception is that the form controls are still accessible.

10. Choose **Review→Protect→Unprotect Sheet**.

11. Unprotect the worksheet using the password: **abc123**

    Now you will unlock some of the cells so the names and ID numbers can be edited if necessary.

12. Select the **range A7:C19**, right-click, and choose **Format Cells...**.

13. Click the **Protection** tab, uncheck **Locked**, and click **OK**.

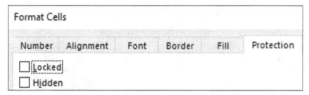

    Now you will hide the formula that calculates the final grades.

14. Select the **range H7:H19**, right-click, and choose **Format Cells...**.

15. Click the box next to **Hidden** to add a check so the cells are both Locked and Hidden; click **OK**.

16. Choose **Review→Protect→Protect Sheet**.

17. Type **abc123** for the password.

18. Check the box beside **Select Locked Cells**, which automatically adds a check to Select Unlocked Cells as well, and click **OK**.

19. Retype **abc123** and click **OK** to begin protection.

    Notice the Formula Bar is now blank but the results of the formulas still display in the range.

20. Type the letter **a** and notice the warning that pops up.

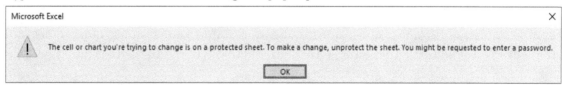

21. Click **OK** to close the warning.

22. Choose **File→Info→Protect Workbook→Mark as Final**.

    The warning box lets you know the file will be marked as final and saved.

23. Click **OK**. Another message box appears to provide more details about the process; click **OK** to close that message.

    Notice you can no longer edit any of the workbook content, the Ribbon is collapsed, and Marked as Final *appears above the Formula Bar.*

24. Close the file without making any other changes.

Self-Assessment

 Check your knowledge of this chapter's key concepts and skills using the online Self-Assessment Quiz.

The Microsoft Office Specialist Exam and This Text

Statistics show that people with a certification are more marketable and earn more than those who are not certified. Obtaining a certification is a way to show employers that you have a specialized skill and have demonstrated ability in a particular area. This complete learning solution meets all the objectives to prepare you to take the Microsoft Office Specialist (MOS) exam for this subject area.

In the following tables, each exam objective (left column) is associated with a reference to the most prominent location(s) in your learning solution that deal with that objective (right column). You might use this table as you prepare for a MOS exam.

For more information on MOS certification, go to: certiport.pearsonvue.com/Certifications/Microsoft

ASSOCIATE EXAM		
OBJECTIVE		**TEXT LOCATION**
1	**Manage Worksheets and Workbooks**	
1.1	Import data into workbooks	
	1.1.1 Import data from .txt files	Importing and Exporting Data, p. 228
	1.1.2 Import data from .csv files	Importing and Exporting Data, p. 228
1.2	Navigate within workbooks	
	1.2.1 Search for data within a workbook	Other Navigation Methods, p. 38
	1.2.2 Navigate to named cells, ranges, or workbook elements	Creating Names for Cells and Ranges, p. 64
	1.2.3 Insert and remove hyperlinks	Inserting Hyperlinks for Navigation, p. 364
1.3	Format worksheets and workbooks	
	1.3.1 Modify page setup	Customizing the Page Setup, p. 122
	1.3.2 Adjust row height and column width	Adjusting Column Width and Row Height, p. 27
	1.3.3 Customize headers and footers	Headers and Footers, p. 136
1.4	Customize options and views	
	1.4.1 Customize the Quick Access toolbar	The Quick Access Toolbar, p. 4, *and* DYS E15-D5, p. 374
	1.4.2 Display and modify workbook content in different views	Adjusting View Options, p. 90
	1.4.3 Freeze worksheet rows and columns	Adjusting View Options, p. 90
	1.4.4 Change window views	Adjusting View Options, p. 90
	1.4.5 Modify basic workbook properties	Editing Document Properties, p. 161
	1.4.6 Display formulas	Display and Print Formulas, p. 62
1.5	Configure content for collaboration	
	1.5.1 Set a print area	Printing Options, p. 136
	1.5.2 Save workbooks in alternative file formats	Exporting, p. 341
	1.5.3 Configure print settings	Printing Worksheets, p. 36
	1.5.4 Inspect workbooks for issues	Inspecting Your Workbook, p. 368

2		**Manage Data Cells and Ranges**	
2.1		Manipulate data in worksheets	
	2.1.1	Paste data by using special paste options	The Office Clipboard, p. 9
	2.1.2	Fill cells by using AutoFill	Entering a Series Using AutoFill, p. 34
	2.1.3	Insert and delete multiple columns or rows	Insert and Delete Rows, Columns, and Cells, p. 54
	2.1.4	Insert and delete cells	Insert and Delete Rows, Columns, and Cells, p. 54
2.2		Format cells and ranges	
	2.2.1	Merge and unmerge cells	Cell Alignment, p. 30
	2.2.2	Modify cell alignment, orientation, and indentation	Cell Alignment, p. 30
	2.2.3	Format cells by using Format Painter	Formatting Text Using Font Group Settings, p. 13
	2.2.4	Wrap text within cells	Cell Alignment, p. 30
	2.2.5	Apply number formats	Creating Custom Number Formats, p. 119
	2.2.6	Apply cell formats from the Format Cells dialog box	Creating Custom Number Formats, p. 119
	2.2.7	Apply cell styles	Cell Styles, p. 115
	2.2.8	Clear cell formatting	Cell Styles, p. 115
2.3		Define and reference named ranges	
	2.3.1	Define a named range	Creating Names for Cells and Ranges, p. 64
	2.3.2	Name a table	Table Name, p. 277, *and* DYS E11-D2, p. 279
2.4		Summarize data visually	
	2.4.1	Insert sparklines	Creating Sparklines, p. 198
	2.4.2	Apply built-in conditional formatting	Conditional Formatting Using Graphics and Custom Rules, p. 132, *and* The Quick Analysis Tool, p. 260
	2.4.3	Remove conditional formatting	Conditional Formatting Using Graphics and Custom Rules, p. 132
3		**Manage Tables and Table Data**	
3.1		Create and format tables	
	3.1.1	Create Excel tables from cell ranges	Excel Tables, p. 139, *and* Working with Tables, p. 274
	3.1.2	Apply table styles	Table Style Options, p. 278
	3.1.3	Convert tables to cell ranges	Excel Tables, p. 139
3.2		Modify tables	
	3.2.1	Add or remove table rows and columns	Insert and Delete Table Rows and Columns, p. 274
	3.2.2	Configure table style options	Table Style Options, p. 278
	3.2.3	Insert and configure total rows	Total Row, p. 278
3.3		Filter and sort table data	
	3.3.1	Filter records	Excel Tables, p. 139, *and* Apply a Sort or Filter, p. 191
	3.3.2	Sort data by multiple columns	Excel Tables, p. 139, *and* Apply a Sort or Filter, p. 191

4	**Perform Operations by Using Formulas and Functions**	
4.1	Insert references	
	4.1.1 Insert relative, absolute, and mixed references	Using Relative and Absolute Cell References, p. 79
	4.1.2 Reference named ranges and named tables in formulas	Creating Names for Cells and Ranges, p. 64
4.2	Calculate and transform data	
	4.2.1 Perform calculations by using the AVERAGE(), MAX(), MIN(), and SUM() functions	SUM, AVERAGE, COUNT, MAX, and MIN, p. 77
	4.2.2 Count cells by using the COUNT(), COUNTA(), and COUNTBLANK() functions	SUM, AVERAGE, COUNT, MAX, and MIN, p. 77
	4.2.3 Perform conditional operations by using the IF() function	The IF Function, p. 130
4.3	Format and modify text	
	4.3.1 Format text by using RIGHT(), LEFT(), and MID() functions	Using Functions to Modify Text, p. 220
	4.3.2 Format text by using UPPER(), LOWER(), and LEN() functions	Using Functions to Modify Text, p. 220
	4.3.3 Format text by using the CONCAT() and TEXTJOIN() functions	Using Functions to Modify Text, p. 220
5	**Manage Charts**	
5.1	Create charts	
	5.1.1 Create charts	Create Charts to Compare Data, p. 70
	5.1.2 Create chart sheets	Move and Size Charts, p. 105
5.2	Modify charts	
	5.2.1 Add data series to charts	Selecting Chart Data, p. 98, *and* DYS E4-D1, p. 100
	5.2.2 Switch between rows and columns in source data	Edit Chart Data, p. 107
	5.2.3 Add and modify chart elements	Chart Tools, p. 74
5.3	Format charts	
	5.3.1 Apply chart layouts	Selecting Chart Data, p. 98
	5.3.2 Apply chart styles	Chart Design, p. 75
	5.3.3 Add alternative text to charts for accessibility	Inspect a Workbook for Accessibility, p. 370, *and* DYS E15-D4, p. 371

EXPERT EXAM	
OBJECTIVE	**TEXT LOCATION**
1 **Manage Workbook Options and Settings**	
1.1 Manage workbooks	
1.1.1 Copy macros between workbooks	Storing and Sharing Macros, p. 325
1.1.2 Reference data in other workbooks	Create Cell References to Other Worksheets, p. 52
1.1.3 Enable macros in a workbook	Changing Macro Security, p. 220
1.1.4 Manage workbook versions	Manage Workbook Versions, p. 378
1.2 Prepare workbooks for collaboration	
1.2.1 Restrict editing	Protecting Workbooks, p. 376
1.2.2 Protect worksheet and cell ranges	Protecting Workbooks, p. 376
1.2.3 Protect workbook structure	Protecting Workbooks, p. 376
1.2.4 Configure formula calculation options	Protecting Workbooks, p. 376
1.2.5 Manage comments	Working with Notes and Comments, p. 366
1.3 Use and configure language options	
1.3.1 Configure editing and display languages	Configure Editing and Display Languages, p. 250
1.3.2 Use language-specific features	Configure Editing and Display Languages, p. 250
2 **Manage and Format Data**	
2.1 Fill cells based on existing data	
2.1.1 Fill cells by using Flash Fill	Merge and Modify Text with Functions and Flash Fill, p. 221
2.1.2 Fill cells by using advanced Fill Series options	Additional Charts and Chart Tools, p. 236
2.2 Format and validate data	
2.2.1 Create custom number formats	Creating Custom Number Formats, p. 119
2.2.2 Configure data validation	Controlling Data Entry with Data Validation, p. 99
2.2.3 Group and ungroup data	The Outline Feature, p. 255
2.2.4 Calculate data by inserting subtotals and totals	The Outline Feature, p. 255, *and* Subtotals, p. 257
2.2.5 Remove duplicate records	Remove Duplicates, p. 295
2.3 Apply advanced conditional formatting and filtering	
2.3.1 Create custom conditional formatting rules	Conditional Formatting Using Graphics and Custom Rules, p. 132
2.3.2 Create conditional formatting rules that use formulas	Conditional Formatting Using Graphics and Custom Rules, p. 132
2.3.3 Manage conditional formatting rules	Conditional Formatting Using Graphics and Custom Rules, p. 132

3	**Create Advanced Formulas and Macros**	
3.1	Perform logical operations in formulas	
	3.1.1	Perform logical operations by using nested functions including the IF(), IFS(), SWITCH(), SUMIF(), AVERAGEIF(), COUNTIF(), SUMIFS(), AVERAGEIFS(), COUNTIFS(), MAXIFS(), MINIFS(), AND(), OR(), and NOT() functions	Nested Functions, p. 228
3.2	Look up data by using functions	
	3.2.1	Look up data by using the VLOOKUP(), HLOOKUP(), MATCH(), and INDEX() functions	Introducing Lookup Functions, p. 252
3.3	Use advanced date and time functions	
	3.3.1	Reference date and time by using the NOW() and TODAY() functions	Using Date Functions, p. 176
	3.3.2	Calculate dates by using the WEEKDAY() and WORKDAY() functions	Using Date Functions, p. 176, *and* Calculations Using Date and Time, p. 131
3.4	Perform data analysis	
	3.4.1	Summarize data from multiple ranges by using the Consolidate feature	Summarizing Data, p. 345
	3.4.2	Perform what-if analysis by using Goal Seek and Scenario Manager	Scenario Manager, p. 203, *and* Goal Seek, p. 206
	3.4.3	Forecast data by using the AND(), IF(), and NPER() functions	NPER Function, p. 198
	3.4.4	Calculate financial data by using the PMT() function	PMT Function, p. 195
3.5	Troubleshoot formulas	
	3.5.1	Trace precedence and dependence	Trace Precedents and Dependents, p. 232
	3.5.2	Monitor cells and formulas by using the Watch Window	The Watch Window, p. 235
	3.5.3	Validate formulas by using error checking rules	The Watch Window, p. 235
	3.5.4	Evaluate formulas	The Watch Window, p. 235
3.6	Create and modify simple macros	
	3.6.1	Record simple macros	Recording Macros, p. 323
	3.6.2	Name simple macros	Recording Macros, p. 323
	3.6.3	Edit simple macros	Recording Macros, p. 323

4	**Manage Advanced Charts and Tables**	
4.1	Create and modify advanced charts	
	4.1.1 Create and modify dual-axis charts	Additional Charts and Chart Tools, p. 236
	4.1.2 Create and modify charts including Box & Whisker, Combo, Funnel, Histogram, Map, Sunburst, and Waterfall charts	Additional Charts and Chart Tools, p. 236
4.2	Create and modify PivotTables	
	4.2.1 Create PivotTables	Creating PivotTables, p. 202
	4.2.2 Modify field selections and options	Changing Value Field Settings, p. 208
	4.2.3 Create slicers	Filtering with Slicers, p. 304
	4.2.4 Group PivotTable data	Formatting PivotTables, p. 299
	4.2.5 Add calculated fields	Creating Calculated Fields, p. 214
	4.2.6 Format data	Formatting PivotTables, p. 299
4.3	Create and modify PivotCharts	
	4.3.1 Create PivotCharts	Creating PivotCharts, p. 217
	4.3.2 Manipulate options in existing PivotCharts	Creating PivotCharts, p. 217
	4.3.3 Apply styles to PivotCharts	Creating PivotCharts, p. 217
	4.3.4 Drill down into PivotChart details	Creating PivotCharts, p. 217

Index